Jim –

To a quality guy who has brought so much to the Hawthorne team.

And as a friend, I hope our paths never diverge too far.

Thanks for being the insightful, creative, whole person you are.

Tim

MAY 12, 1997

The Complete Guide to INFOMERCIAL MARKETING

Timothy R. Hawthorne

Foreword by Nancy Edwards

Senior Manager, Marketing Initiatives and Research • Nissan Motor Corporation, U.S.A.

Printed on recyclable paper

NTC Business Books
a division of *NTC Publishing Group* • Lincolnwood, Illinois USA

Library of Congress Cataloging-in-Publication Data

Hawthorne, Timothy R.
The complete guide to infomercial marketing / Timothy R. Hawthorne
p. cm.
Includes bibliographical references and index.
ISBN 0-8442-3445-1 (alk. paper)
1. Television advertising. 2. Infomercials. I. Title.
HF6146.T42H36 1997 96-43356
659.14'3--dc20 CIP

Published by NTC Business Books, a division of NTC Publishing Group
4255 West Touhy Avenue
Lincolnwood (Chicago), Illinois 60646-1975, U.S.A.

Manufactured in the United States of America.

7 8 9 0 QB 9 8 7 6 5 4 3 2 1

Contents

Foreword

Capture Their Attention . . .

- Why does only one in ten infomercials succeed?
- Aren't infomercials just for low-end products?
- How could we possibly keep people interested in a 30-minute commercial?
- Who watches infomercials, and when?
- Won't an infomercial damage the brand?
- Can you really make a fortune overnight in infomercials?
- Can my general ad agency make an informercial?
- Should we give up regular TV advertising and just run infomercials?
- Should we make a 20-minute, 5-minute, or 2-minute infomercial?
- Do we have to use a celebrity?

Create Interest . . .

Here's a book dedicated to a subject in which those who succeed rarely want to tell others how to! And because you know that fortunes can be won or lost in this business . . . and mostly lost . . . . it sure would be helpful to know how to minimize the risk.

Tim Hawthorne to the rescue. He has put together an in-depth perspective, from how past events shaped the infomercial business to how the infomercial business will shape the future of advertising. Plus, the book is a step-by-step guide to making an infomercial, including how to decide if an infomercial is right for your product, the special considerations in creating and producing a long-form commercial, the inside track on media, how to prepare a pro-forma, even how to avoid committing infomercial suicide, and much more.

For anyone in the infomercial supply and distribution business, for advertising agencies, for consumer products or service companies, for any student of marketing, advertising, or the art of the infomercial . . . there's something in here for you.

Direct Response TV is probably one of the most effective and efficient forms of media available in the marketing mix. It's accountable and measurable. This is good. It's also scary if you're a big-brand marketer who has spent multimillions on regular broadcast media. Get over it. With the information in this book, you can create a successful infomercial. There is nothing more satisfying than watching the phones ring off the hook after your first airing. Imagine being able to see exactly which time slots are pulling today, so you can change your media selections tomorrow. Knowing precisely what your cost per call was by minute, by day, by week, by station, by whatever way you can think of to slice it! Thousands of people interested in your product actually calling you! Knowing the names and addresses of all those customers! A marketer's dream come true?

The whole landscape of advertising is changing, with the customer controlling when, where, how and what kind of advertising information they will be exposed to. How are infomercials part of this future? The infomercial is the foundation of where interactive advertising is headed. If infomercials weren't captivating and entertaining, people wouldn't sit and watch them like they do. Infomercials stop channel surfers in their tracks because they are engaging and they provide information . . . lots of it . . . to viewers . . . when and where they want it. It sure sounds a lot like what's needed to "hook" the internet surfer . . . sure sounds a lot like what's needed to capture the attention of the interactive TV viewer. INFOTAINMENT is the next wave, and infomercials are the springboard. Read more in Chapter 15.

Instill Desire . . .

If only this book had been written when Nissan's Marketing Initiatives group was trying to get our company to make an infomercial. We needed plenty of advice because it was a totally new way of thinking about how to market. And there were lots of preconceived notions (mostly negative) about infomercials. Fortunately, we found Hawthorne Communications to help us launch the concept, and as it worked out, they had exactly the expertise we needed. We had a million questions embarking on this new media venture for our company, and Tim and his crew taught us the why's, what's, and how's of the business. Well, fortunately for everyone else, in this book Tim Hawthorne has published his expertise and invaluable words of wisdom.

Motivate Them to Action . . .

Buy this book, read it, and hide it from the competition.

Nancy Edwards
Senior Manager, Marketing Initiatives and Research
Nissan Motor Corporation, U.S.A.
Gardena, California
October 1996

Acknowledgments

It is with deepest appreciation that I express my thanks to all of the many people who made this book a reality.

To Bob Moore, Gene Silverman, Mark Ratner, Thomas Kelly and John Prechtel, all of whom have worked closely with me in this business for many years and helped me in innumerable ways.

To my editors Kathy St. Louis, Rich Hagle, Elizabeth Pasco, Steve Niemela, M.K. Jones, Laura Grooms, Maggie Argiro and Diane Frank.

To many of my staff, past and present, including Lori Macrander, Penny Waldren, Cyndia McBeth, Sandra McClure, Carol Tripp, Connie Main and Dana Miner.

And also for their significant contributions: Jim Hall, Jeff Glickman, Dean Schirm, Sarah Ledger, Bonnie Gould, Joel Rappin, Roger Silber and Grace Carpenter.

A special thanks to Tom Stone for manifesting a good idea and to Laya Schaetzel for her untiring support.

Introduction

More than a decade ago, I addressed a group of Direct Marketing Association members in Dallas, Texas, which turned out to be the first of many presentations I would give about long-form advertising, also known as infomercials.

As I stepped up to the microphone that day, before I could say one word, a leathery hand shot into the air. An older gentleman wearing a bolo tie and western shirt was marching to the aisle microphone. He didn't wait for me to acknowledge him.

"I want you to know that I sell my beef steak through direct mail," he barked. "And I'm here to tell you that your TV infomercials are a lot like the longhorn cattle I raise. They make a point here and a point there," (gesturing to indicate the two ends of a longhorn's headgear) "but there's just a lot of bull in between! They should be banned from the television airwaves!"

As an active advocate of infomercials through the years, plenty of marketing executives have confronted me with similar accusations. To them, I seemed to represent a reincarnation of the sleazy, door-to-door snake oil pitchmen—the consummate "bad guys" in old black-and-white Westerns. To professionals trained in traditional advertising methodology, infomercials were perceived as tools that were used only by fast-buck artists who gobbled up half-hour time slots to peddle pots, pans, and potions to vulnerable late-night television viewers. I may as well have been speaking Greek.

Accountability versus Image

Countless times, I've presented my slide show on the "Power of the Half-Hour"™ infomercial to groups of advertising executives and drawn skeptical stares. Their eyes begin to wander, especially when I describe the mathematics of infomercials and how we measure their results.

The mere mention of concepts such as cost per order (CPO), cost per lead (CPL), media efficiency ratio (MER), and ad allowables, which are everyday measurement tools of infomercial marketers, elicits a great deal of audience leg-crossing and coffee-sipping. After all, we're talking about bean counting and *advertising accountability*. To many agency executives, advertising accountability is a new concept.

Traditionally, 30-second spot advertising does not require the measuring tools needed to determine if a typical ad campaign is working. It is largely for this reason that 30-second spots have long reigned supreme as *the* television commercial format favored by Madison Avenue advertising executives.

In stark contrast to a 30-second commercial project, everyone involved in an infomercial knows immediately whether or not their 30-minute program is working. That's one of the reasons major ad agencies are still apprehensive about going the infomercial marketing route: that looming specter of accountability. Meanwhile, many Fortune 500 marketing executives are thinking that this accountability sounds pretty good.

Let's face it. Most ad agency executives would rather spend $30 million in a spot television campaign that looks pretty but does not have to give quantifiable results. Now, are they going to spend $500,000 for infomercial production and another $50,000 for a media test, and face the possibility of having to tell their boss and client in as little as two weeks that the show failed? In contrast, as long as their old standby 30-second spot makes a good impression, the creative looks good, people talk about it, and the awareness factor of the commercial is high, then the spot is considered a success. No one even *thinks* about sales.

But pretty commercials don't necessarily mean increased sales. According to a *Wall Street Journal* report, seven out of the top ten most popular commercials for 1993 didn't increase sales for the product. In some cases, sales for the product decreased during the time the commercials aired.

For good reason, more and more advertisers are demanding accountability for their ad expenditures. Accordingly, infomercials are destined to become an accepted component in advertisers' marketing mix. As this happens, advertising executives everywhere will be required to measure the results of their advertising campaigns.

A New Way of Thinking

Many advertisers have a preconceived negative impression of infomercials and their products dating back to the "Old West" and legendary traveling salesmen pitching miracle potions. In addition, integrating infomercials into their clients' media mix means learning a whole new media strategy that includes measurement and accountability (which places winning or losing squarely on their own shoulders). Now, figure in yet another old school of thought that creates resistance to the idea of long-form advertising. Many account executives have learned to distrust infomercial effectiveness because they've been taught that viewers would reject the required investment of time and attention.

Actually, the opposite is true. For centuries, sales people who work face-to-face with prospects have understood the old maxim: "The more you tell the more you sell." They know that the longer the salesperson can talk to a prospect, the greater the chance of a sale.

Salespeople using printed materials and the telephone concur. Direct-mail marketers understand that the more product information you get somebody to read, the greater the chance of converting the prospect to a customer. The same is true for outbound telemarketing professionals. Furthermore, the television viewer deliberately *chooses* to watch an infomercial because he or she is attracted to it while channel surfing. Infomercials don't intrude on people's awareness nearly as abruptly and unavoidably as do traditional spot commercials.

The individual who watches an infomercial has, in essence, raised his or her hand and said, 'I'm interested in your product." It follows that infomercial viewers are more likely to become customers than those whose entertainment time is interrupted by a 30-second commercial.

Well Worth the Effort

Before I began making infomercials, I worked for 11 years as a television documentary producer/writer/director. After producing hundreds of documentaries for network affiliates and prime-time reality magazine shows in Los Angeles, I moved to Fairfield, Iowa, a small Midwestern town that seemed a safer place to raise a family. When I arrived, I was interested in starting an industrial production company. After networking with the local business community, I soon discovered the potential for that particular endeavor looked grim.

Then one evening I was invited to a dinner hosted by Ed Beckley, an entrepreneur who would change my professional outlook, career, and life. His "no down payment" real estate educational seminars were well-attended across the country, riding the wave of "creative real estate financing" first popularized by Robert Allen in the 1970s.

Beckley produced a television "documentary" about creating personal financial independence, complete with tag pages that listed when and where people could attend free introductory lectures on real estate investing. He purchased half-hour time periods on broadcast stations, viewers attended the free seminars, and many would gladly pay $495 for intensive weekend seminars that further explored the topic.

I approached Beckley about producing his next half-hour documentary, but it wasn't until he heard of the recent success of real estate colleague Paul Simon that I heard from him. A small ad agency called Media Arts had produced a show that was selling Simon's "home study course," consisting of his book and audiotapes, directly on television by having viewers call a toll-free number. Simon's direct response television (DRTV) program was an enormous success. Beckley wondered if I might do the same for him.

I jumped right in and oversaw Beckley's first 60-minute long-form infomercial. Our first test program aired on a small satellite network in late December 1984 and resulted in profits nearing $27,000! All my experience as a producer, writer, and director had not prepared me for the staggering success of that one evening. It opened up a truly dynamic, all-new marketing channel—the long-form infomercial.

Since then, I've gone on to produce dozens of successful infomercials, as well as some that haven't worked. In this book, I'll show you how, why, and where to go for infomercial expertise. I'll give you step-by-step formulas to help you determine whether or not an infomercial is right for your product, goals, and budget. And, I'll openly share with you what I've learned from my mistakes and the secrets of my success.

Timothy R. Hawthorne

CHAPTER

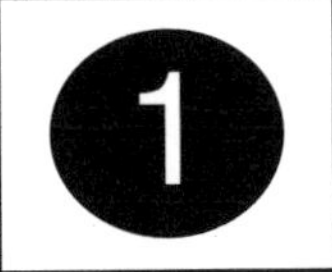

The Power of the Half Hour™

It's past midnight. You can't sleep. You've been worrying about the new product introduction, brand identity, and market share. You grab a couple of cookies and a glass of milk and turn on the tube. Suddenly, there's a likable, credible-looking guy staring you in the face. He's excited!

> Folks! I've got a secret—a secret that can make you money. In the next 30 minutes, I'm going to show you how to get in on one of the hottest direct marketing vehicles ever invented. I'll show you how to select hot products, make commercials that wake up hundreds of telemarketing operators to take orders for your product. Find out how you can make not 10, not 20, not even 50, but $100 million or more in just months. So stay tuned . . .

Then the announcer says, "Welcome to long-form TV—the ultimate direct response vehicle—with your host, Tim Hawthorne. Now sit back, relax, and experience the latest and hottest tips on how to make a fortune in infomercial marketing."

(Music flourish. Fade to black.)

Infomercial Persuasion: How and Why It Works

At 12:30 A.M., I bet I got your attention. Odds are 50 percent of the readers of this book would not change channels. And after a half-hour, I'd have gotten up to 15 percent of you to call and order my product. It's called an infomercial.

Infomercials, also called long-form television commercials, are 30-minute programs designed to motivate viewers to request more product information, place an immediate order, or purchase a product at a retail outlet. The body of the program informs, entertains, builds credibility, explains product benefits, and handles anticipated objections. Several two- to three-minute ads within the infomercial further explain benefits, demonstrate the product, present the offer, and give a toll-free number and other ordering information. Infomercials are aired on national cable networks and local broadcast stations in all 212 markets nationwide. What infomercials do better than any other marketing medium is, in the immortal words of Charles Revson, "Create demand."

Some infomercials may appear silly or tacky to you or me, but guess what? There's a good chance they were crafted particularly to create that image. Why? Because a particular product or audience might not warrant a million-dollar production. Also, the product may be directed at an unsophisticated audience that enjoys an entertaining pitch and whose demographics show an inclination to buy similar products and can afford the price.

Many of these programs—the silly and the sophisticated—have at least one thing in common: they sell products like crazy. Why? Because they respond to the needs, demands, and tastes of their audiences. They provide product information that is important to their audience in a way that is interesting to that audience. How do we know? Because the audience votes—with its orders and its money.

All of these infomercials, at least the successful ones, have one more thing in common. They embody the basic idea that drives all successful infomercials and explains why they have become such an incredibly powerful selling medium:

> The more you tell, the more you sell.

Study after study has reported that the buying public wants more information about the products and services it buys. The character and

EXHIBIT 1.1

Philips's award-winning "The Great Wall" infomercial, produced by TYEE, Portland, Oregon, uses high production values to present its high-end CD-i (compact disk-interactive) system in the most appealing light for its target audience.

sophistication may vary with the product and audience, but buyers do want to know more. And that's what infomercials do—and, of course, sell.

Infomercials in Your Media Mix—A Powerful Combination

Corporate brand managers sometimes tune out when they're presented with the potential advantages of infomercials because they don't want to dump their traditional advertising formats. I'd react the same if, in fact, that was the intention of an infomercial proponent. Frankly, in most cases it would be folly to eliminate spot commercials from a media mix and *replace* them with an infomercial-only campaign. Spots will always have a place in the mix. Over and over again, we've seen the two advertising formats work together beautifully.

Advertisers who have comfortably used traditional spot commercials but are new to the long-form genre must understand the difference between the probable outcomes of their general advertising versus infomercials. Thirty-second spot advertising is usually intended to affect consumer thinking, awareness, and attitude about a product or service. What direct marketers try to do—and what infomercials do so effectively—is lead viewers to the next stage, which is to take action. Infomercials can generate direct and immediate over-the-television sales, inspire viewers to call for more product information or directions to "the store nearest you," or simply send people racing to their nearest mass merchant to buy your product. (See Exhibit 1.2.)

Following are five fundamental reasons to add infomercials to your overall media mix:

1. A half-hour program allows enough time to fully educate and excite an interested audience about your product because they have 30 minutes to take the viewer step-by-step through the persuasion process. Again, the more you tell, the more you sell.
2. The half-hour can be the most effective selling medium when combined with the reach and efficiency of spots. In contrast to spot commercials, your long-form programs will be accountable and measurable.
3. When focused around the same message, long-forms will synergize the entire media campaign and the results will be exponential.
4. Long-form infomercials represent a unique tactical marketing tool—one that will delight retailers and rattle the competition.
5. There is a tremendous potential to produce "breakthrough creative." The entire long-form format begs for head-twisting programs that increase brand identification while making sales.

This is not an argument for or against 30-second spot advertising. Instead, it is a logical case for including both the half-minute and the half-hour program in the same media mix. The results can be quite spectacular, as Exhibit 1.2 illustrates.

Long-form commercials are effective because they tell a product's story in a way that awakens consumer interest, powerfully positions a product, develops a strong emotional tie with viewers, and produces an immediate stream of sales and leads. The content of the program creates greater viewer receptivity to picking up the phone and ordering when the actual commercials appear. And it creates easier viewer identification and understanding of a product when viewers see it in retail stores. Exhibit 1.4 lists examples of infomercials' profitability effectiveness.

EXHIBIT 1.2 How Spot Advertising Compares to Infomercials

30-Minute Infomercial	30-Second Spot Commercial
A full half-hour "theater."	A 30-second "blur."
The most *effective* selling medium.	The most *efficient* reach medium.
Attracts an interested audience from a huge channel-surfing universe.	No way to measure viewers' interest while watching regular programming.
Created as freestanding, sponsored programming.	Dependent upon before-and-after host programming for viewers.
Creative focuses on many product features and benefits	Creative focuses on just one or two features and/or benefits.
Each rating point equals interested prospects.	No correlation between ratings and interested prospects. Ratings reflect only the host show's audience.
Infomercial show ratings are a true measurement of interested prospects.	Rating points eroded due to approximately 39% of viewers who zap commercials.
Enables measurement of resulting direct and/or retail sales.	Difficult to measure spot ad's connection to retail sales.
Content features rich product information in a compelling format.	Little content, mostly imagery within a non-reality-based presentation.
Twenty to 25 minutes of total audience viewing time.	Fifteen to 30 seconds average viewing time.
Fifty percent average recall, up to six weeks later.	Twelve to 15% next day unaided recall.
A new, outside-the-box marketing opportunity.	An old, safe, and conservative marketing tool.
Unique and different—only a $650-million media market.	Clutter crisis—a $35-billion media market.
Due to time duration, maximum impact.	Due to brevity, minimum impact.
Average CPM per 30 seconds of $3.50.	Average CPM per 30 seconds of $10.
Average production budget between $150K to $750K for 30 *minutes*.	Average production budget between $150K to $750K for 30 *seconds*.
Creative breakthrough opportunity unlimited.	Tough breakthrough potential—170,000 commercials aired this year.
Precise accountability.	Little accountability.

EXHIBIT 1.3

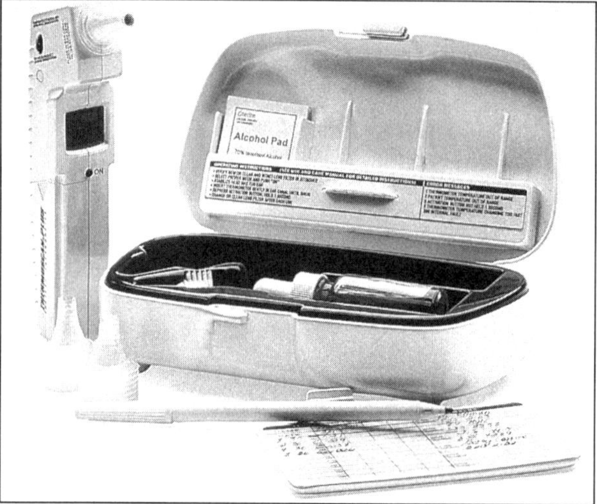

The Thermoscan thermometer infomercial created by Hawthorne Communications generated direct sales and also drove consumers into stores to buy at retail.

EXHIBIT 1.4 Infomercial Profitability Effectiveness

- Creating product sales up to $120 million in just one year and two to five times that if the product is available at retail stores.
- Reaching millions of new customers and presenting a complete product story for an average of 30 cents per viewing household.
- Enhancing, supporting, and filling in where other advertising avenues, particularly spot television, leaves off.
- Generating qualified leads for as little as five dollars per lead.
- Producing annual revenues of more than $25 million for many companies.
- Reducing advertising costs per order and avoiding escalating print and mail costs.
- Rapidly and cost-effectively introducing a new product, or reviving an undermarketed but potentially profitable product.

Over the years, infomercial marketing has firmly embraced time-tested product categories that sell well (see Chapter 3). Infomercial agencies have at their fingertips creative formulas that have proven to stimulate response, as well as historical databases that help predict which media time slots are priced for maximum profitability. Infomercial experts have honed the format and media buying to such a fine degree that immediate sales feedback now allows *daily adjustments* in creative and media strategies, a luxury (or necessity?) that traditional advertising has never provided.

Obviously, infomercial marketing is becoming an increasingly well-respected advertising venue. Today, a great many Fortune 500 companies have followed in the footsteps of earlier infomercial entrepreneurs and benefited from the proven sales and creative strategies of long-form television advertising. However, we should remember that this level of professionalism and acceptance did not appear overnight. In truth, it was about 50 years ago, long before the word *infomercial* had any meaning at all, that the groundwork was being laid by some of the most determined—not to mention successful—people in the annals of salesmanship. The advent of commercial television was integral in this building process, as was the changing regulatory environment. Today's long-form commercial successes are a result of lessons learned all along the way. In the next chapter, we'll take a brief look at the infomercial's rollicking ride from there to here, a testimony to the enduring Power of the Half Hour.™

CHECKLIST

✔ Need to broaden your advertising reach? Consider the potential revenues in airing 30-minute infomercials on national cable networks and broadcast stations in all 212 markets nationwide.

✔ Do you want to sell while you sleep? Millions of households are still watching at midnight, 1:00 A.M., and even 2:00 A.M., and reruns are the weak competition.

✔ Would your product lend itself to an advertising message that provides in-depth information and evokes an emotional response?

✔ Could your television spot ad campaign use a boost? Infomercials and spot ads heighten the effectiveness of your total media mix.

✔ Does your advertising require more time to fully explain product points that will set it well apart from competitors' products?

- ✔ Are you ready to have immediate feedback regarding your advertising effectiveness, not to mention your advertising expenditures?
- ✔ Do you need to build a name for yourself and your product? Infomercials are proven to be effective at promoting brand name and image.
- ✔ Do you need to "create demand"? Long-form commercials do it best.
- ✔ Does "The more you tell, the more you sell" make sense to you?

CHAPTER

A Short History of Infomercials:

From Evolution to Revolution

The Early Years: 1946–1950s

My father was fond of saying, "There's nothing new under the sun." As the following history demonstrates, infomercials are no exception.

Commercial television was launched in the late 1940s and early 1950s by a handful of broadcasters who desperately sought programming to fill their air time. In those days, a typical television station ran only a few hours of network shows in the morning and then again in the evening.

At the same time, in places like Chicago, Philadelphia, and Atlantic City, ad men such as Al Eicoff and Lester Wunderman and entrepreneurs such as the Popeil and Arnold families recognized the profit potential in this new television medium. They were sales, marketing, and advertising experts who had already made their names pitching products on radio, through the mail, in newspapers, or live and in person at state fairs or on Atlantic City's boardwalk.

Together, these sales innovators created the first of what would later be called infomercials. Their television commercials ran anywhere from 5 to 30 minutes or more and featured evangelistic, often outrageous, product presentations. The same fast-paced sales techniques, honed before thousands of fair goers and seaside vacationers, provided a new breed of television entertainment, which—as it happened—also sold products by the millions.

There were no toll-free 800 telephone numbers and no credit cards. A "call to action" was intended to persuade viewers to send a check or scurry on down to Walgreens. Families in cities across America huddled around their new Philco TVs, entranced by the exciting demonstrations of the latest, one-of-a-kind, "must-have" gadget. It was a time of freedom of expression, prosperity, and growth in a new commercial industry, which, as we've learned, would inevitably come under regulatory scrutiny that mandated change. (Exhibit 2.1 shows an early infomercial.)

EXHIBIT 2.1 The "Vita Mix" Show

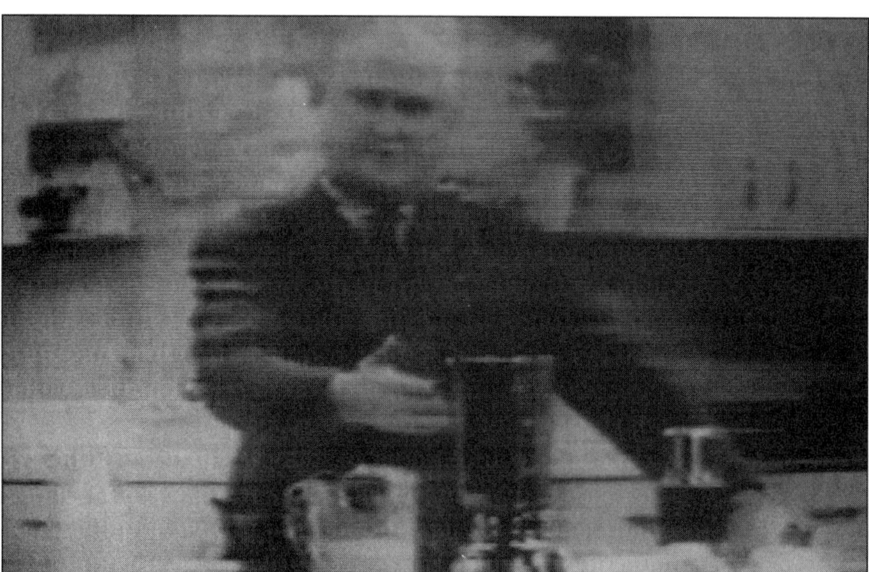

The "Vita Mix" show was among the first infomercials to hit the airwaves in the early days of television.

1962–1984: Limits Offset by Opportunities

As the "Golden Age of Television" took hold, major advertisers began to compete for 60-second time slots that sponsored entertainment programming. Infomercial pioneers were dismayed to find that less and less long-form infomercial media time was available, and what was still available cost a lot more than in the "good old days."

When the quiz show scandals of the late 1950s struck, all eyes turned to the rapidly growing television medium, its crass commercialism and apparent ability to corrupt American youth. Television programming and its sponsors had greatly disappointed the American public, whose trusting eyes and ears had once watched and earnestly believed in what appeared on their black-and-white living room Philcos.

In an effort to stem the tide of public dissent and help salvage commercial television, in 1962 the Federal Communications Commission (FCC) slapped new regulations on the boob tube. From then on, broadcast television stations were permitted to sell a maximum of 12 to 14 minutes of commercial time per hour.

Riding the Waves of Regulations and Innovations

How did the new regulations affect the originators of long-form television advertising? Then, as now, they adapted. A determined bunch, long-form advertisers such as Eicoff and Wunderman adapted to the new FCC regulations by running two-minute direct response commercials. Positioned as "key-outlet" direct response spots, they tagged their brief product demonstrations with the names of three to six major retailers that currently carried the showcased product.

Meanwhile, in 1968, AT&T introduced the next revolution in direct response television (DRTV)—the WATTS line, or toll-free 800 number. Suddenly, a commercial could run nationwide with a centralized inbound phone reception center taking orders from across the country. What a bonanza this innovation from the telecommunications industry gave to DRTV!

The ban on cigarette advertising in 1970 created an enormous gap in broadcasters' ad revenues. Television media time became plentiful and inexpensive as broadcast stations hustled to fill up the commercial air time that was once dominated by cigarette advertisers. Short-form (60-, 90- and 120-second) direct response television commercials multiplied. Products such as records, books, tools, kitchen gadgets, pest control, and arts and crafts proliferated. Any mass-market consumer items that could be demonstrated, provide immediate solutions, and be entertaining were prime candidates for short-form DRTV ad campaigns.

For approximately 25 years, DRTV commercials remained a breed apart from general awareness television advertising. Direct response spots were notorious for being low-budget productions that featured hard-sell, rapid-fire pitches and wildly exaggerated demonstrations and claims made by gregarious hosts relentlessly driving home the sale. As a result, the credibility of DRTV ads left much to be desired among consumers, and deservedly so. Unfulfilled or late orders happened too often, and many of the products that *were* delivered were of such poor quality that purchasers were left disgruntled and disenchanted with the whole business.

In the early 1970s, *Reader's Digest* dared to apply classic general television advertising concepts to short-form DRTV ads in support of its direct mail subscription campaign. One of the first television support campaigns specifically designed to drive direct at-home response, it was executed with style and substance. Thanks to *Reader's Digest*, DRTV spot advertising regained some face and, in the process, succeeded in waking up Madison Avenue advertising executives to this "new" mode of advertising. They began to see the potential benefits of television advertising that actually provided *measurable* response and still maintained their Fortune 500 clients' image-enhancing style of traditional high-quality spot ads.

Record and audio tape clubs, book continuity programs, magazines, and insurance pioneered the upscale DRTV commercials of the 1970s. Time-Life, Columbia House, Publisher's Clearinghouse, Liberty Mutual Insurance, *Rolling Stone, Newsweek, Time,* and *Playboy* covered the airwaves. What's more, they weren't restricted to late-night fringe-time, low-brow hours, but appeared throughout the day and prime time evening.

Creatively, except for their 800-number direct response ordering component, most DRTV short-form ads were virtually indistinguishable from general advertising. The new breed of DRTV programs were shot on 35mm film (providing superior production values) and employed experienced union models and actors in compelling

EXHIBIT 2.2

Reader's Digest's breakthrough campaign of the early 1970s showed how DRTV commercials could project style and substance—and generate response.

fictional story settings. DRTV had finally earned the respect of the advertising "establishment."

The Arrival of Cable

Meanwhile, all was quiet on the long-form front. Only the evangelists for God and nonprofit organizations (WorldVision), not products, were taking advantage of the Power of the Half Hour™ on Sunday mornings. Savvy ad agencies spent millions in media time for these causes, which generated donations that well exceeded their media investments. Though officially designated as religious or not-for-profit programming, there's no doubt that the evangelists borrowed techniques for closing their "sales" from the best boardwalk pitchmen of the 1950s.

The rebirth of long-form advertising was in part due to the advent of upstart, advertiser-supported, national cable networks, such as The Cable Health Network (now Lifetime), USA Network, and Satellite Program Network (now dead).

EXHIBIT 2.3 An Early Sharper Image Multiproduct Commercial

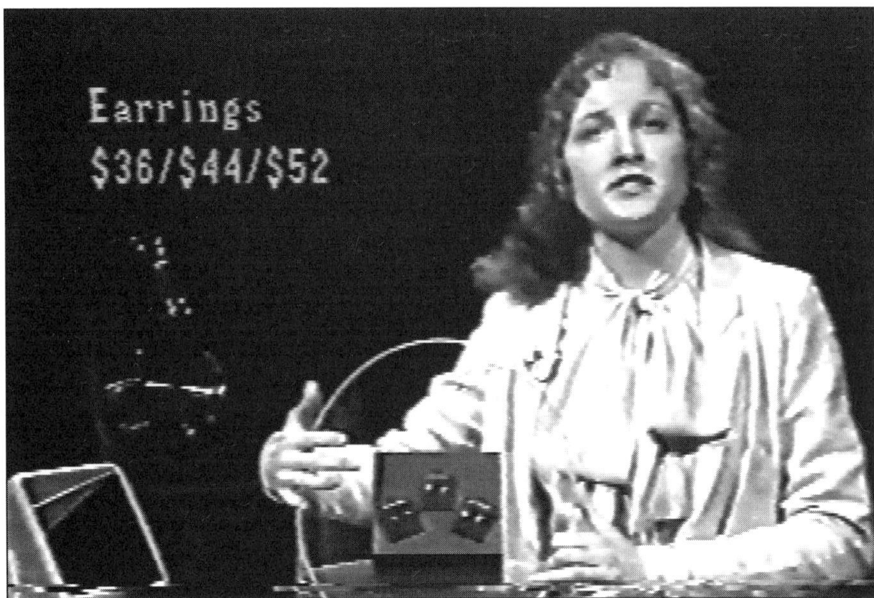

Catalog giant *The Sharper Image* launched the first multiproduct infomercial in 1983.

In the late '70s and early '80s, these fledgling networks were wired into only a small percentage of TV households in the U.S. and were thus ignored by most major advertisers. Like the pioneering broadcast TV stations 50 years ago, they hungered for ad revenues.

Because they weren't subject to FCC rules regulating broadcast commercial time, these cable networks welcomed the cash-up-front advertising revenues from half-hour commercials in the early 1980s.

In 1983, *The Sharper Image* catalog pioneered the multiproduct infomercial on cable, a good three years before Home Shopping Network launched the same format nationally, 24 hours per day, to great success.

Meanwhile, a few risk-taking broadcast TV stations, still under commercial time regulations, began to air infomercials disguised as TV talk shows and "documentaries" for such products as hair restoration formulas and real estate investment seminars.

Most of those infomercial campaigns bear no resemblance to today's programs. They typically ran in a limited number of markets at any one time or had brief runs on cable. It wasn't until the summer of 1984 that infomercials were *officially* born.

1984: The Modern Infomercial Emerges

During the Reagan administration and the accompanying "deregulation fever," the FCC determined that it was time to allow the marketplace to self-regulate TV advertising on broadcast stations. Then in June 1984, the FCC officially removed any commercial time constraints.

The decision to deregulate television advertising was well-founded. If a television station began selling more than 12 to 14 minutes of advertising per hour, viewers would shun the station's programming, which would lower their viewership/ratings and their commercial rates. It would not be in the financial interests of broadcasters to increase commercial time sold.

What wasn't expected from this ruling was how entrepreneurs would use their limited long-form experience on cable to conceive a new billion-dollar industry. Annual sales from this new long-form advertising format have skyrocketed from approximately $10 million in 1984 to nearly $1.5 billion in 1997.

The modern infomercial era really began in the fall of 1984, when Herbalife generated millions of dollars in revenues through their weekly Sunday evening motivational pep rallies on USA Network. It was then that I founded Fairfield Television Enterprises to produce infomercials.

EXHIBIT 2.4 Gross Sales of Products Generated by Infomercials, 1984–96 (in millions)

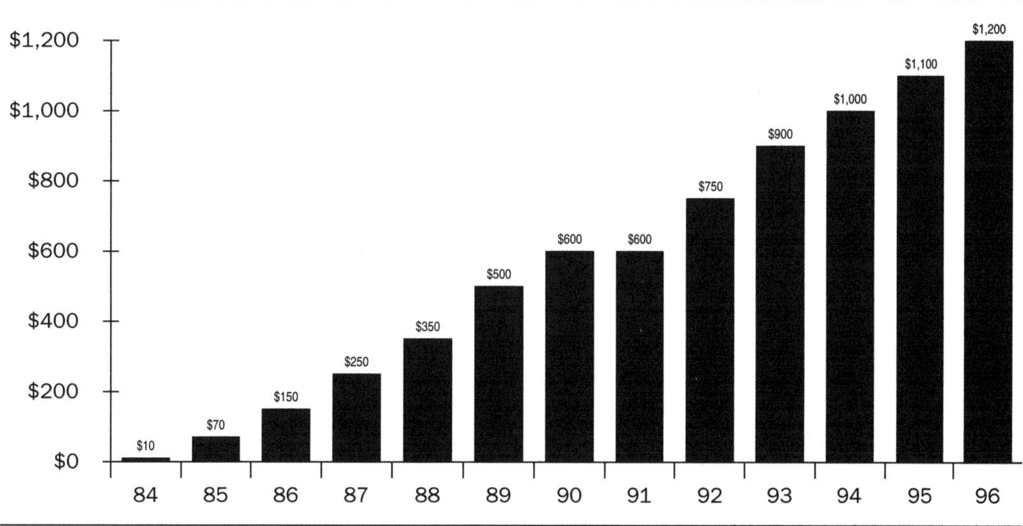

Source: Hawthorne Communications, Inc.

Time Takes Its Toll: The Price of Change

The road to widespread infomercial advertiser and consumer acceptance has been fraught with obstacles. Since they began, long-form television marketers have had to face down accusations of being boardwalk pitchmen of dubious reputation; adjust to regulation, deregulation, and re-regulation by federal agencies; and regain the confidence of a disenchanted TV-viewing audience. Through it all, infomercial advertisers have adapted and thrived and will continue to do so in spite of ongoing challenges, such as those that exist today.

For example, in 1985, an advertiser could purchase cable air time at an average cost of $250 per half hour. Therefore, it was very easy to have a success ratio of $5 in revenue for every media dollar spent. A 10-to-1 ratio was typical with a hot show. Media time on the same cable channels currently is going for as much as $45,000 a half hour. The industrywide cost of media time has ballooned an average of 500 percent. These prices reflect phenomenal increases in numbers of cable subscribers.

In addition, average production budgets have surged from $30,000 per half-hour infomercial in 1985 to $250,000 per show today. Both increases reflect a heated-up competitive marketplace. In 1984, there were 5 infomercials on the air; today an average of 175 infomercials barrage broadcast stations and cable networks during any one week and nearly 500 per year.

Corporate America Plunges into Long Form

You may be surprised and encouraged at how many major advertisers have already entered the infomercial fray. Because of the tremendous growth and positive effects of self-regulation in the infomercial industry, major institutions and Fortune 1000 corporations are already taking advantage of this successful and proven marketing channel (see Exhibit 2.5).

Many well-known retailers, financial institutions, publishers, insurance companies, and manufacturers have used infomercials to showcase their products, as the following sample list shows.

EXHIBIT 2.5 Corporate America goes Long Form

800 Flowers	Fuji	Prodigy
American Airlines	General Motors	RCA
Apple	GTE	Redkin
Arista	Hyatt	Revlon
AT&T	Hoover	Schering Plough
Bank of America	Kodak	Sears
Bell Atlantic	Lexus	Sega
Bissel	M & M Mars	Slim Fast
Black & Decker	Magnavox	SmithKline Beecham
Blue Cross Blue Shield	Mattel Toys	Sony
Braun	MCA Records	State Farm
Buick	MCA Universal	Target
Century 21	McDonalds	The Disney Channel
Christian Children's Fund	MGA/UA	Time-Life
Club Med	Microsoft	Toyota
Coca Cola	Mormon Church	Toys-R-Us
Corning Ware	Nissan	Troybuilt
Dayton Hudson	Nordic Track	UpJohn
Direct TV	Norelco	US Health Care
Estee Lauder	Panasonic	Visa
Fidelity Investments	Paramount	Volvo
Fischer Audio	Pepsi	VW
Fisher Price	Phillips	Wal-Mart
Ford	Playboy	Warner Music
	Procter & Gamble	Weight Watchers

Source: NIMA International/Hawthorne Communications

A Quiet Revolution: Retail-Driving Infomercials

A quiet revolution toward retail-driving infomercials began in the 1990s, marked by a number of significant events:

- In 1990, Time-Life Music successfully entered infomercial marketing as the first Fortune 500 company, and Fitness Quest simultaneously launched new products through infomercials and at retail.

- In 1991, infomercial media costs continued to inflate at a frantic pace due to increased competition for limited "avails" (available time slots), while front-end profits and success ratios decreased and reliance on back-end sales (see Chapter 11) increased. Saturn broadcast the first image-only infomercial (without an 800-number mechanism).
- In 1992, Ross Perot debuted an infomercial designed to educate the nation regarding the details of his United States' presidential campaign. Retailers acknowledged the immense impact infomercials have for "as seen on TV" product categories. Juicers sold through infomercials flew off retail shelves. Major advertisers began seriously considering infomercial campaigns: Braun, Redken, GTE, and Volvo debuted successful infomercials. Corporate infomercials demonstrated their ability to drive sales at retail while paying for part or all of their TV media air time with direct response television sales.

The 10-year history of infomercials has proven that millions of viewers will watch from 5 to 30 minutes of well-produced commercial advertising. Our research shows that consumers are hungry for product information. They are growing increasingly skeptical of commercial advertising. Established brand names are less important to consumers these days. Today, it takes a typical company $150 to $200 million to create a brand. In comparison, after investing approximately $100 million in research and development on her color cosmetics line, Victoria Jackson spent just $15 million in media to create a brand—solely through infomercials—that is now earning tens of millions annually.

When you look all the way back to the 1940s and get a sense of those classic salesmen pitching their wares at fairs and on boardwalks, and then make the leap to the 1990s and infomercial marketing, it's hard to imagine the connection. You have to remember there is no more effective way to sell than person-to-person, as Al Eicoff and the others did way back when. It allows for the greatest flexibility in responding to—and fulfilling—the individual's needs, which is, after all, the essence of sales. But since the event of a mass mail delivery system and electronic media, technology has molded and distanced our selling techniques and strategies from in-person need fulfillment. We've traded off the ability to close a higher percentage of individuals one by one, to close a lower percentage of a mass audience. Thankfully, long-form television advertising provides us with a terrific way to deliver our in-depth sales messages to a vast population of information-hungry consumers.

CHECKLIST

- ✔ Accept and appreciate the infomercial format's colorful beginnings. What went on 50 years ago built the foundation for the tremendous profits you can achieve with the new breed of infomercials.
- ✔ Be prepared to adapt to the ever-changing media environment. Infomercials are still evolving as a viable marketing channel.
- ✔ Look at its history and consider the many uses of long-form advertising.
- ✔ Do your homework on the current infomercial marketplace by consulting with experts in the field.
- ✔ Technology is always introducing new creative ways to apply infomercial selling techniques. Keep your eyes open!
- ✔ Keep these points in mind, and the rewards from your infomercial campaign can be astronomical.

CHAPTER

Determining Product Viability

"The Product is King." Before you even begin to think about the power and glory of your first infomercial, you need to find out whether or not your product or service is right for long-form advertising on television.

How do you determine whether an infomercial will work for you? From my experience in managing more than 150 infomercial campaigns, I have found a number of important criteria to help you determine whether infomercial advertising is right for your product. Even the most successful infomercial products do not satisfy all of the categories' criteria, but all of them are strong in at least a few of them.

We will occasionally find products that have grossed as much as $80 to $120 million in just one year using infomercial advertising. Other products are estimated at grossing between $30 million and $50 million per year. These obviously are dramatic success stories—the exceptions. There might be eight to ten products currently in this category. There is, however, always room for more big winners.

The first weight-loss infomercials appeared in 1986, as did those for skin care and cosmetics. Kitchen gadgets, arts, crafts, auto care, and self improvement, all debuted to huge success in the late 1980s and early 1990s. Now, long-form commercials are used successfully to sell a

EXHIBIT 3.1

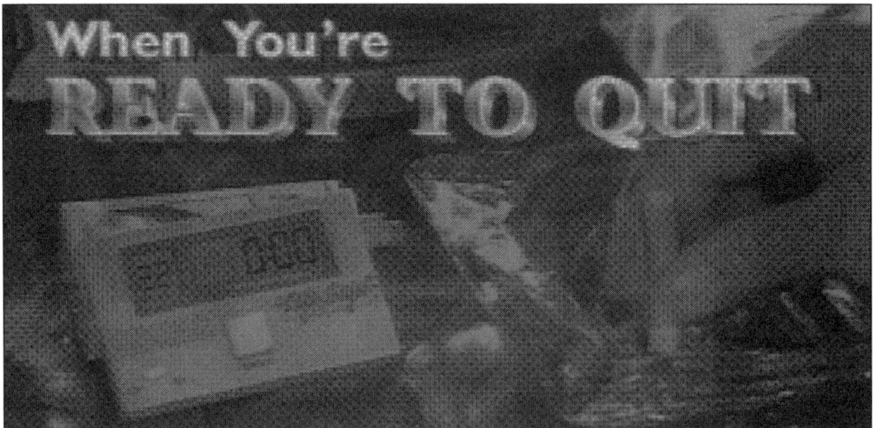

Self-improvement infomercials for products such as DietMate and Life Sign's Stop Smoking programs became popular in the mid to late 1980s.

much wider range of products, including entertainment, telecommunications, pet food, fitness equipment, and even automobiles. All of these product categories, and a variety of other consumer goods and services, have profited through infomercials.

But along with all these winners are the losers. We estimate that less than 1 in 10 infomercials succeeds, partly because the potential profits to be made in this market are so great and partly because it looks so easy to the uninitiated. Unfortunately, many of these marketers have products that are unsuitable for the format. Unsuccessful programs can also be due to a poorly produced program (see Chapter 7) or an ill-executed media strategy (see Chapter 8).

What do you have to lose? You could lose it all—your entire production and media dollar investment. That's why a reputable infomercial advertising agency won't take your product on unless they feel it has an excellent chance of success.

Hot Infomercial Products and Categories

In years past, we've seen some truly exceptional results from marketers whose products were new to the infomercial format. One of these happy campers launched an infomercial for "juicers," resulting in a retail sales increase for the category from $10 million to $380 million in one year. Another—a manufacturer of a name brand hand blender—doubled its sales. And an electronics corporation saw its inventory at retail stores sold out in the fourth quarter of 1993.

Following is a list of product categories and types that have proven to be successful using an infomercial format. When available, approximate gross dollar sales from all sources per product are included (from the 1995 Jordan Whitney *Greensheet Annual Review*). Longer-running shows will show much larger gross amounts.

Apparel

One product category that has had great DRTV success is jewelry, accessories, apparel, and sunglasses—for example, BluBlocker sunglasses. Television sales of jewelry, designer apparel, and other accessories are most often sold on home shopping channels. Retail apparel stores also run long-form advertising on local-access television channels. For instance, Fred Hayman of Beverly Hills, owner of his designer retail store on Rodeo Drive, has successfully marketed Fred

Hayman apparel and accessories via home shopping and long-form advertising.

Automotive

Automobile polishes, waxes, safety and security devices, and car-washing tools have sold well (Exhibit 3.2). In 1995, the leaders in this category included DuraShine ($30 million from all sources), Touchless ($17 million), and DuraLube ($40 million). Other successes include Nissan's "The Art of Buying a Car," and Toyota Tercel's "I Want a New Car."

EXHIBIT 3.2

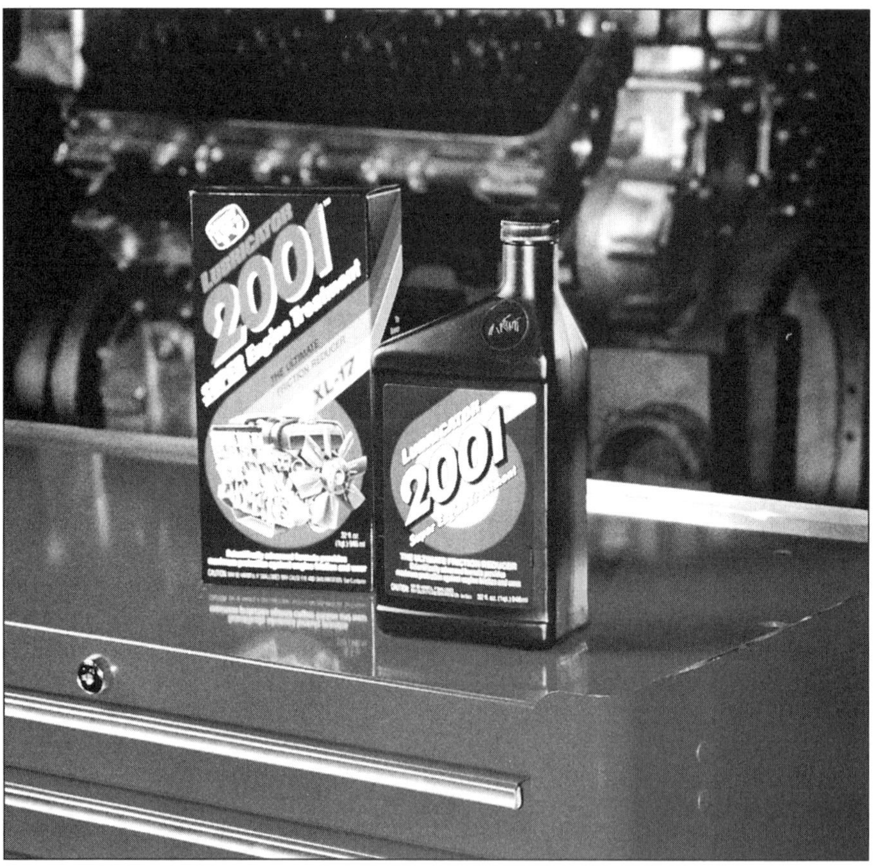

Script to Screen produced this name-brand infomercial for Turtlewax, Inc.'s "Lubricator 2001."

Beauty and Personal Care

Acne treatments, skin care products/regimens, wrinkle treatments, cosmetics, hair care products, teeth whiteners, hair replacement systems, toothbrushes, and hair gadgets have sold well through infomercials. Successes include Murad skin solutions and care ($80 million), Victoria Jackson color cosmetics and instruction ($200 to $300 million), and Principal Secret ($150 million from all sources). Backend and catalog sales contributed greatly to the gross sales of the preceding infomercial products. Other winners are Perfect Smile teeth whitener ($35 million) (see Exhibit 3.3), Perfect Hair ($35 million), Ionic Toothbrush ($7 million), and Sonicare.

Business Opportunities

Infomercials have proven ideal for marketing business opportunities, such as investment programs, real estate, retirement planning, coupon clipping, network marketing, party planning, home-based business,

EXHIBIT 3.3

Guilty-Renker's "Perfect Smile Teeth Whitening System" infomercial was launched when consumer interest in these products was on the rise. The smiling Wheel of Fortune co-host Vanna White served as spokesperson.

EXHIBIT 3.4

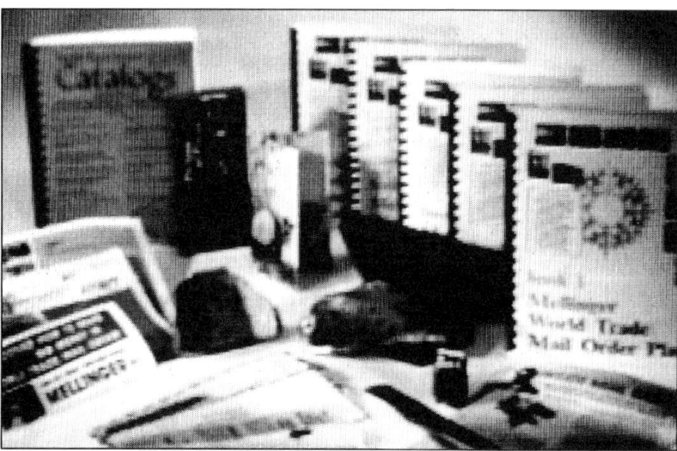

The Mellinger World Trade program expanded on the proven "how to make money" product category.

franchises, lottery systems, contests, and credit cards. Examples include Money Making Secrets, Carleton Sheets, William McCorkle, and the Mellinger World Trade Marketing Course.

Diet, Health, and Fitness

Infomercials have been successfully used for weight loss products and programs, exercise programs, fitness equipment, nutrition, stop-smoking programs, vitamins, remedies, anti-insomnia solutions, anti-cellulite, pain relief, energy boosters, hearing aids, and eyesight improvement systems. These include Healthrider ($200 million), Gravity Edge, Jake Ab & Back Plus ($90 million), Jake Hip and Thigh Machine ($60 million), Power Walk Plus ($25 million), Farewell to Fat ($20 million), ABFlex ($100 million +), Susan Powter ($50 million), Flex & Blast (9 million—TV), Cholestaway ($10 million—TV), AB Roller Plus, EZ Krunch, Workout Warehouse, Six-Day Bio Diet, Aspen Wellness Diet, and Chromatrim.

Fund-Raising and Nonprofit

Nonprofit organizations have successfully used infomercials for donation solicitation. These include Christian Children's Fund, World Vision, and Saint Jude's Hospital.

EXHIBIT 3.5

Nonprofit organizations such as the Christian Children's Fund have been very successful in using infomercials to communicate their mission to supporters.

Kitchen and Electronics

Kitchen items and home electronics marketers have found infomercials very effective in selling bread bakers, food dehydrators, pasta makers, dessert makers, exotic cookers (woks, etc.), knife sets, mixers/ blenders, pressure cookers, roasters/broilers, steamers, slice and dicers, and even home computers.

Examples include Apple's "The Martinetti's Bring Home a Computer," Philips CD-I, Amway "Queen Cookware," Ronco Electric Food Dehydrator ($125 million), Chef's Super Slicer ($50 million), Smart Chopper ($10 million+), Royal Diamond Cookware ($35 million), and Popeil Pasta Maker ($95 million).

Leisure Time

Leisure items that have sold well via DRTV include autographed baseballs, baseball card collections, books on tape, sporting (golf, fishing, tennis) goods and accessories, videotapes, audiotape/CD music clubs or sets, travel clubs, games, toys, travel packages. These include Helicopter Lure ($12 million), Drivemaster ($1.2 million), Killer Bee

EXHIBIT 3.6 Amway International

Corporate giant Amway International marketed its line of "Queen Cookware" via an infomercial produced by Script to Screen.

(golf product) ($4 million), Slice Buster, "Sounds of the 70s," "Dick Clark's Rock 'n Roll Era" (Exhibit 3.7), "Dance Mix USA," Peter Rabbit Videos, Preview Vacation Bargains, Travel Perks, and James Bond videos.

Home and Garden

Infomercials have also successfully sold home and garden products such as all-purpose cleaners, build-it-yourself kits, chamois, cleaning tools, dusters, exotic plants, ladders, garden tools, home restoration, fertilizers, pet care, security devices, specialized cleaners, super glue, vacuums and rug-cleaning machines, workbench tools, emergency first aid supplies, water purifiers, orthopedic beds, mattresses, pillows, and painting systems. Winners include Smart Mop ($108 million), Power Foam ($40 million), and Kal Kan Pedigree Puppy Food.

EXHIBIT 3.7

Time-Life Music's "Dick Clark's Rock `N Roll Era" collection infomercial launched in 1995 by Hawthorne Communications.

Self-Improvement

Infomercials work well for self-improvement products such as teaching aids, instruction on relationships and parenting, crystals, correspondence schools, astrology, memory improvement techniques, handwriting analysis, self-confidence builders, national vocational schools, learn-to-play-piano courses, and how-to-succeed instruction.

Some examples are "Personal Power" ($160 million+), "Making Love Work" ($48 million), "Memory Power" ($48 million), "Passion, Profit & Power" ($19 million), "Men Are From Mars . . ." ($7 million), "Mathemagics" ($3 million), Quick Study Videos, "Dianetics," "Hidden Keys to Loving Relationships," "Hooked on Phonics," and "Where There's a Will There's an A."

Services

Marketers of products such as brokerage services, prepaid legal services, funeral insurance, IRAs, and life insurance have also found infomercials profitable. Some examples include Fidelity, Bank of America, and Blue Cross/Blue Shield.

900 Services

Pay-per-call services have flourished using infomercials, including Psychic Friends Network ($250 million), Your Psychic Experience, and Psychic Connection.

Is Your Product Right for Direct Response Television?

Just about any product has a shot at being successful in direct response TV, but some products are clearly better than others. The first step is to evaluate the suitability of your product in the marketplace, and you can begin that process yourself.

To help in this process, we developed a ten-item system for ranking products that are unavailable at retail and primarily use a one-step offer. This rating guide is shown in Exhibit 3.9. Each item can be ranked "Strong," which is worth three points in the ratings; "Good," which is worth two points; or "Fair," for one point. To use the rating system, review each of the ten items and determine if your product is

EXHIBIT 3.8

The phenomenally lucrative "Psychic Friends Network" series of infomercials hosted by Dionne Warwick sell psychic readings via a pay-per-call 900 prefix number.

worth three, two, or one points on that item. Then enter that rating in the "Rating Score" column at right. When you are done, add up the ratings and get a total. If your total is 20 or more, you have a reasonable chance for success in direct response TV. If it is 25 or more, you may have a very hot product.

Once you complete this form, the next step is to get an expert opinion on your product. If you scored 20 points or more on this self-rating system, you should contact a reputable infomercial ad agency or infomercial marketer and get a preliminary opinion on DRTV marketing feasibility.

The following is a line-by-line explanation of the 10-Point Product Rating Guide:

- Item 1: If your marketing goal is to sell your product directly over the television in a one-step offer, the larger the markup ratio, the greater your chance of success. Markup ratio is determined by dividing *retail price* by *cost of goods.*
- Item 2: Television has the unique ability to reach a mass audience. Its most significant disadvantage is an inability to precisely target specific demographics (much better accomplished via direct mail). Thus, the greater your product has mass appeal, the greater its success potential.
- Item 3: Consumers purchase products to affect change in their lives—to move from a before state to an improved after state. The more your product can visually demonstrate this change and/or use compelling, real people testimonials to support it, the greater your opportunity for profits.
- Item 4: All new infomercial DRTV campaign tests are marketing gambles. Increase the odds on your wager by marketing a product that has some marketplace history.
- Item 5: Everybody loves a deal. Enough said.
- Item 6: Infomercial scripts are often based on simply stating the consumer's *problem;* then the *solution* provided by your product. The bigger the problem that your product can solve, the faster you're headed for the "Infomercial Hall of Fame." Solving a *potential* problem (e.g. personal/home security products) does not generate as much response.
- Item 7: The lower the price ($29.95 minimum), the more accessible your product is to the masses.
- Item 8: Television viewers who are most willing to pick up the phone to order, are also those most influenced by a persuasive, charismatic (but credible!) on-camera product spokesperson.
- Item 9: Upsells and backend marketing can generate 30 percent to 50 percent of your revenues. The more related products you have available for upsell/backend campaigns, the wider your advantage in the infomercial marketplace.
- Item 10: Typically, less than 1 percent of all infomercial viewers actually order the product. If your product is available at retail or soon will be, you can dramatically drive retail sales by capitalizing on the huge *awareness* advertising you create with a successful infomercial.

EXHIBIT 3.9 Top 10 Reasons You Might Have a Good Infomercial Product ©.

Item #	Strong (3 Points)	Good (2 Points)	Fair (1 Point)	Rating Score
1.	Product has 5-to-1 markup or better	Markup less than 5-to-1 but more than 3-to-1	Markup 3-to-1 or less	
2.	Product has mass market appeal	Product has solid research indicating mass appeal	Product appeals to upscale consumer or niche market	
3.	Product easily demonstrable (kitchen gadget, car wax, etc.) "Magical Transformation"	Benefits endorsed by testimonials only (success product, audio tapes)	Product can't be demonstrated and testimonials are weak	
4.	Product has proven retail or direct sales	There is a successful product in the same category	There is no sales history for this product category	
5.	Ratio of value to price very attractive	Value good but price relatively high	Perceived value low, price high	
6.	Product solves a real problem	Product solves a potential problem	Purely preventative product	
7.	Price $49.95 or less/or lead generator	Price $99.95 or less	Price $100 or higher	
8.	Charismatic product expert	Celebrity participation	Non-celebrity talent with proven track record	
9.	Good upsell or back-end potential	Limited upsell or back-end potential	No upsell or back-end potential	
10.	Product is available at retail stores everywhere	Hope to get retail distribution from infomercial demand	Product will not have retail distribution	

Total Rating Points: ______

Rating Types of DRTV Formats

Many clients or product owners are confused about which DRTV option is best for them: infomercials, short form or live home shopping. The fact is they are often complementary. But take note, many products will work in one DRTV channel and not the others.

For example, jewelry is the back bone of TV home shopping sales, comprising as much as 40% of Home Shopping Networks annual revenues. But rarely, if ever, has jewelry been successful in short form or infomercials. On the other hand, self-development products (Tony Robbins) work extremely well in infomercials, okay on QVC and not at all in short form.

To understand why, it's necessary to review the nature of short form and live home shopping.

Short form DRTV commercials are generally 60, 90, or 120 seconds long. Because they are brief DRTV messages, the product needs to be easily understood in this time. Many infomercial products won't work in short form because it takes 8 to 10 minutes to fully explain the product features and benefits. Or if your product sale requires creating an emotional bond ("improve your relationships" self help course) to make the sale, short form will not cut it.

Think about the classic short form products you've seen over the years and how the products' benefits are quickly understood: classic rock music CD's, Clint Eastwood movie collection, Ginsu knives, miracle polishers/cleaners, unique tools, Thigh Master, and so on. Of note, 90% of all short form products are priced at or below $29.95.

Television home shopping (QVC, HSN, Value Vison) is live, 24 hours per day, 365 days per year product pitching. The traditional format has an on-camera host describing a single product's benefits and features for 5 to 15 minutes, on average. Top grossing product categories are jewelry, electronics, fashion and beauty products.

Many products work on home shopping but would fail in short or long form. One major reason is lower marketing costs. Because TV home shopping channels lease their own satellite transponders, their marketing distribution costs are minimal, generally no more than 10% of sales. Consequently they can successfully profit from hawking goods with markups as small as 2 to 1 (50% gross margin).

On the other hand, short and long form marketers must pay as much as 50% of sales for marketing distribution (cost of TV media), thereby requiring product markups of 5 to 1 (80% gross margin) to ensure success.

What should you do? If your product meets all infomercial success criteria, use this DRTV channel first. Then, capitalizing on the high visibility and great ratings long form provides, launch simultaneous short form and TV home shopping campaigns. Of course, you have many other marketing channels to open up (retail, international, etc.) as your campaign progresses, discussed in detail in Chapter 11 on aftermarketing.

Here's a brief "one-glance" checklist for determining which DRTV channel to use first. As in anything, there are exceptions to every rule.

Infomercials

- price point above $30
- need time to understand the product story: features, benefits, uses
- need time to create an emotional bond with viewers
- need to establish consumer recognition in marketplace
- want to drive retail, direct mail, international and all other aftermarketing channels
- failed in short form and home shopping

Short Form

- price point below $30
- products purpose easily understood in one minute or less
- one camera shot sells it all (Ginsu cuts a beer can in half)
- product appropriate for a very hard sell: kitchen gadgets, etc.
- music, videos and continuity products
- limited budget of $100,000 or less

TV Home Shopping

- average to low gross profit margin
- jewelry, electronics, fashion and other proven winners

- closeout stock deeply discounted from retail
- limited product in inventory
- proven winner in short form and infomercials
- product has celebrity spokesperson willing to go live

All Things Considered—Truth in Advertising

In an infomercial, you should put your best foot forward in terms of what a product should be able to do and yet be honest and forthright about its potential for success when used by the consumer. The FTC has required that you be very careful not to oversell the product's magical transformation capabilities in an infomercial. Potential consumers need to understand what their realistic chances for success are. Most infomercial testimonials are "best case" and therefore require an on-screen disclaimer that says "results may vary." But these disclaimers don't necessarily cause a dramatic decrease in sales. Infomercials can still succeed, while upholding the standard of truth in advertising.

CHECKLIST

Use the following checklist to get a handle on the viability of your product for infomercials:

- ✔ Is your product unique?
- ✔ Does your product have a fascinating story to tell about its development and/or use?
- ✔ Does your offer appear as an incredible value—a bargain that can't possibly be missed?
- ✔ Does your product have a history of successful, proven sales?
- ✔ Is the product's markup on cost of goods at least five to one?
- ✔ Does your product have high demand among a mass-market audience? Or can it be targeted to the demographics specific to various vertical cable TV networks?

- ✔ If your product is already available in stores, will a half-hour of demonstration, information, and image-building enhance your sales?
- ✔ Does your product appeal to impulse buying? Does it hit hot buttons? Does it fulfill a dream or solve a common problem?
- ✔ Does your product offer include premiums and bonuses that can motivate impulse buying?
- ✔ Can the product be demonstrated in a visually interesting manner? Can you demonstrate—in an eye-catching and educational fashion—all its purposes and benefits?
- ✔ Does your product have the potential for back-end sales? That is, can you sell related products to your TV customers? Or, will the initial order of your product lead to ongoing consumption or resubscription to your product?

CHAPTER

Infomercial Strategies

You've decided your product is right for an infomercial. What now? There are so many elements in an infomercial campaign that demand specialized knowledge, contacts, and expertise, it's probably best to begin by choosing one of the following two options:

1. Strike a deal with an infomercial/DRTV marketer who will either buy your product wholesale or pay you a royalty of 3 to 10 percent of sales. Using an infomercial/DRTV marketer is a low risk/low return option. These direct marketing firms source their own product, buy their own media, do their own fulfillment and outbound telemarketing. They have an estimated 80 percent share of the infomercial marketplace, and seven of the top ten shows.

2. Pay an infomercial advertising agency for production and media. This option allows you to keep all the profits. Using an agency is the high risk/high return option. Infomercial advertising agencies provide an alternative for product owners who don't want to share their gross sales, as they would have to do with an infomercial/DRTV marketer.

Keep in mind that you're getting into a business that is much like the movie industry, where only one out of ten movies makes money on release: the same hit ratio holds for infomercials.

Who Does What?

Newcomers to infomercial marketing are usually in the dark about what goes into a long-form advertising campaign. Once acquainted with all that is required, they are usually more than happy to hand over their projects to one of the two project management businesses noted above. The chart in Exhibit 4.1 gives an overview of the intricacies of the infomercial process.

Which Format Is for You?

One of your first decisions will be to select a format for your infomercial. Should it be a talk show? Documentary? Lecture format, storymercial, or demonstration show? The predominant infomercial formats are reality-based. Everything in these infomercials is real: real people demonstrating a real product, real testimonials, real product users, and so on. The hot new format, though, is the storymercial, where the body of the show is fictional. Here's a complete list of creative formats to choose from.

Talk Show

Al Eicoff's and Frank Cannella's 1983 "New Generation" hair restoration infomercial was the first to use a talk-show format. This format remains a tried-and-true concept for low budgets and nondemonstrative products. Inphomation's successful "Psychic Friends Network" program is a sample of how this genre has been refined today. "Judge Wapner's Family Legal Guide" (Exhibit 4.2) is another.

Demo Show

Bob Warden (of *Galloping Gourmet* fame) brought the demo show back to the future in 1987 with his Vacuum Sealer. A staple of 1950s DRTV sales, this format is used successfully for lower budget, highly demonstrative products. They generally don't require a celebrity. Success here

EXHIBIT 4.1 Who Does What?

	Inventor	Manufacturer	Product Sourcer	Infomercial/ DRTV Ad Agency	General Ad Agency	Independent Infomercial Producer	Outbound Telemarketer	Media Buyer	Infomercial Marketer	Fulfillment House
Develop Product	✓	✓	✓			✓			✓	
Assess Product			✓	✓		✓			✓	
Assess Competition	✓	✓	✓	✓	✓	✓			✓	
Pricing & Markup	✓	✓	✓	✓	✓	✓			✓	
Set Goals	✓	✓		✓	✓	✓			✓	
Determine Budget				✓	✓	✓			✓	
Determine Audience				✓	✓	✓			✓	
Business Plan	✓	✓	✓	✓		✓			✓	
Set Timeline				✓	✓	✓			✓	
Set Show Format				✓		✓				
Celeb/Spokesperson				✓		✓				
Write Show Script	✓	✓		✓		✓				
Testimonials	✓			✓		✓				
Find Merchant Bank	✓	✓	✓	✓		✓			✓	
Show Production				✓		✓				
Off-line Editing				✓		✓				
On-line Editing				✓		✓				
Music				✓		✓				
Graphics				✓		✓				
Promote Show				✓		✓				
Test				✓				✓	✓	
Track Results				✓				✓	✓	
Inbound Call Handling				✓			✓			
Buy Media				✓				✓	✓	
Tape Duplication				✓						
Tape Distribution				✓				✓	✓	
Rollout Campaign				✓				✓	✓	
Outbound Calls				✓			✓		✓	
Continuity				✓					✓	✓
Backend				✓			✓			✓
Retail Program				✓	✓					
Warehouse Product				✓					✓	✓
Fulfill Orders				✓					✓	✓
Handle Returns				✓					✓	✓
Track Activities, Status Financial				✓	✓				✓	
Ancillary Programs, Short Form, etc.				✓					✓	
Future Planning				✓	✓				✓	

*See Glossary for explanation of above vendor categories.

EXHIBIT 4.2

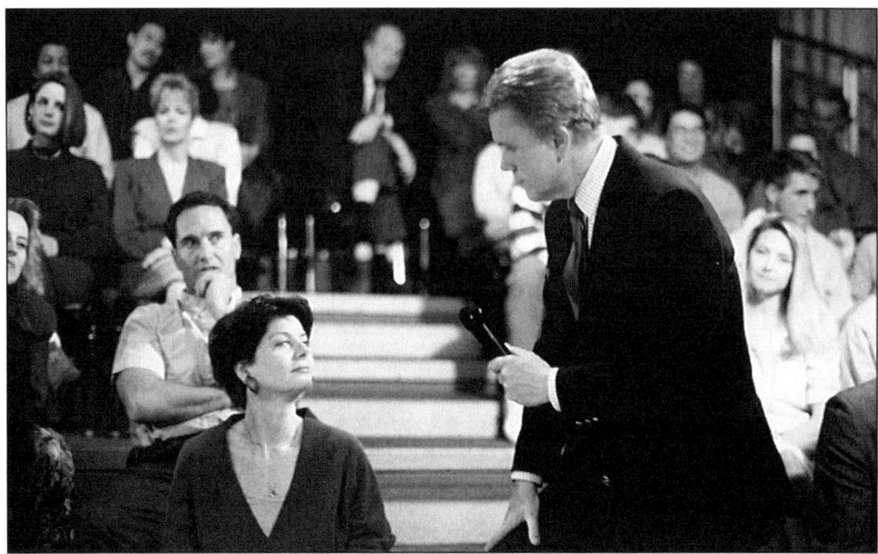

"Judge Wapner's Family Legal Guide" talk-show format infomercial with host Doug Lewellyn aired in 1992.

is driven overwhelmingly by fascination with product demonstration and the presenter's personality.

Lecture Format

Paul Simon was one of the first to use the lecture format, often called the "evangelist show," in 1984. Ed Beckley, Gary Cochran, and Susan Powter later took the format to new heights. This tends to be a low-brow, low-budget approach. Success rests entirely on the evangelistic presenter's ability to be credible, inspiring, and motivational. A good evangelist can sell anything! Since product quality is stressed less than the presenter's personality, this format has the least credibility.

Mass Rally

In 1984, Herbalife made millions bringing together thousands of company distributors in a gigantic auditorium with glitz, glamour, and hyperbole. The mass rally format's "big event" programming creates a commonly shared experience and credibility through mass activity. Historically, this has a lower demographic appeal, but there's room for improvement. The format would have a different, more acceptable flavor, for example, if Ford Motor Company produced it.

Live Auction

In 1986 one of the first live-auction multiple-product infomercials aired. A San Jose flea market sold three or four products per half hour by having an actual audience bid up the displayed product's price, then discounting the price significantly for home TV buyers. This is another low-budget, low-brow, yet entertaining format. Today, several cable networks appear to be successful in using auctions to sell products.

Multiproduct Home Shopping Knock-Off

The multiproduct home shopping format has been attempted many times, both QVC style (laid-back, cool) and HSN style (down-home, chatty). It has never worked for a canned, non-live infomercial. It can be produced upscale or downscale. Even though the home shopping format is risky, expect more attempts at making it work.

Game Show

Forget the game show format. Home Shopping Network tried it in 1989. Maybe in a few years—with truly interactive TV—it might work.

Telethon

Infomercials using the telethon format tend to be as fake and deceptive as the early "investigative reporter-style" Blu-Blocker infomercial in 1987. They use low-budget, low-class productions and are fair game for FTC investigation.

Sitcommercial

Shooting for funny and entertaining, plumber Ralph Ringer and his nutty family attempted to sell Bell Atlantic's call-waiting service using a "sitcommercial" format similar to a situation comedy. Poorly conceived and implemented as a selling medium, it missed the mark entirely. When done well, this format can be very effective. But be very careful: there is danger everywhere.

Documercial

Infomercials with a *60 Minutes* bent are called documercials. This is the most credible format going, although it may be described as the least entertaining. American consumers are hungering for more real product information and more and more Fortune 500 companies are delivering the goods through documercials. This format requires bigger budgets and more time to produce, but offers the most upscale positioning of all the formats.

Video Magazine

The *PM Magazine* version of the documercial is the video magazine. It is more downscale, entertaining, faster paced, and uses moderate budgets. Former *PM* host Jim Caldwell of Future Thunder Productions does it as well as anyone.

Storymercial

TYEE started the storymercial trend with Soloflex. In a storymercial, drama heightens emotion and pulls the viewer in. The storymercial in our industry essentially means a fiction-based format. It has definite upscale potential but can be risky if not done exactly right. The storymercial's softer sell appeals to major brand name advertisers. Generally structured as one to three fictional vignettes in a half hour, their appeal is based on our natural desire to experience the resolution of conflict. (See Exhibit 4.3.)

Brandmercial

The most exciting wave of the future is the *brandmercial*! This is a new hybrid infomercial—where an authentic brand image is created, right along with the *selling mechanics* of DRTV. Brandmercials for Apple Computer and Nissan are exemplary uses of this new breed of infomercial, which is designed to generate leads and/or sales by using an arresting high creative level and production imagery that reflects powerful brand positioning. (See Chapter 15.)

Featuremercial

Coined by a Hawthorne Communications Creative Director, Perri Feuer; it uses behind-the-scenes footage of the making of a TV show or feature film to boost box office sales and television ratings.

EXHIBIT 4.3

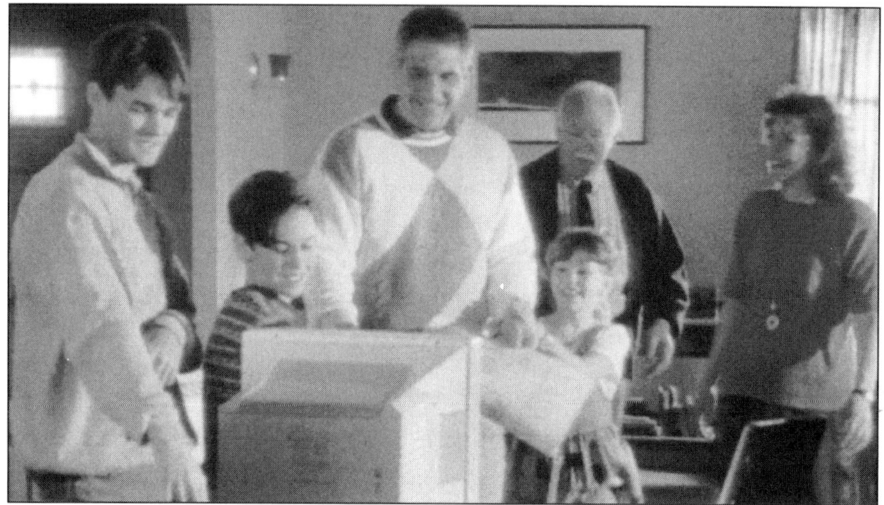

"The Martinetti's Bring Home a Computer," created for Apple by Hawthorne Communications and TYEE, combines both storymercial and brandmercial formats very successfully.

Undoubtedly, every conceivable long-form format will be attempted in the next few years—especially by those madcap Madison Avenue copywriters. I'm sure we'll see music videomercials, mysterymercials, continuing dramamercials, soapmercials, suspensemercials, comedymercials, home videomercials, cartoonmercials, and action-heromercials (Schwartzeneggermercials).

The best formats will rise to the top, but only if the makers know your product and target audience well. (See Chapter 5.) Increasing numbers and types of vertical-market cable channels will help them reach the right demographic for your product.

Classic Offers

Three different types of infomercials are aired regularly: the classic one-step offer, the two-step offer, and retail-driving shows.

One Step

The classic one-step offer infomercial has dominated the industry for 12 years. It's usually used to sell such products as exercise equipment, kitchen appliances, cosmetics, and diet programs priced between $29.95 and $495. The traditional one-step infomercial sells unique products—not available at retail stores—directly to television viewers. Because of today's high cost of media air time, the success rate for one-step offers has fallen from one-out-of-two to one-out-of-ten. These days, infomercials that employ one-step offers are considered high-risk ventures—that is, if the show itself is the only profit-making element.

One-step infomercial marketers have adapted to the increased media costs by attracting customers with the one-step offer and marketing profits on the back end. Back-end programs may include outbound telemarketing, direct mail, continuity programs, home shopping appearances, catalogs, on-line programs, and more. Obviously, high media costs have not deterred one-step marketers: Eighty-five percent of the infomercials on the air today are one-step offers.

Two Step

Reacting to the squeeze on one-step offers, advertisers have begun turning toward two-step offers (or lead generators). Major financial service companies such as Bank of America are using the two-step approach to successfully generate leads from infomercial viewers. If your product is priced over $300 and your one-step infomercial doesn't work, consider changing your offer to generate a lead. You can't get a more qualified lead than someone who has already watched 30 minutes of your sales presentation. Out of more than 175 successful infomercials running now, only 10 to 15 are lead generators. By 2000, I believe 50 percent of all infomercials will be lead generators.

Driving Retail

The retail-driving infomercial is an interesting hybrid of direct response and image awareness marketing. Ninety-nine percent of infomercial viewers will not buy directly in response to television (average infomercial response rate is between .1 and 1 percent). But these millions of nonpurchasing infomercial watchers are primed to purchase the product at retail or through catalogs, their preferred buying channels. Corporations such as Braun, Mattel, and Magnavox, that traditionally marketed strictly through retail, are using infomercials to drive their retail sales.

EXHIBIT 4.4

Magnavox's storymercial was designed by TYEE to generate leads and drive retail.

Infomercial Retail Strategies

Like the many other myths related to long-form advertising, conventional advertising "wisdom" has typically viewed infomercials as competition to sales at retail stores. We know now that view is far from the case. Infomercials boost retail sales. Typically, we project average retail sales increasing anywhere from two to five times the sales generated directly over television.

Another reason infomercials don't compete with retail sales has to do with price. The product on television is typically more expensive. We purposely add premiums to the TV offer so the viewer pays $10 more on television than if he or she bought it at retail. Of course, there's $10 more value with the infomercial product, too. Millions of infomercial viewers will see a product on television for $59.95 and won't buy it. But if they see it at their local KMart for $49.95, they snap it up.

And that's why the number of people who buy a product at retail will always be significantly greater than those who buy through an infomercial: there are many more retail outlets than there are television stations or opportunities to watch an infomercial.

Remember "juicer mania" in 1991? Juicers went from a $10 million retail category to $380 million in one year because of infomercials.

There were as many as five different juicer infomercials on-air at one point, all of them selling lots of product through direct-over-television sales, as well as driving retail sales dramatically. To this day, juicers are still a popular appliance.

Philip's Electronics' compact disc interactive system is another example. Philip's tried to sell its CD-I for two years, spent $12 million in spot television and print, and could not move the product at retail. After the company conceded the failure of spot commercials for its product, Philip's created a $6 million infomercial campaign that cleared retailers' shelves in just three months.

What about My Other Advertising?

Infomercials effectively supplement a company's existing advertising media mix. Working in concert with your other advertising avenues, infomercials can bolster consumer awareness of your product and provide more information and product benefits than are often possible in other media. By running infomercials on national cable and broadcast television, a product's story and benefits can be shared with millions of additional prospects. Direct sales are made in direct proportion to the number of television viewers. The cost per lead (CPL) or cost per order (CPO) can usually match or beat other direct marketing channels, such as direct mail or print ads.

As you plan through your infomercial campaign, there are a number of springboards built in to further bolster the success of your program. *Back-end* direct marketing works off your infomercial, often resulting in profits that are two to seven times those of up-front sales. *Continuity programs, upsells, cross sells, list management,* and more build in profits well beyond your initial expectations. (See Chapter 12.)

CHECKLIST

- ✔ For best results, begin by selecting either an infomercial/DRTV marketer (low risk/low return) or an infomercial advertising agency (high risk/high return) to plan and manage your infomercial campaign.
- ✔ If you have a great hard goods product that can be sold in a one-step offer—don't hesitate to get into this explosive marketing

channel—the window of opportunity is still open, but not for long. If you do opt for this traditional one-step infomercial direct-sell offer, plan to offset high media costs by making profits on the back end.

- ✔ If your product is priced over $495, chances are the one-step infomercial offer won't work. In this case, go for the two-step offer designed to generate leads.
- ✔ Don't be afraid to use your infomercials to drive retail sales. More and more Fortune 500 companies are doing just that with great success.
- ✔ Carefully consider the right format for your infomercial (talk show, demonstration, storymercial, etc.). Check out results of past shows and trust the experience of your infomercial agency.
- ✔ Use infomercials to enhance and supplement your company's existing advertising media mix.
- ✔ If you represent a company that can use 30 minutes to tell your product's story in a fascinating way to generate leads, promote image, or drive retail sales, look seriously at launching an infomercial—now!

CHAPTER

Identifying Your Target Audience

Since 1984, thousands of infomercials have been produced. In 1995, television direct response sales—including 24-hour home shopping and 60- to 120-second spots—earned more than $4 billion. More than $1 billion of those revenues will be generated by infomercials, surpassing the once dominant short-form direct response television format.

Most infomercial products have a life cycle of 9 to 18 months. But a select few don't burn out and are still on the air two to five years after rollout. The reasons for such endurance include a quality product, imaginative production, and shrewd media buying. And don't forget the importance of smart, focused targeting.

Ninety-nine percent of all households in the United States (95.8 million of them) have televisions. The challenge in this era of increasingly targeted marketing is in selecting winning products to be direct marketed via this most massive of all mass marketing channels—the home television.

Learn from Others' Experience

You already know a little something about your product. Chances are, if you've come this far, you have an idea of what kind of customers are likely to buy your product. Now, you need to do a bit of digging and probing to narrow down your ideal infomercial marketing avenues. A good place to start is in the past. How about examining my picks for the "Top Ten Infomercials of All Time"?

- Soloflex Heroes—an upscale demonstration format advertising fitness equipment
- Jetstream Oven—a classic in-studio demonstration of a kitchen appliance (see Exhibit 5.1)
- Victoria Jackson Cosmetics—demonstration of cosmetics in a talk show setting
- Richard Simmons' "Deal-A-Meal"—talk show/demonstration/documercial for a diet plan

EXHIBIT 5.1

American Harvest's Jetstream Oven show, hosted by company president David Dornbush (shown here with celebrity Vickie Lawrence) is the classic demonstration infomercial and has proven broad audience appeal.

- Amazing Discoveries' Auri Car Wax—dramatic demonstration of a car care product
- Time-Life's "Rolling Stones" Music Collection—a documercial on pop music icons
- Lifesign Stop Smoking—a documercial on how to quit smoking
- Anthony Robbins' Personal Power—a documercial talk show on motivational topics
- "The Martinetti's Bring Home a Computer"—storymercial lead generator for Apple's Performa computer
- Healthrider—a breakthrough demo show including music video montage sequences

Some of these programs, or updated versions of them, have been running for years. You've probably even seen most, if not all, of them. Does your product or infomercial bear any resemblance to these programs? If so, find out everything you can about the production, the media buys, the strategies, and the history of the similar program. And, try to follow their proven lead!

Research and Focus Groups

One way to try to predict the effectiveness of advertising is through focus groups. The use of focus groups comes from traditional image advertising. Infomercials have some similarities with and many differences from traditional image ads. Therefore, focus group research has both benefits and limitations when applied to infomercial research.

First we have to make the distinction between the two elements of an infomercial that relate to research and focus groups:

- The offer package
- The creative concept

The offer package involves testing the product price, bonuses, "call now" motivators, packaging, and premiums in front of focus groups before the actual production. Is the product and price point attractive enough to motivate someone to pick up the phone? The knowledge you gain from this kind of testing is extremely useful.

The creative concept is much more difficult to test for infomercials. It's almost impossible to use storyboards to communicate to a focus group what a 30-minute viewing experience will be like, create a feeling for the product, and determine whether or not they're going to buy that product. This is because execution can make all the difference. Focus group feedback of a rough video edit, though, can sometimes provide helpful insights. But the true test of an infomercial is in the real marketplace—on air.

Testing Response to Your Infomercial

You can, however, run tests of two or more versions of your infomercial to determine which works best.

That's why we advise clients to budget a $40,000 media test and to reserve $20,000 to $50,000 just for re-edits. After the $40,000 test, you not only see the results, but you can call viewers and ask, "What did you like about the infomercial? What product benefits do you recall the most?" The answers can help you craft a more effective infomercial. You might use A/B split testing to test the offer, as well. Testing different price points and premiums is easy. Just run two or more versions in the same time slots under the same conditions—as close to identical as possible. Warning: be sure to test just one variable—say, the premium—at a time.

You can even use inquiries from people who don't buy the product. Call them to find out why they didn't place an order. This provides excellent immediate feedback that allows you to understand exactly what needs to be adjusted in the selling message. Why not use it?

Where Are Infomercials Playing?

Infomercials now run on more than 44 major cable networks, many reaching over 60 million homes. They air on over 900 broadcast stations in every television market and often attract ratings of one to four percent of the total TV homes. There are several 24-hour-per-day infomercial networks on the air today, more are on the horizon.

Infomercials are not just for night owls (although 15 percent of all homes have their televisions on at 1:00 A.M.!). Infomercials routinely air between 7:00 A.M. and 6:00 P.M., seven days a week, with the heaviest rotation on weekends. *Fifty million* households per week tune in.

Targeting Your Demographics

Where is the best place to find your target audience out there in TV-Land? It seems much easier to locate specific kinds of viewers/buyers since cable television has made its mark!

- Have a financial product? Run your show on CNBC.
- Have a yuppie-appeal product? Try Nick-at-Nite.
- Have a youth-oriented or entertainment product? Use VH-1.
- Have a female-oriented product? Make a beeline to Lifetime.
- On broadcast television, if you have an upscale product such as an expensive golf club, consider running on Saturday and Sunday daytime only.
- Have a downscale product? Late night, Friday through Sunday, is the way to go.

Granted, these are pretty broad demographic/psychographic strokes. Accordingly, my recommendation is: If you want to maximize sales by running a show in every U.S. television market—select a product with broad appeal.

Consider the following when contemplating your ideal viewing audience:

- Infomercial product purpose and position self-selects your viewer/prospect demographics.
- 45 percent men, compared to 55 percent women, frequently buy infomercial products.
- The average age of infomercial customers is 35 to 45 years old.
- Consider the average income/education of your prime prospect.
- Look to broadcast for mass appeal.
- For narrowcasting, consider CNBC, Lifetime, VH-1, and sport channels for specific vertical audiences.

- Consider latenight versus weekend time slots—when will your customers be watching?
- Consider *prime-time buys*—which reach more women and broader audience but come with a higher cost per order, versus *fringe air times*—which reach a smaller audience comprised of more men than women but are more cost effective. Which makes the most sense for your product?

When Are Infomercials Paying Out?

Timing, as they say, is everything. That may be a stretch in some cases, but should not be ignored when seeking your infomercial target audience. Depending upon the nature of your product, some infomercials won't work on any channel at particular times of the year. The opposite also holds true: Some infomercials have a much better chance at zeroing in on their buyers, say, in the summertime or during the holiday season. Exhibit 5.2 shows which infomercial products traditionally sell best at different times of the year.

The Flip Side of Cable

Hang onto your couch cushions: According to a study of cable subscribers, two-thirds (68 percent) of cable subscribers surf through channels (flip through the channels until something catches their eye) while they watch television. Of those who surf, two-fifths (43 percent) mostly watch one program but flip channels during commercials; one-quarter (26 percent) truly surf for all it's worth, and 7 percent of all adults watch multiple programs at the same time. Channel surfing is a national pastime.

On the average, surfing subscribers flip the channel 7.2 times in a half hour. One in ten (12 percent) surfing subscribers scan their channels 11 or more times per half hour. Premium subscribers (flipping channels an average of 8.1 times per half hour) are more active than basic-only subscribers, who report a mere 6.3 flips per half hour. Since infomercials rely heavily on capturing surfers for their audience, you have just 2 to 10 seconds to get a viewer's attention. So don't let your infomercial production flag for even a moment.

Cable and the remote control have brought a new equality to all

EXHIBIT 5.2 Hot Infomercial Products by Season

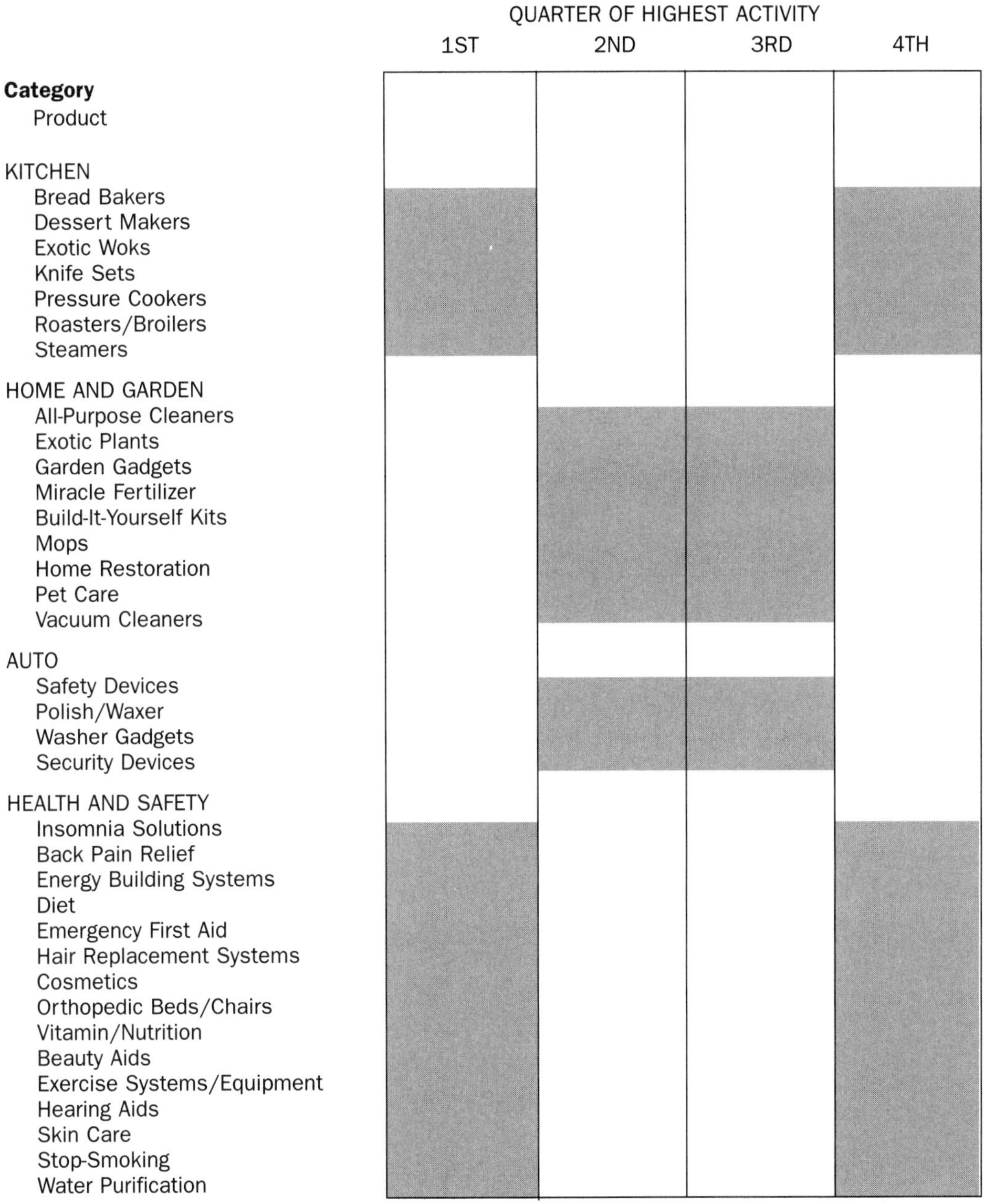

Category Product	QUARTER OF HIGHEST ACTIVITY 1ST	 2ND	 3RD	 4TH
KITCHEN Bread Bakers Dessert Makers Exotic Woks Knife Sets Pressure Cookers Roasters/Broilers Steamers	■			■
HOME AND GARDEN All-Purpose Cleaners Exotic Plants Garden Gadgets Miracle Fertilizer Build-It-Yourself Kits Mops Home Restoration Pet Care Vacuum Cleaners		■	■	
AUTO Safety Devices Polish/Waxer Washer Gadgets Security Devices		■	■	
HEALTH AND SAFETY Insomnia Solutions Back Pain Relief Energy Building Systems Diet Emergency First Aid Hair Replacement Systems Cosmetics Orthopedic Beds/Chairs Vitamin/Nutrition Beauty Aids Exercise Systems/Equipment Hearing Aids Skin Care Stop-Smoking Water Purification	■			■

EXHIBIT 5.2 (Continued)

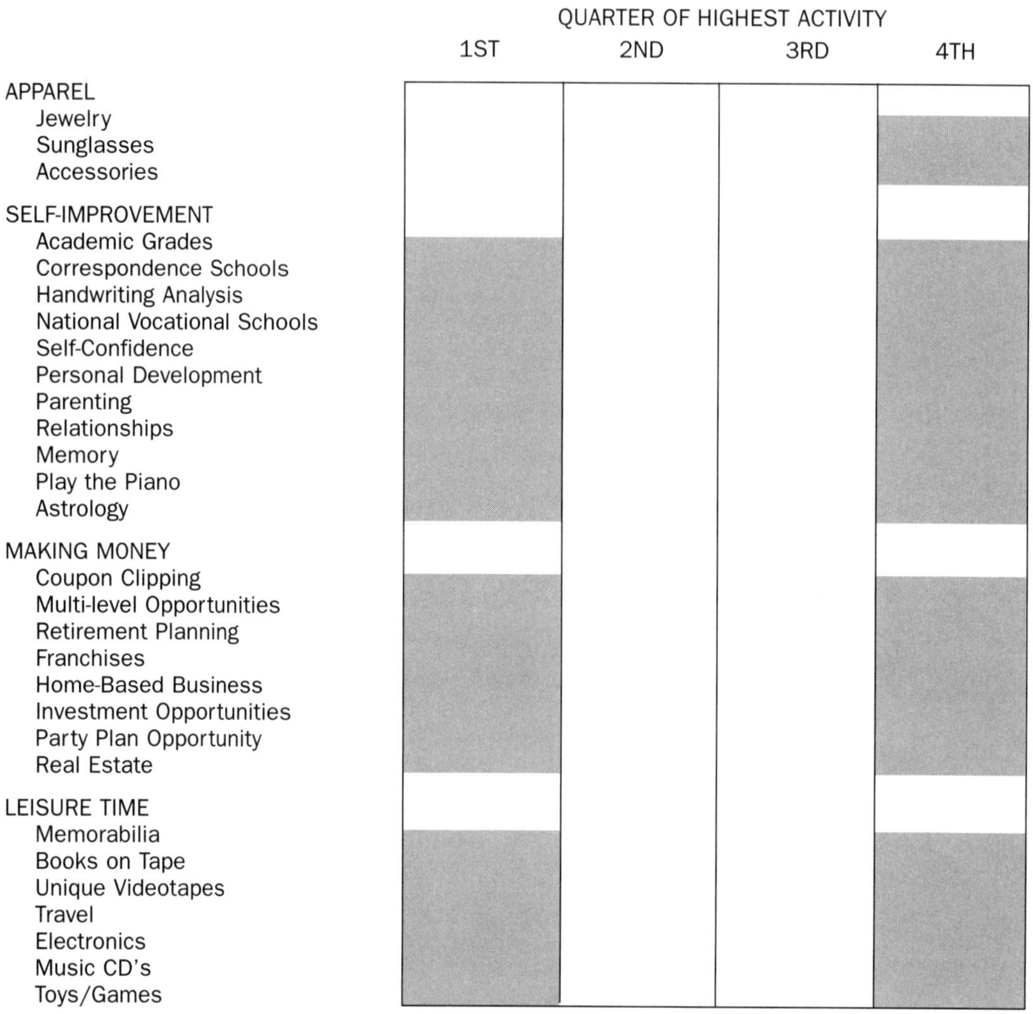

QUARTER OF HIGHEST ACTIVITY

1ST 2ND 3RD 4TH

APPAREL
- Jewelry
- Sunglasses
- Accessories

SELF-IMPROVEMENT
- Academic Grades
- Correspondence Schools
- Handwriting Analysis
- National Vocational Schools
- Self-Confidence
- Personal Development
- Parenting
- Relationships
- Memory
- Play the Piano
- Astrology

MAKING MONEY
- Coupon Clipping
- Multi-level Opportunities
- Retirement Planning
- Franchises
- Home-Based Business
- Investment Opportunities
- Party Plan Opportunity
- Real Estate

LEISURE TIME
- Memorabilia
- Books on Tape
- Unique Videotapes
- Travel
- Electronics
- Music CD's
- Toys/Games

Source: Hawthorne Communications

the different networks. The wider variety of available channels creates a favorable environment for surfers. Every one of those channels now becomes fair game for surfing, which benefits infomercial advertisers because they have the opportunity to be seen more often by more viewers.

The more challenging aspect of increased numbers of cable channels and surfers is: How do you find and buy air time on the channel that not only has the viewers you're looking for, but can hold onto them long enough for them to catch your infomercial and respond? The answer lies in doing your homework: by asking the experts and by calling the networks (see Broadcast and Cable listings in the Appendices). Keep in mind that not all networks accept long-form infomercial advertising. Most important, you maximize success by crafting the most compelling infomercial message ever to hit the air waves. This brings us to the all-important creative process, which will be covered in the following chapter (Chapter 6).

CHECKLIST

- ✔ For a winning, long-running infomercial, be smart when you're looking for your target audience.
- ✔ Remember: surfers are the bane of 30-second image advertising but a boon to infomercial marketers.
- ✔ Check out my favorite infomercials of all time. Find out everything you can about their production, media buys, long- and short-term strategies. Learn how they managed to find—and land—their ideal audience.
- ✔ Conduct focus group research on the *offer package* as well as the *creative* concept of your infomercial.
- ✔ Run tests on infomercials you've created to determine what works and what doesn't; then adjust or tweak them to deliver better results.
- ✔ Because of the increasing number of cable channels and surfers, remember your infomercial has only two to ten seconds to capture a viewer's attention.
- ✔ Keep in mind that not all cable networks or broadcast stations accept long-form infomercial advertising.
- ✔ Proliferating cable networks means better targeting opportunities but smaller audiences.

CHAPTER

Infomercial Creative Components

I was on a one-year leave from college and traveling through Africa. I was going somewhere; I don't remember exactly where. Maybe Gondar, Lalibela, or Massawa. The bus station, a large dusty square in the center of town, could only be reached by walking a gauntlet of peddlers and merchants, squatting next to their foods and wares. Sandals made from discarded tires, walking sticks, cigarettes, colorful shawls, fruits. Shouts of, "Foreigner, buy this!" I wanted none of it. I just wanted to find and board my old, diesel-smoking bus and depart for a cool refuge in the Abyssinian Mountains of Ethiopia.

Divine Inspiration

As I wound my way through that market maze 25 years ago, I learned a memorable lesson in direct marketing. A hand was thrust in front of me, holding a beautiful traditional earthenware plate with six moist, glistening sections of an orange.

> "Mister," the woman said, "Wouldn't you like to try some wonderfully sweet orange?"

She was beautiful; maybe 18 or 19 years old, draped in a flowing white cotton highland dress splashed with traditionally colorful Ethiopian Coptic designs.

> "Just picked this morning!" she said. "So fresh. Please, try a sample. They'll make you love life!"

I bought one.

After what seems like a lifetime later, I have never forgotten the beautiful woman selling oranges as her ancestors must have done for 2000 years.

It was my first encounter with a classic direct marketing pitch.

Infomercial Creative: The Guiding Light

We don't call it "the pitch" today. It's "the creative." What role does "creative" play in infomercials? Creative guides the entire infomercial process from concept to rollout and beyond. Words, images, people, pictures, emotions, sales, action, attention, market research, product information, value, and much more are the province of the creative minds behind infomercials. Their job is to gather together all these pieces and provide an intelligent, solid framework from which an infomercial is born.

Long-term success in selling stems from answering one basic question: What need does this individual have that I have the capability to fulfill? As long as the infomercial marketers focus on this goal, the commercial exchange of goods and services becomes a natural, three-dimensional process, much like life itself. These dimensions are characterized by the fundamental energies of *need* (motivation), *response* (presentation), and *result* (relationship). How do these manifest themselves in the selling process?

As marketers, we identify an individual's *desire for more* as needs; needs that motivate and initiate the buying impulse. Need for more security (power, control, confidence, self-preservation, fear-of-loss); more wealth (greed, acquisition, something-for-nothing, bargain hunger); more love (vanity, glamour, self-esteem, exclusivity, conformity, guilt) and, of course, the need for more pleasure (sex, pain relief, power tools and kitchen gadgets!). It's these basic needs that fuel the selling opportunity. Such needs seek fulfillment and we are here to present solutions and, in the process, establish a relationship.

As direct marketers, our job is to identify qualified, motivated prospects and make our presentation for a close. If we've done our job, we will fulfill the prospect's need. The prospect will become a customer and we are now in a relationship. The third dimension of the selling event becomes manifested.

Twenty-five years ago, I bought an orange on a dusty square in Ethiopia—and I didn't even know I wanted one. But great presentation and a unique promise motivated me to buy. Two decades later, I can still remember loving life as I tasted that orange while the bus bumped along the mountain roads. That's selling!

Meticulous Engineering of the Creative

Novice infomercial producers have a treacherous minefield to navigate toward success. However, meticulous engineering of the creative pays off in a big way.

When you're writing a traditional documentary or corporate communications video the purpose of your script is primarily to present information in an orderly fashion. But when your goal includes presenting information *and* motivating someone to take immediate action, you're in an entirely new stratosphere of scripting and crafting.

Because channel surfers might discover your infomercial at any point during the program, every single moment of your 30-minute script is important. That's a lot of moments that must be crafted to perfection.

Channel surfers and other sedentaries are the viewers who initially watch and respond to infomercials. We have from 2 to 10 seconds to catch their attention, that's all. Throughout your entire 30 minutes, you have to figure out a way to snag a viewer's attention at any point along the way. You can't let up for a moment. Just as there is a science to writing and laying out successful catalogs and direct mail letters, great infomercials require their own special kind of art and science. A keen knowledge of the factors critical to an infomercial's success is imperative.

Key Success Factors for Infomercial Creative

The most important key success factor for the infomercial is the time that you take to talk about the product. The more time viewers spend with the commercial message, the more likely they are to buy. The more you tell, the more you sell. The longer they watch, the longer you're in a relationship, and the greater the chances of closing the sale. While time is the greatest asset you have working for you—right out of the gate—with infomercials, it is the complex set of creative elements that fill that time that makes or breaks your program. Your creative determines how much time your viewer gives to your message.

Creative Fundamental—Selling Cycles

In the first segment, which is 8 to 10 minutes long, we tell the entire story about a product, and then we give people a chance to order the product.

This is the basic long-form selling cycle—8 to 10 minutes—and is repeated (though not verbatim) three times. Is there something magical about an 8–10 minute segment? Why not two 15-minute cycles? A few reasons. First, in my experience, it only takes 8 to 10 minutes to cover virtually any product's major selling points. Second, North American viewers are accustomed to 8 to 10 minutes of network program entertainment before commercial interruption. Third, research indicates about half of infomercial viewers watch 20 minutes or more; the other half watch 10 to 20 minutes or less. By completing a selling cycle in 10 minutes, viewers who only watch that amount get the opportunity to order. Fourth, the all-important channel surfer might join an infomercial in progress, 10 or 20 minutes in. A short selling cycle can inform and move a late arrival to order even at the program's end. Fifth, repetition can reinforce selling points.

No matter what creative format you use, whether documercial or storymercial, the basic content of each selling cycle is the same.

Here are three content outlines.

- A.I.D.A.: capture their Attention; create Interest; instill Desire and motivate them to Action.
- Compose a symphony of 8 to 10 one-minute movements comprised of product features, benefits, uses (demonstrations), credibility (testimonials), guarantees, offer details, requests to order.
- Finally, the classic "problem/solution." Remind viewers of a common problem and how your product solves it.

During the second 8- to 10-minute segment, tell people the same story—with the benefits and features—in a different fashion. Then give viewers another opportunity to order. Do this one more time in the third segment. About 2 to 5 percent of the viewers are motivated to order after watching just the first segment. Another 2 to 5 percent order after the second segment or ordering opportunity, but the majority of viewers will wait to order until after the third segment. Fundamental knowledge of selling cycles, along with the following items, are essential when crafting the creative for a successful infomercial.

Infomercial Creative "To Do" List

1. Create a sense of urgency to buy. Although you have 30 whole minutes to romp around in, you must remember that you have only seconds to attract viewers at any point during the infomercial. Tried and true "Order Now Motivators" are old tricks of the trade, though certainly not effective for all products. Some classics in infomercials include, "If you call within the next hour you'll receive a special bonus!" or "Two for one!" or "Immediate discounts!" or "The first 100 callers will receive . . ." and, of course, Ron Popeil's famous, "If you promise to tell a friend about the dehydrator . . . ." They might not work for your product, but they're a good place to start.

And, remember, whatever you offer, you must deliver. What if that's not possible? Then don't make the offer. Leave it out.

2. Establish presentation and product credibility. Whatever the product, it's important to remember that an infomercial's success is based on credibility. It is a purchasing decision that is emotionally sparked but rationally concluded. Infomercial creatives need to attract viewer attention through entertaining and well-paced story lines or information. Once attracted, prospective buyers must trust in the quality and promise of the product being sold.

3. Use a *true believer* as the commercial spokesperson. After the quality and the benefits of each specific product, the presenter is most critical to the success of the majority of infomercials today. A powerful on-camera product presenter can absolutely make the difference between success or failure. The only way to increase the power of that presenter is if he or she has used the product and believes in it. That combination of professional skill and personal conviction—the real true believer—will produce a powerful statement for your product and its benefits.

Again, however, use this approach only if it's right for your product.

4. Product is king. Don't stray too far from the all-important product. All your copy should tie back to product features, benefits, and uses. Identify the primary buying motivator: *love* (self-esteem, vanity), *security* (power, fear of loss), *acquisition* (greed, wealth), *pleasure* (pain relief, entertainment).

5. Showcase an irresistible offer. Surprise them. Build value. Give them more than they expected. But wait, there's more! (You don't have to say it, but do it in what you're offering.) People love a bargain. Bonuses, premiums, discounts, coupons. "Free" is the strongest word in direct marketing. But don't give them too much; it's confusing and damages credibility. (Why are they giving me so much? What's the catch?) During the scripting, I encourage my writers to compile their list of hooks, content points, and key selling words, phrases, and images. Every product has unique properties that are critical to the essence of communicating the product's benefits. For example, how could you possibly resist buying Time-Life Music's "Rolling Stone Collection," which is digitally remastered, unavailable in stores, *and* compiled by the editors of *Rolling Stone* magazine? (Exhibit 6.1.) It's a once-in-a-lifetime offer!

6. Emphasize information/content over entertainment. Don't *over*-entertain and *under*-sell. The entertainment factor should never take the viewers so totally away from their real world that it hampers their ability to make a rational decision to buy. For example, Bell Atlantic produced "The Ringers," a fictional sitcommercial, to generate leads. But it was too entertaining. A reality-based infomercial could have generated at least twice as many leads at half the production cost. People order when logic justifies an immediate response. Too much entertainment distracts them from making a logical decision.

7. Pacing is everything. Novice infomercial writers don't get it. It's a symphony of sight and sound: benefits, features, uses, success stories, credibility builders, expert testimony, research, guarantees, offer details, call to action. Repeat the cycle three times in a half hour. One short line, then a broad paragraph. Seven-second sound bytes, 15-second voice-over. Sell the benefits, tell a joke. It's not only what you say, but when you say it. If you crowd the viewers, back off. Inhale, exhale.

Keep viewers interested, pleasingly off-balance, anticipating. Be unpredictable, yet believable. Pace it. Rhythmically move between on-camera spokesperson, cover footage, brief testimonial inserts, appropriate digital video effects. Spice with music when appropriate.

8. Create a high perceived value for the product. The strength of direct response television has always been its positioning as a personal—not universal—message to the television viewer. Infomercials take the time to outline specific solutions to individuals' problems. You know your target audience well. Surprise them. Offer an attractive premium, something for nothing, easy payments, discounts on upsell or cross-sell products. Give a little and get a lot back. Your relationship with your customer will be off to a great start.

9. Mention the product name whenever possible—at least three times a minute. Much like in-person sales, where your goal is to use the prospect's name three times in the first 30 seconds, make sure you repeat the product name over and over again. For example, *Braun's* hand blender infomercial must include the words: *Braun's* superior quality, world-class *Braun* products, *Braun's* renowned craftsmanship, and so on. There's power in names.

EXHIBIT 6.1

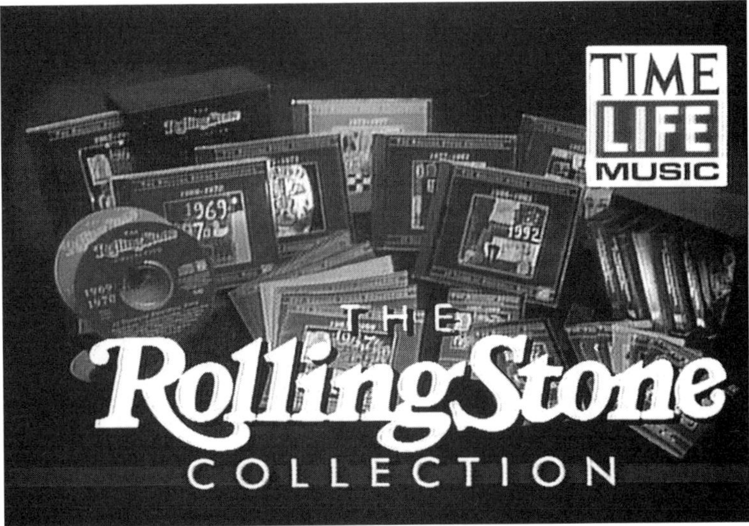

Time-Life Music's "Rolling Stone Collection" infomercial exemplifies an irresistible offer.

10. Complete a full sales cycle before doing your call to action. Capture their Attention, create Interest, instill Desire, and finally motivate them to Action (AIDA). When you've done your work of establishing a relationship with the viewer, building credibility, and demonstrating the product benefits, you've earned the right to give price, payment terms, and to ask them to call now! If you ask for the order too soon—before minute 6 at minimum—you aren't respecting the viewer's right to information before making a buying decision. You'll lose the sale.

11. Call to action (CTA). The CTA closes the AIDA cycle and the sale. They are the commercials within the infomercial, a minimum of 2 minutes in length inserted three times throughout the program. In the call to action, review all the highlights of your product, then urge viewers to call. Recreate a miniature experience of the emotions you evoked in the show body. Refresh viewers' memories just before you ask them to order. Display the toll-free number on screen for as much of the time as possible. Keep the mailing address up for twice the time

EXHIBIT 6.2

An example of a "tag page," or "billboard," from American Harvest's Jet Stream Oven infomercial CTA.

it takes to read. Preferably the announcer should state the 800 number and mailing address a minimum of two times. Payment terms, credit cards, C.O.D., and guarantee policy should also be visible on the tag page and stated, if time allows. Showcase the installment price, if it's a multi-pay offer, but be sure to graphically show the full payment price. (See Exhibit 6.2.)

12. Capture and maintain the audience's interest. Keeping a viewer's attention for 30 minutes is no easy task. This is why the best infomercial writers have documentary backgrounds. They've spent years cultivating the skill of packaging information in an entertaining fashion over time—30 minutes of time. They most easily adapt to long-form copywriting by learning and incorporating the basics of direct marketing into their documentary writing skills repertoire. You've done your job well if you've kept the viewer's attention for 8, 18, or 27 minutes. You're moving in only one direction now—toward a climax of closing the sale. Don't blow it!

13. Make it easy to understand. Paint word pictures. Good documentary writers know this rule well. Use 25-word paragraphs, seven-second sound bytes. Use colorful adjectives. No million-dollar words. The ear listens while the eyes watch and the combined experience is infinitely more powerful if you don't state the obvious—that which the eyes are seeing. Your audio track is married to, yet separate from, the video. Be specific, not general. Use photo captions, subheads, on-TV-screen support graphics, flip charts (a la Ross Perot). Simple offer, simple order graphic page.

14. Choose excellent talent. Often a personality, celebrity or non-celebrity, will be intimately connected to a product. The talent might be a major product asset; either the spokesperson knows the product pitch better than anyone, or millions of dollars already have been spent on associating the product with the specific celebrity. If you are doing an infomercial for Sprint, for example, using Candace Bergen is only logical. Infomercial talent is the individual who must create a relationship with the home viewer for 30 minutes! That's incredibly valuable time which we entrust to the celebrity to achieve a positive relationship with viewers and gain their trust. We buy from people we like. Therefore, the writer and creative team need to know who's available and who's right for hosting the show even before concepts can be decided. (See Exhibit 6.3.)

EXHIBIT 6.3

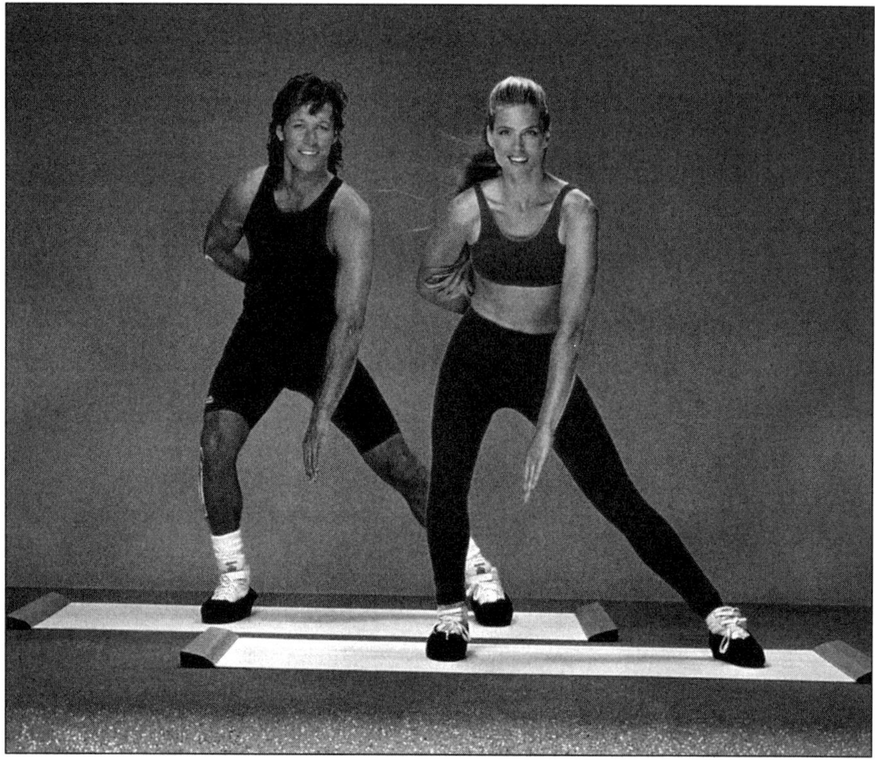

Supermodel Kim Alexis, shown here in Fitness Quest's "Slim Slide" infomercial, stops most channel surfers with her dynamic stage presence.

In the past many celebrities wouldn't touch infomercials. Recently it appears that the tide is turning. Celebrities are useful in infomercials for two reasons: First, their appearance on screen will stop the remote control zappers and zippers long enough (2 to 10 seconds) to capture their interest. Second, they give credibility to the product. If your product presenter doesn't have vivid personality, as Susan Powter or Mike Levey do, and/or your product or company name is not a household word, consider using a celebrity.

15. Craft a script that emphasizes benefits and answers objections. Writing an infomercial is like having a half-hour conversation with a mute person who can't respond except with his or her dialing finger. You must anticipate the viewers' every response to your ongoing monologue. You must anticipate and answer the objections that will typically arise. And you must get them to agree with your common-sense statements as often as possible. The more they agree, the more they're in a relationship. Remove their doubts—with a smile. Move them from fear and skepticism to trust. Be credible. Use expert testimonials and endorsements. Be honest, sincere, and genuine. Tell them why they need your product now, why the price is a great value, and why they should get it from you. Sell the sizzle. Folks want to know the benefits—what the product can do for them.

16. Sell the benefits; close with emotion. Emotion will always win out over intellect. Don't ever ask someone, "What do you think?" Instead ask, "How do you feel?" Use emotional, evocative language and visual images. Be enthusiastic and passionate. Inspire excitement. Be entertaining and humorous (within reason). Create the emotions that they will feel when using your product. Give them a taste and they will want it all. Let them know you like them. Logic justifies, but emotion buys.

17. Be powerful and real. Your purpose is to motivate immediate action. You want the viewer to pick up the phone and order right now or to go to a local retail outlet now. Communicate your enthusiasm for the product. Don't *let* the sale happen; *make* it happen.

18. Use quality product shots. It seems basic, but the perceived quality of your featured product depends greatly on what it looks like on the infomercial. Make sure the colors are bright, edges are sharp, and that the product is angled for just the right presentation. The best scriptwriting in the world can't override a lousy product image on screen. Make sure the photographer is experienced in shooting commercials and achieving your desired commercial effects. Even a pricey, high-quality piece of fitness equipment will look like something from a swap meet unless it's placed in the right setting, under the best lighting conditions.

19. Create graphics and montage that make sense. Support your strongest images with *simple* on-screen graphics where appropriate. Avoid obscure imagery that can sidetrack your viewers' attention from your message. The quality and variety of computer-generated special effects these days is enticing, especially for the computer graphic artist. Stick to your theme and remember your audience. Use montage: quick cutting of images is as old as filmmaking—and still effective. It always holds attention. But don't think you have to do it MTV-style (50 to 300 cuts per minute!). Slower is OK. Again use crisp graphics that enhance, rather than detract from, your message. Use bullet points to graphically list your benefits.

20. Employ affecting music. Use background music to emotionally communicate your message. Make it fit what you're selling. The music accompanying a talk show format infomercial on beauty tips would likely be soft and soothing, not at all like the upbeat score used for a Tony Little exercise video (see Exhibit 6.4).

Then, of course, there's the music for an infomercial for music products. In this case, the most critical creative element in music infomercials is the music track itself. When marketing music CDs and cassettes, the maxim is: let the music do the selling. While visual components help, it's the music that sells music products on infomercials.

EXHIBIT 6.4

Tony Little's infomercial for his "Wonderball" exercise program employs upbeat music to generate and inspire energy among his viewing audience.

21. Present gripping and real testimonials. Quality testimonials can boost response by 20 to 50 percent. They should be real people, real product-users, and truly interviewed, not scripted. Photos and videotape of potential testimonials and product experts should be gathered during pre-production to determine the strength of the product's testimonial component. Testimonials are not required for success, but if you've got 'em, use 'em. If they're incredibly strong and emotional (Deal-a-Meal), go with a documercial format. If they're weak (verbally or in appearance) or nonexistent, a storymercial might be your preferred format. Or, you may have to bite the bullet, delay production, and take a year to collect a fat file of gushing testimonial letters.

Testimonials talk directly to the viewer, not the masses. Give viewers testimonials they can relate to. They, too, must be true believer spokespersons. Great testimonials create immediate response. Very few infomercials have achieved success without them.

22. Generate high emotional appeal. Nobody turns the channel when a real-life infomercial testimonial-giver is crying. Poignancy sells better than any emotion. Happiness (ecstasy, joy, fulfillment) is second on the bestseller list. Then humor. The emotional infomercial will always outsell the dry. It's empathy at work. Viewers can't help it. And if they empathize, they're connected. You've created a relationship. This is a classic advertising technique.

Create a dialogue with your customers. Get them involved. Demonstrate the product. Give them a sample and they'll want it all. Appeal to their five senses and you appeal to their emotions.

23. Emphasize the "magical transformation." Weight loss products, cosmetics, kitchen gadgets—they all transform something. Incorporate before-and-after photos. The more dramatic the change, the better. The customers don't want our *products*, only what they can do for them. They want the profits, not the mutual fund; they want the compliments and approving looks, not the skin cream. The product isn't really king; what it does for the customers is king. Give them the dream, the magical transformation. State the before, but give them the after.

24. Ask for the order. Earn the right to ask for the order, but don't be shy. There's a right time and place. Everybody dislikes salespeople who haven't earned the right to ask for the order.

25. Remember to sell all the time. No moment or element of the script should have any purpose other than to sell your product. Period.

The Creative Meeting

What an agenda. Send out for lunch! The creative men and women have their work cut out for them. Keeping the above criteria in mind, the creative team meets and meticulously designs the program by analyzing, in-depth, the following categories:

1. Product—What are we selling?
2. Offer—Direct sale, lead generator or retail driver?
3. Product changes—Is it ready and packaged for TV sales?
4. Demos—Who are we selling to?
5. Product features—What makes this product better than others?
6. Benefits—Brainstorm what it will do for the consumer.
7. Objections—Brainstorm why the consumer will resist.
8. Psychological needs—What are the deepest needs to be fulfilled?
9. Concept—What is the principal theme of the program?
10. Expand the benefits vision—Take the primary benefits to a universal level.
11. Theme headline—What will attract the target audience?
12. Strategy—Summarize how to implement the concept.
13. Elements—What scenes must be included? Product shots, testimonials, experts, etc.?
14. Format—Documercial, storymercial, or other alternatives?
15. Opening—How do we grab our audience in the first seven seconds?
16. Show title—How can we make the show title catchy, different, yet reflect the show's content?
17. Audience retentives—What specific tactics will we use to keep the audience watching?

18. Call to action—What are the mandatory components and how will they be delivered?
19. Talent—Who is the ideal spokesperson or celebrity?

Selecting Your Writer

What are the essential criteria for a good infomercial writer? The best writers have scripted a few winners—and a lot of losers. This is a trial-and-error business. We all keep learning as we watch our own—and our competitors' infomercials.

Ideally your scriptwriter should have documentary experience as well as short-form commercial experience. Background in 30-second image spots or even two-minute direct response spots is not enough to guarantee infomercial success. Pacing, rhythm, and timing—staples in infomercial marketing—are significantly different between short- and long-form commercials.

It's rare, very rare, that a first-time infomercial scriptwriter will create a winner. The best writers will have experience in numerous disciplines: documentaries, image spots, industrials, talk shows, and direct mail. They understand infomercial fundamentals of formats and formulas. Infomercial copywriting is far more demanding and exacting than spot writing, and success or failure is immediately measurable. Let your scriptwriter take the time to do it right. Four to six weeks for a 35-page, 30-minute script isn't asking too much.

How to Assess the Script

As you read their script, ask a few questions on each page. How are we capturing the viewer's attention at each moment? Are we creating desire and building motivation? Are we honest, sincere, credible? Are we creating a positive relationship and trust with the individual viewer, and earning the right to ask for the order? And lastly, have you moved the viewers with emotion and convinced them with logic? If you find scriptwriters who can do this, hang on to them. They are like gold. The future of on-line and television advertising in the interactive age will be long-form and they, like all of us in infomercials, have a jump start on the 30-second spot copywriters. Madison Avenue just doesn't know it yet. Where spot advertising has become image-driven and thus a director's medium, infomercials are content-driven, and thus the province of the writer—all the more reason why infomercial professionals and newcomers to the industry must have a clear concept of infomercial copywriting fundamentals.

Creating the Creative

The creative goal is simple: construct a half-hour viewing experience that informs, entertains, and keeps the viewer watching as long as possible in order to generate an immediate response. There are four primary stages to script development: creative briefs, concepts and treatments, offer scripting, and body scripting.

Creative Briefs

Often given short shrift by entrepreneurial infomercial clients and inexperienced producer/writers anxious for results, crafting the creative brief is a critical stage. Simply put, this stage determines your entire infomercial's positioning, format, look, and feel. Your success or failure is incubated here. Give it the time it requires.

During the creative brief phase, your writer and researcher should first gather existing resources—advertising materials, marketing research, demographic studies, preexisting film or tape footage, testimonial files, expert opinion, celebrities or talent already associated with the product—all your product assets—in order to thoroughly understand the product's history.

Second, a clearly defined unique selling proposition (USP) needs to be carefully crafted and a demographic target decided upon. Remember, only 30 percent of TV viewers are DRTV shoppers. Are enough of your product's demo target among those? If not, then your offer may change from a one-step, direct product sale to a lead-generator intended to drive retail. At this stage, an associate producer should be making testimonial pre-interview calls. The results of all your research should be summarized in the creative brief document.

Allow a minimum of one to two weeks for this all-important phase. Well begun is half done.

Concepts and Treatments

Scriptwriting can be a lonely job. But in this stage, an experienced creative team effort is essential. I gather a creative staff of ten infomercial pros who collectively have written and/or viewed hundreds of successful and failed infomercials. This collective consciousness absorbs the writer's creative brief in order to develop several viable concepts for presentation to the client. Infomercial concept development is not nearly as creative or free-wheeling as image spot conceptualizing. In the midst of the television commercial clutter, makers of image TV advertising have unfortunately reduced their marketing goals to impact, impression, frequency, and recall. This method of persuasion and motivation does work for delayed purchasing of product but lacks accountability. And because it plays more on the viewers' emotions (read "entertaining") versus their intellects, it has a wider field of creative concepts and images to play in. Infomercials have to play more by the rules. Budget, image, format, talent, testimonials, and product characteristics all need analysis before determining concept and treatment.

Offer Scripting

Script the call to action (CTA) first, then script the show body to synchronize with the offer. Not vice versa. The offer is not an afterthought! It's the most critical part of your infomercial—when the viewer is asked to make a decision. It's an exercise in clarity. You'll discover how you need to describe and place the product benefits and features in condensed time. And, remember, the consumer needs to understand the logic of ordering your product.

By contrast, one of Madison Avenue's favorite tactics, associating products with sex, seems almost insidious when compared to an infomercial's appeal to logic.

Body Scripting

The infomercial copywriter's primary goal is to motivate an immediate response. The secondary goal, and nearly as important, is to keep the viewers watching as long as possible. As the viewing minutes add up, the chances of closing the sale increase dramatically. The more you tell, the more you sell. Decades ago, every door-to-door salesperson knew this instinctively.

The key to great infomercial body scripting is to get viewers' attention. And keep it, for every moment of every minute. The only way to do this is to think—for every paragraph, on every page of copy—how am I getting and keeping their attention? Here are some ways to get attention:

EXHIBIT 6.5

"The Great Wall" infomercial produced by TYEE for Philips Electronics' CD-I system broke new ground with unusual and arresting visuals.

Visual Grabbers. Take a cue from Madison Avenue. Beautiful, startling visuals get attention (see Exhibit 6.5).

Problem and Solution. This is a classic opening for DRTV spots. State a common problem and then tell viewers you have a solution. They'll watch to discover it.

Be Personal. Talk to the individual. Use "you," not "him/her/them." Testimonials may look like the viewer or, better yet, the viewer may aspire to look like them.

Tell a Story. Stories take time and command people's attention from beginning to end. This is why storymercials work—for a full half hour. It's problem/solution again. Or conflict and resolution in three acts. People seek resolution and happy endings. But stories can also be told by hosts, talk show guests, product presenters, and testimonials. Testimonial features (two- to four-minute real-life stories) are very effective.

Show the Process. The mind is curious. People love watching a process of making or changing anything. A recent hot kids' video was a documentary on building roads. It included big machines pushing lots of dirt around. Go figure. In 1990 the Daily Mixer hand blender infomercial sold $50 million of product based on viewers' fascination with watching skim milk whipped into cream. Just remember, professionally presented *process* peaks and retains interest.

Ask Questions. If you ask a question, viewers are naturally wondering about at that moment, they'll wait for the answer.

Present a Challenge. For example, lighting a car hood on fire. The viewer's response is, "Oh, my! What's going to happen?" Of course, there are many more sophisticated ways to do this.

Use a "Holder." Atlantic City pitchmen did it 70 years ago. Promise people a great deal up front—something free, perhaps, if they'll stick around until the end of the commercial. Gary Cochran did it best in infomercials by offering viewers $100 if they watched his entire half-hour pitch. He ended up giving callers a $100 discount. Tacky tactic, but it works.

Pacing. You're structuring four audio/video tracks: visuals, voice-overs, on-camera spokespeople/testimonials/actors, and music. How you pace these tracks proves your mastery of the infomercial symphony. Surprise people again. Don't drone on. Keep your dialogue snappy, your voice-overs and testimonial cuts brief (maximum 15 to 20 seconds). Cut/cut/dissolve. Again, remember AIDA: Get attention, create interest, then desire, then motivate them to action. Move it.

Present the Dream. Again, Madison Avenue ad executives excel at this. Give viewers a beautiful image of their lives transformed after using the product.

Be Specific. It's easier to write in generalities; but generalities don't sell. Work harder and be specific. Similarly, it's easier to write long-winded explanations than to be precise and to the point. Cut the extra words and get down to essential selling points.

Take Time to Do It Right

Creating a successful infomercial is not as easy as it looks at first glance. It takes time to craft an infomercial effectively. Research alone can take as many as four weeks. During every moment of an infomercial, you have to keep the attention of the audience. I use all my selling skills, all my scriptwriting skills, all my visual directing skills. That is why the scriptwriting phase, which is the most critical, can take six weeks.

The production itself requires another two to three months. That may seem like a lot of time, but hiring qualified specialists and allowing them to do their jobs right will save you money in the long run. Traditional ad agencies have struggled with the infomercial format because there are different rules of persuasion for 30-minute commercials versus 30-second spots. The very first sitcommercial proves the point. It was, as you will see, a classic boondoggle . . .

Bell Atlantic commissioned their traditional agency to create an infomercial for their add-on phone services: call waiting, call forwarding, and so on. Bell's agency spent $750,000 on a well-known Hollywood sitcom writer to craft a situation-comedy infomercial.

The plot revolved around an Archie Bunker-style family called "The Ringers." Ralph Ringer, a plumber, tried for 30 minutes to keep peace in his family by introducing them to the add-on Bell Atlantic phone features. The concept was unique, innovative, and entertaining, but the infomercial was unable to create sufficient response. It violated a basic selling rule. The writer had placed Ralph, a fictional character, in the role of asking for the order. Periodically, Ralph stepped out of character, turned to the camera, and described the phone features available. He asked the viewing audience to "call the 800 number on your screen now." Those experienced in infomercial marketing recognized the blunder immediately. Few viewers will do the bidding of a fictional character—especially when it requires making a purchase. This is one of the lessons the Madison Avenue copywriters must learn in the emerging era of interactive advertising.

The American population truly craves information, as evidenced by the enormous success of *60 Minutes*. The need extends to information about products. Infomercial producers can fulfill this need. The great infomercials of the future will not be the wildly creative accomplishments of television directors so much as the success of competent producer/writers who understand how to structure product information in fascinating and entertaining ways.

Don't Try This

To help make sure your infomercial succeeds, here are some pointers on what *not* to do in your infomercial creative:

1. Don't just create a general topic information program and then throw two or three DRTV commercials into it. You must sell benefits all the time. For example, don't do a talk show about *all* types of insurance. Talk specifically about the insurance you're selling.
2. Don't think that a celebrity spokesperson guarantees success. It doesn't. In a recent survey, 57 percent of infomercial customers said their purchase was not influenced by celebrity endorsements. Remember: the offer and the copy rule supreme.
3. Don't try to entertain too much. Sure, make it glitzy, fun, exciting, and fast-paced—but you're selling all the while.
4. Don't spend lots of money if you can convey the same message with less. Today, the average cost to produce an infomercial is $250,000, with brand-name companies spending up to $1,000,000 to produce a hot infomercial. Can it be done for less? Remember, the old adage of "test cheap" still holds true.

Problem Solving

There are several things you can do to an infomercial to increase response, everything from doing a whole new creative to changing the length of time the 800 number is on. If the initial script and production were poorly executed, the more you change it, the greater the potential for lifting response. But if you begin with even a decent infomercial, just some subtle changes can help things dramatically. There have been instances of this.

A classic example involves a friend of mine who sent me a copy of an infomercial another agency had done, which he told me had a 70 percent inquiry rate (viewers who called but did not order). He was unfamiliar with some of the basics that cause inquiry rates to get that high. I watched the infomercial and discovered the very simple problem: The 800 number came up before people knew what the offer was. Delaying the 800 number until after viewers understood what they were buying dropped the inquiry rate in half and doubled the productive response. Unfortunately, the show's creators were unaware of some of the basics that most infomercial professionals understand.

Create Dynamic Rhythm

If your show body is slow in pace, pick it up during the commercial. Use a voice-over spokesperson. If your show body is fast-paced, slow the commercial down. Use an on-camera spokesperson.

As you can see, very minor changes can increase response dramatically. The harsh reality is: if you're unaware of the basic formulas, you will fail. As Claude Hopkins said in 1922, practice "scientific advertising." Anyone who has been in the infomercial business for three years or more is at least familiar with these success formulas. And yet knowledge of formulas doesn't guarantee success. Great creative usually breaks or bends a rule or two and can rarely sell a product the public doesn't want. But these formulas provide a good foundation and starting point.

CHECKLIST

- ✔ Long-term success in selling stems from answering one basic question: What need does this individual have that I have the capability to fulfill?
- ✔ Infomercials give you one ultimate advantage: Time. The more you tell, the more you sell.
- ✔ The creative brief stage determines your entire infomercial's positioning, format, look, and feel.
- ✔ Budget, image, format, talent, testimonials, and product characteristics all need analysis before determining concept and treatment.
- ✔ Employ the AIDA formula: create attention, interest, desire, and action.
- ✔ When it's appropriate to the product, use a true believer as the commercial spokesperson.
- ✔ Script the call to action (CTA) first, then script the show body to synchronize with the offer.
- ✔ Logic justifies, emotion buys.
- ✔ Balance entertainment with information and credibility.

- ✔ Always say, "Call Now!"
- ✔ Remember the "eight movements of the symphony": selling cycles, benefits, features, uses, credibility, guarantees, offer details, call to action.
- ✔ Product is king.
- ✔ A script can be 30 to 40 pages long; give creative the time it takes.
- ✔ Stop the channel surfers by catching their interest at any point in your infomercial.
- ✔ Balance entertainment and information so that neither overshadows the other.
- ✔ Direct testimonials to your viewers, up close and personal, one on one.
- ✔ Don't let the sale happen; make it happen.
- ✔ Review product benefits during the CTA for at least one minute.
- ✔ Pace your infomercial appropriately.
- ✔ A product offer pitched by the right celebrity can mean a 15 to 20 percent increase in response.
- ✔ State the offer details verbally and clearly to encourage direct sales and avoid inquiry calls.
- ✔ Use premiums and bonuses whenever possible. They'll lift response 10 to 25 percent.
- ✔ Say the phone number and address a minimum of two times in the tag.

CHAPTER

Producing an Infomercial

Following a working agreement between your company, your agency of record and/or your infomercial agency—and preceding the commencement of creative work—there is a marketing strategy meeting. Typically, in attendance are you (the client), and your agency's account manager(s), creative director(s), and creative team. At this time, the client presents as much information about the product or service as possible. This is also the time when the offer (price, premiums, upsells, payment plan, etc.) is structured.

The Creative Strategy

The foundation for any infomercial is the creative strategy, outlined in the creative brief. It spells out the marketing and advertising objectives and the tone and manner of the show. It defines the primary and secondary target audience, lists the most important features and benefits of the product/service, addresses executional considerations, states the product offer(s) and the communication message that is to be conveyed by the show. The creative strategy is based on marketing and product information provided by you, the client, at the marketing strategy meeting. Once the creative strategy is agreed upon, work begins on the script treatment.

Production Schedule

A proposed production schedule is presented along with the creative strategy. This schedule gives the overall time framework for the production of the show. It is refined once a creative treatment is completed. However, an accurate, working production schedule cannot be put together until script approval.

Show Treatment

The treatment is a written overview that presents the creative concept and structure that will support the tone and manner of the show. It gives descriptions of the visual presentation, examples of key copy points, and talent requirements. If celebrity talent is called for, recommendations are included. The treatment will be accompanied by an estimated budget for the production of a show based on this treatment. The treatment is the blue print for the show's script and should clearly reflect the creative strategy. As such, the treatment and the estimated budget must be agreed upon and approved before beginning to write the actual script. (See Chapter 8.)

The Script

First Draft

The first draft of the script is the infomercial in written form. It is built upon the script treatment and will have all spoken copy (audio) and indicate who is delivering this copy. It will also describe the setting or location where action takes place and describes what is happening visually (video). All elements of the show—the opening, three body segments, the three calls-to-action, testimonials, etc.—are placed where they will appear in the show. The creative team puts a great deal of time and effort into creating a script that will capture and hold the target audience and, most importantly, sell your product or service.

Before you receive the initial script, it should be thoroughly reviewed, rewritten, and polished several times.

Second Draft

Following your reading of the first draft, there is a script meeting between you and the creative team. Your candid comments, suggestions, and recommendations are encouraged at this time because it is less expensive to make changes on paper than during or after production. Based on the outcome of this meeting, the script is revised and a second draft is submitted for your approval. Generally, the second draft is the basic script with a few minor changes.

Shooting Script

The shooting script, which incorporates all changes, is the script that will go before the cameras. Once you've approved a shooting script, a final estimate for the cost of producing this script is presented for your approval. The complete, award-winning Nissan Altima infomercial script is included in Appendix F.

Graphics

Creating on-screen graphics is a very time-consuming process. Therefore, if visual effects, such as computer graphics or animation, are planned for the show, this is the time to begin their design and creation. By starting on them at this stage of the creative/production process, there will be sufficient time to produce the desired graphics and have them approved. This avoids delaying the other steps in the production and completion of the show.

Pre-Production

This is the planning and organizational work that goes into producing any infomercial or short-form commercial and may be the most important element in the overall production. The reason? With proper preproduction, most shooting and editorial problems will be eliminated. In addition, it's much more cost effective and efficient to make decisions at a desk rather than in a studio or editing suite, where you're paying a complete crew by the hour.

EXHIBIT 7.1

Some infomercial locations, like this one produced by Script to Screen for Taylor Made Golf starring golf pro and broadcast network commentator Gary McCord, are more challenging than others.

Preliminary Pre-Production

The first steps in pre-production begin once a script treatment is approved. The producer and assistant producer will start searching for and negotiating with actors, announcers, production crew talent, and/or production sources. They will start investigating locations and begin the selection process required to obtain the best individuals for product testimonials. This ongoing process lasts until the entire production crew, talent, and testimonials are selected.

Show Pre-Production

Once revisions are made to the first draft of the script, the pre-production process involves dealing with locations and/or sets, necessary equipment and crew, travel arrangements, scheduling of the production and, with the director's input, the shooting of the show. Aspects of show pre-production continue up until the actual day of shooting.

Final Pre-Production

A day before rehearsal, a final pre-production meeting is held to go over all aspects of the shoot and to ensure that there are no loose ends. Everything from crew arrival time to props to how the director plans to shoot the script is covered at this meeting. In attendance is the client, director, producer, assistant producer, and any other personnel that are essential to the shoot. This is the last chance to make decisions before they become expensive afterthoughts.

Production

The actual video taping (or filming) of the various elements that will be edited together to form the completed show is the *production*. Keep in mind that your show will be shot in pieces (i.e., the host/presenter portion, product demonstrations, testimonials) and not in sequential order. Rarely are commercials or television shows of any kind shot in one long, continuous sequence. For example, the testimonials may be shot first and the host/presenter scenes or demonstrations last. Even scenes with the host/presenter are generally not shot in the order in which they will appear in the show. Logistics such as the lighting, camera positioning, and location dictate the order of shooting. The production phase is completed when everything needed for the show has been shot and is on film or tape and "in the can."

Original Music

Most infomercials use music to set the mood, add impact, and enhance various portions of the show. This is best accomplished by creating original music customized to fit your particular show. Once the shooting is finished, the producer will meet with a composer to discuss music requirements The composer will then begin creating musical themes which are presented to your agency for approval. The selected music is then fully orchestrated and presented to the client for approval. When the off-line phase of post-production (see below) is finished and approved, the composer adjusts the music to match the various portions and video action of the show. The final music track is added to the show during sweetening (see below).

EXHIBIT 7.2

American Harvest's infomercials are on custom-designed indoor stages, where the logistics of the production such as lighting are well under control.

EXHIBIT 7.3

The crew in the Hawthorne Communications online editing suite combines all audio elements, such as voice, sound effects, and music during this sweetening session.

Post-Production

Post-production occurs after all the videotaping or filming has been completed and consists of three major phases: off-line editing, on-line editing, and sweetening.

Off-Line Editing

This process assembles the show elements in their proper order. In creating the off-line edit (a preliminary edited version of the show), the editor uses notes taken during taping to select the best versions (takes) of the scenes and edits them together to create the pacing, flow, and mood of the show. Off-line editing is the decision-making phase of post-production and the best time to make editorial changes. The creative director and producer must work closely with the editor, and it's imperative that the client contributes at this point. In many cases, depending on the complexity of the show, various stages of the off-line edit are sent to the client for comments and approval. When all elements have been assembled exactly as they will appear in the completed infomercial, the client gives final approval. Graphic and typographical elements that will be superimposed over various scenes, including how-to-order information, often are not on this final off-line edit version. Changes made after off-line editing are difficult, time consuming and expensive. Therefore, the editing process cannot continue without client approval of the final off-line edit.

On-line Editing and Sweetening

Following client approval of the off-line edit, the production moves into the on-line editing suite, where the on-air version is created. During on-line editing all graphics elements are added to the show. A separate audio mixing session called sweetening then occurs, which meticulously combines all audio elements, such as voice, sound effects (SFX), and music. The client's final approval of the on-line edit gives the go-ahead for the show to be dubbed and sent to the stations.

Infomercial Project Sample Timeline

The Appendix to this chapter is an average 20-week timetable for the execution of an infomercial. This chart details the significant action steps required in creative, production, telemarketing, and fulfillment in preparation for a successful infomercial test. The complexities of your particular show will affect this schedule and require modifications for your specific needs.

Common Client Production Questions

The following section responds to typical questions clients ask agencies about infomercial production.

Life

How long can I expect my show to run successfully? If a show is successful, the average life span of the program in its original form is about 9 to 18 months. If the show is not aired too often or does not have wide exposure, the product could continue indefinitely. Conversely, a heavy broadcast schedule with a great deal of exposure could shorten the life of a show.

Wear-out

What happens when my show starts to wear out? After about one year of broadcast exposure the original show would be re-created to give it a fresh appearance and feel, but with the same creative platform to assure continued success.

Creative Input

How much input do I have in the creative process? This is up to you. When you hire an infomercial agency, you are obviously paying for their talent and ability to create a successful show. However, you have the most intimate knowledge of your product. The ideal creative process is a marriage of an agency's television advertising, marketing, and sales skills with your product expertise. You are encouraged to provide as much input as you want to give.

Production Time

How long does it take to produce an infomercial? It generally takes about four months from the original creative concept to the final

EXHIBIT 7.4

Superstar Dionne Warwick lends a great deal of credibility to the very successful "Psychic Friends Network" series of infomercials, produced by Inphomation Communications.

on-line master. However, the availability of celebrity talent, traveling to different locations, and special visual effects can increase production time to six months.

Approvals

Is there a formal approval process for production? Definitely. Your approval is not only asked for at every major decision point of production (creative brief, creative treatment, celebrity selection, scripting, budgets, graphics, off-line editing), it is *required* before moving onto the next phase of production.

Budgeting

How does the budgeting process work? Initially you determine a cost range that fits your budget for the production of your infomercial. Then your agency should develop creative concepts that can be produced within these budget parameters. An estimated production budget is presented for your approval, along with the show treatment. Then upon approval of a final script, when all the specifics and requirements involved in the production of your show are known, a final production budget is submitted for your approval. (See Chapter 8.)

Talent

Do I need a celebrity for my infomercial? If so, how do you choose one? Celebrity talent is not for every show. There are many successful shows that use good non-celebrity presenters. The advantages of using celebrities are that they lend credibility to the show and help capture channel surfers. In addition, the right celebrity creates an instant connection between the show and the viewer. Therefore, each program is carefully tailored for the best match-up between the celebrity, product, and show format. Always select a celebrity who is well-known, respected, and admired by the target audience. Of course, budget has a great deal to do with the choice of celebrities.

What will my production cost? Production costs can range anywhere from $150,000 to more than $800,000, depending on the creative design of the infomercial. (By comparison, the current average cost of a 30-second commercial is over $200,000.) It's absolutely possible to create a half-hour show for $50,000. And remember: You get what you pay for.

CHECKLIST

- ✔ Be sure you have a *working agreement* among your company, your ad agency of record, and/or your infomercial agency regarding participation in the production process.
- ✔ Plan to attend the *creative input meeting,* with the agency account manager, creative director, and creative team.
- ✔ Present detailed information and input regarding your product and long-term goals to your infomercial agency.
- ✔ Understand, approve, and trust your agency's creative strategy; it will provide the framework for the entire program.
- ✔ Pay close attention to the proposed production schedule and have your products ready for distribution by air time.
- ✔ Give your approvals promptly at various stages of the process to avoid delays.
- ✔ Make recommendations for script revisions and speak up if it does not meet your expectations, before you are presented with the final shooting script.
- ✔ Good graphics are costly and take time. Be patient.
- ✔ Stay involved throughout the pre-production process, when you can still make inexpensive changes. Attend the final meeting.
- ✔ Don't expect sequential shooting. Your infomercial will be shot in the most cost-efficient order, not as it will appear in its final form.
- ✔ Work closely with the creative director, producer, and off-line editor in the post-production stage.
- ✔ With your approval of the final on-line editing and sweetening, your infomercial will be dubbed and sent to television stations.
- ✔ Infomercial competition is heating up. Create the best production your budget allows.

APPENDIX CHAPTER 7

Infomercial Project Sample Timeline

	Creative & Production	Media	Telemarketing	Fulfillment	Misc.
Week 1	• Creative "think-tank" meeting • Review product and market research	• Agency dept. coordinator meeting with client • Campaign product, position and goals provided to media for developing test strategy	• Agency dept. coordinator meeting with client	• Agency dept. coordinator meeting with client	
Week 2	• Develop creative concept • Initial positioning, pricing, packaging • Determine offer elements: premiums, guarantee, upsells	• Media test proposal research	• Research telemarketing needs	• Research fulfillment needs	
Week 3	• Develop creative concept	• Media test proposal research	• Create and send RFP to telemarketing houses	• Create and send RFP to fulfillment houses	
Week 4	• Finalize treatment • Commence scripting	• Media test proposal written			
Week 5	• Scripting • Develop preliminary budget	• Media test proposal written	• Review RFP's and make recommendations to client • Coordinate multiple telemarketers if necessary	• Review RFP's and make recommendations to client • Coordinate multiple fulfillment houses if necessary	

	Creative & Production	Media	Telemarketing	Fulfillment	Misc.
Week 6	• Scripting • Develop music concepts • Design graphic elements and animation • Design sets • Testimonial research and scheduling	• Secure client approval on media test proposal	• Client's legal department reviews and signs service agreements	• Client's legal department reviews and signs service agreements	
Week 7	• Scripting • Scout locations • Testimonial research and scheduling	• Media proposal distributed to the buyers		• All product info gathered from client: pricing, payment and delivery methods, shipping and handling charge, weight of product, payment methods, upsells, etc.	
Week 8	• Scripting • Assemble shooting schedule	• Buyers negotiate and purchase test media	• Opening deposits paid to telemarketing house	• Opening deposits paid to fulfillment house • Relay all client information to fulfillment house • Work with the client and the fulfillment center on merchant account set up for credit card authorization	• Determine how to handle multiple shipments, "check holding," PO Box requirements and MO discrepancies • Determine parameters for inventory levels, returns, C.S., pick and pack, etc.

	Creative & Production	Media	Telemarketing	Fulfillment	Misc.
Week 9	• Finalize positioning, pricing and packaging • Finalize script, talent, set, locations, testimonials, budget, shoot schedule and crew	• Buyers negotiate and purchase test media	• Write telemarketing scripts; secure client approval; provide to telemarketer	• Set up fulfillment house with designated telemarketer (including electronic transmission, hard copy of orders and layout of program.) • Test modem between telemarketer, fulfillment house and agency	
Week 10	• Initial legal review	• Buyers negotiate and purchase test media		• Train fulfillment customer service operators to receive calls for checking on order, adding to an order, reordering, canceling an order, or obtaining more information on the product	
Week 11	• Travel and shoot • Graphics and animation in production	• Buyers negotiate and purchase test media	• Review telemarketing screens (hard copy) • Coordinate optional telemarketer services: credit card authorization, label generation, etc.	• Set up all labels, grief letters, and information packages with fulfillment house and the client • Set up all reports for specific management needs	
Week 12	• Travel and shoot • Graphics and animation in production	• Buyers negotiate and purchase test media			

	Creative & Production	Media	Telemarketing	Fulfillment	Misc.
Week 13	• Begin off-line edit	• Buyers negotiate and purchase test media	• Telemarketing training • Coordinate telephone representative (TR) focus groups and incentive programs		
Week 14	• Off-line edit • Possible focus groups on initial off-line edit	• Finalized media test schedule provided to client for approval	• Send initial off-line edit to telemarketing house to familiarize personnel with the product and offer	• Send initial off-line edit to fulfillment house to familiarize personnel with the product and offer	
Week 15	• Off-line edit completed • Legal review	• Client billed for media test—payable upon receipt			
Week 16	• On-line edit	• Media test dollars received at agency; payment made to stations in advance of broadcast		• Product inventory sent to fulfillment house	• Tape duplication and trafficking form completed
Week 17	• On-line edit completed • Audio/music sweetening • Ship dubmaster to dub house		• Receive telemarketing test transmission and sample faxes		• NIMA self certification form due
Week 18			• Confirm all 800 #'s have been turned on • Insure adequate operator staffing • Perform test calls	• Perform test calls on fulfillment house customer service telephone representatives (TR's)	• Strike broadcast dubs with 800 #'s and voice over; ship to stations

	Creative & Production	Media	Telemarketing	Fulfillment	Misc.
Week 19		• MEDIA TEST—WEEK ONE • Report and evaluate media test results • Provide breakdown of all non-order calls • Call blockage monitoring • On-going call monitoring • Media strategy adjustments	• Verify the accuracy of all reports • Audit telemarketing invoices for accuracy. Make necessary corrections	• Verify the accuracy of all reports • Audit fulfillment house invoices for accuracy. Make necessary corrections	
Week 20		• MEDIA TEST—WEEK TWO • Determine degree of success	• Verify the accuracy of all reports • Audit telemarketing invoices for accuracy. Make necessary corrections	• Verify the accuracy of all reports • Audit fulfillment house invoices for accuracy. Make necessary corrections	

Source: Hawthorne Communications, Inc.

CHAPTER

Infomercial Financial Realities

Let's cut to the chase, shall we?

"How much money can I make or lose on an infomercial?"

The good news is that some products have grossed as much as $120 million in just one year using infomercial advertising. Typical successes gross between $5 and $50 million per year.

The bad news is that only one in every 10 infomercials succeeds, partly because the competition is so intense and because many of these marketers are novices with unsuitable products and poorly produced programs. What could you lose? You could lose it all—your entire production and media dollar investment.

But there's always hope. In this business, most of the participants have a stake in an infomercial's success. A reputable infomercial agency won't take your product on unless you have an excellent chance of success using the infomercial format. No credible company wants to pick up a loser; you'll be told quickly before investing hundreds of thousands of dollars if your product falls into this category. With such learned advice in hand, you have a variety of choices. Listen to the infomercial agency's rationale, learn about successful products and campaigns, and either correct the problem with your product and get an infomercial made, or market your product differently.

Managing Costs

Elsewhere in this book we've covered how to approach infomercials, what is involved and, in some cases, the cost of each step and expected return on investment. This chapter identifies the primary costs of various infomercial components (see the Appendix to this chapter) and provides detailed sample forms and reports you can use to plan, measure, and manage them. The Appendix to this chapter is a completed Program Cost Estimate. Appendix F at the end of this book contains a completed Pro Forma.

Creative

What does it take to craft a great infomercial? Remember, writing an effective script is not a simple, quick task. It's 35 pages of carefully crafted copy. Set aside $20,000 to $40,000 for the scripting phase. (See Appendix F to read the complete script of the award-winning Nissan storymercial.)

Production

Take time to do it right and allot a workable budget. The result will justify your means. Production costs range from $150,000 to $800,000. If you're doing a studio demonstration or a talk show, it's going to be on the low end—figure $250,000. Production revisions can run between $25,000 and $50,000.

It is common knowledge that you can shoot a half-hour at the local cable station for $5,000. However, beware! Do you want your infomercial—and more important, your *product*— to look like it's being offered by "Crazy Eddie." Caveat emptor! Some companies advertise in the *Wall Street Journal* and in *USA Today* promising to produce a show *and* buy 30 infomercial media time slots, all for just $15,000. As far as I know, these companies have never produced a success.

Media

In the U.S., approximately $650 million per year is spent on infomercial media on broadcast TV stations and cable networks. Infomercial media buyers usually pay $300 per 1,000 viewing households per half hour or $5.25 cost per thousand (CPM) per 30 seconds. Infomercials allow you to buy more time for less on a per-minute basis than spot advertising. That's why they're so efficient.

The approximate price of media tests range from $30,000 to $50,000. Once evaluated as a success, an infomercial will "roll out" at from $50,000 to $500,000 per week and make a profit on virtually every media dollar spent.

Celebrity Talent

Celebrities can cost from $5,000 to $1,000,000. The average cost of a celebrity ranges from $25,000 to $100,000. In addition, celebrity talent may get royalties of one to three percent (average) on net sales. For these substantial fees, celebrities also may commit to representing their infomercial clients' products in retail, print, and other promotions.

A celebrity's status and going rates depend on what's happening with him or her at the moment. For example, Cher reportedly did her hair care infomercial for a guaranteed $1,000,000; Meredith Baxter received $500,000 guaranteed; Tom Skerrit earned a guaranteed $50,000. But note: these figures came well before Meredith Baxter starred in a new sitcom, and Tom Skerrit hadn't gained his "Picket Fences" acclaim. Cher was in the spotlight daily, which is not the case right now. So, check with your producer or celebrity broker for current rates. And, remember, a celebrity is not necessarily the best choice for marketing your products on infomercials.

Duplication and Shipping Costs

Every station or cable network that runs your program needs a copy of the infomercial. This means there will be tape duplication and shipping costs. Depending on whether or not every tape needs special editing for a specific 800/888 number, these duplicating costs can vary from $50 to $300 dollars per station. But remember, once a station has the tape, the successful show tape can run repeatedly for many, many months.

Program Refreshing

There have been programs on the air selling the same product with no production changes for as long as two years or more. Those are the exceptions. The rule is that most infomercials need a new version at least every 12 months. So count on additional production and tape duplication costs every year, and perhaps some changes or additions to your product in the form of new bonuses, premiums, and price discounts.

The Appendix to this chapter is a complete sample pro forma showing revenues, expenses, and profit calculations.

CHECKLIST

- ✔ While some products have grossed as much as $120 million in just one year using infomercial advertising, other successful shows are grossing between $5 and $50 million per year.
- ✔ One in every 10 infomercials succeeds.
- ✔ A reputable infomercial agency won't take you on as a client unless your product has an excellent chance of infomercial success.
- ✔ The average cost of quality infomercial production is $250,000, though production costs can range from $150,000 to $800,000.
- ✔ The approximate price of media testing ranges from $30,000 to $150,000. Media rollout costs range from $50,000 to $500,000 per week.
- ✔ Celebrities can cost from $5,000 to $1,000,000 guaranteed.

APPENDIX

Sample Pro Forma

Using the Pro Forma

The attached pro forma was developed by Hawthorne Communications to project revenues and profits for our clients' infomercials and certain aftermarkets. As in all pro formas, it's only as good as the assumptions it's based on. The following commentary will guide you in preparing your own pro forma. Note: any c with a circle around it (to the right of a column) indicates that this number is automatically calculated by the spreadsheet software.

General Information page 1

- Production cost: infomercial production only; the pro forma will amortize this cost over an 18-month period.
- Multiple payments: the number of months to collect full payment in any installment plan you may consider offering (usually two to four payments).

- Product development cost: all costs to bring your product to market, including packaging. The pro forma will amortize this cost over an 18 month period.

Direct Sales

Revenues

- Retail price per unit: your infomercial offer price
- Shipping and handling: what you will charge, not your costs

Expenses

- Cost of goods: cost of manufacturing (or your cost for purchasing the product(s) at wholesale) for core product and packaging
- Inventory costs: warehousing expenses on a per product basis
- Premiums: cost of manufacturing (or your cost for purchasing the product(s) at wholesale) for any premiums or bonuses you're adding to the core product.
- Returns and bad debt percent: can range from 1 to 10 percent; 5 percent is a reasonable average
- 800 service: depending on what services your telemarketer provides, this can average from $1.50 to $2.50 per unit sold.
- Order processing: your cost to pick, pack and ship your product, including shipping customer service.
- Bank card fees/check processing: your credit card merchant account percent and prorated costs per order for electronic check debits and checks by mail processing fees.
- Credit card order percent: typically 90 percent.
- Check/MO order percent: typically 10 percent.
- Customer service: additional customer service personnel or subcontractor costs to handle problems, inquiries and returns. $.50 to $2.00 per unit, depending on your experience.

- Dub cost: every TV station and cable network requires its own 1-inch or Beta SP infomercial dub (duplicate). Depending on how long the infomercial plays on a station, the dub cost will be amortized to an even smaller cost; $.25 is probably more reasonable.
- Royalties: includes royalties on total retail price for celebrities, production partners, product developers, etc. Royalties should never exceed 10 percent; 5 percent is preferred.

Retail Sales

Revenues

- Wholesale price per unit: your wholesale revenue in sales to retail outlets.

Upsell Units/ Direct Units Ratio (page 1, right column)

- For every 100 units sold directly from the infomercial, 10 upsell products will be sold by the inbound telemarketers. Depending on the nature of the upsell product and price, this percentage can be as high as 80%, but averages 25%.

Revenues

- Retail price per unit: of the product(s) sold in the upsell.

Expenses

- (same calculations as above)

Outbound Sales

- Inquiry percent of total inbound calls: if 100 viewers call the 800/888 number, 50 will order the product and 50 will be inquiries (request for more information, problem calls); this percent can be as low as 20 percent, but 50 percent is conservative.

- Inquiry conversion percent: of those 50 inquiries, 20 percent will order the product when called back by the outbound telemarketing company.
- Credit card decline percent: percent of all purchasers using their credit card whose bank will not honor the charge amount.
- Credit card conversion percent: percent of declines that will eventually purchase the product with another credit card or by check, after being called by the outbound telemarketing company.
- Outbound telemarketing: the amount earned per unit sold by the outbound company. Usually between 25 percent and 35 percent of the product retail price.

Media Efficiency Ratio (MER)

- A MER of 2 means for every dollar of media spent, $2 of sales will be generated strictly from direct TV sales. Does not include upsell, outbound or retail sales.

Media Buy

- The assumed amount of media that can be spent per month at the projected MER. Media spending rises and falls according to season and age of the infomercial. Successful infomercials can spend anywhere from $100,000 to $2,000,000 per month.

Retail Ratio

- The Infomercial Retail Multiple (IRM); for every product unit sold direct via the infomercial, 1 (100 percent), 2 (200 percent) or more units will be sold at retail. This multiple can go as high as 5 (500 percent).

All of the above assumptions and their impact on revenues and cash flow are played out on subsequent spread sheets.

Sample Pro Forma

Pro Forma Data Entry & Margin Calculations

GENERAL INFORMATION

Company Name	Sample Pro Forma
Production Cost	$350,000
Beginning Air Date	June 1997
Multiple Payments (months)	2
% Converted to Single Payment	50%
Product Development Cost	$195,000

DIRECT SALES

Revenues

Retail Price/Unit		89.99	
Shipping & Handling		9.95	
Total Revenues		99.94	©

Expenses

Cost of Goods		9.50	
Inventory Costs		0.00	
Premiums		0.00	
Returns & Bad Debt (%)	5.0%		
Returns & Bad Debt ($)		4.50	©
800 Service		2.00	
Order Processing (incl. shipping)		6.00	
Bank Card Fees/Check Processing	2.6%		
Credit Card Order %	90%		
Check/MO Order %	10%		©
Bank Card Fees/Check Processing		2.60	©
Customer Service		1.50	
Dub Cost		0.40	
Royalties (5%)		4.50	
Other Royalty		1.00	
Total Expenses		32.00	©

Gross Margin/Unit **67.94** ©

RETAIL SALES

Revenues

Wholesale Price/Unit		45.00	
Total Revenues		45.00	©

Expenses

Cost of Goods		9.50	
Royalty Percentage	5.%		
Royalty		2.25	©
Returns & Bad Debt (%)	0%		
Returns & Bad Debt ($)		0.00	©
Order Processing		0.00	
Inventory Cost		0.00	
Other Royalty		1.00	
Total Expenses		12.75	©

Gross Margin/Unit **32.25** ©

UPSELL SALES

Upsell Units/Direct Units Ratio

Revenues

Retail Price/Unit		24.99	
Shipping & Handling		3.00	
Total Revenues		27.99	©

Expenses

Cost of Goods		12.00	
Inventory Costs		0.00	
Returns & Bad Debt (%)	5.0%		©
Returns & Bad Debt ($)		1.25	©
Order Processing (incl. shipping)		2.00	
Bank Card Fees/Check Processing	2.6%		©
Credit Card Order %	90%		©
Check/MO Order %	10%		©
Bank Card Fees/Check Processing		0.73	©
800 Service		0.50	
Other Royalty $2/Other (5%)		3.25	
Total Expenses		19.73	©

Gross Margin/Unit **8.26** ©

OUTBOUND SALES

Inquiry % of Total Inbound Calls	50%
Inquiry Conversion %	20%
Credit Card Decline %	4%
Credit Card Conversion %	75%
Outbound Telemarketing	27.00

MEDIA EFFICIENCY RATIOS, MEDIA BUYS, RETAIL RATIOS

Month	MER	Media Buy	Retail Ratio
1	0	$0	0%
2	2	40,000	0%
3	2	150,000	0%
4	2	250,000	0%
5	2.5	350,000	0%
6	2.5	500,000	0%
7	2.5	650,000	100%
8	2.5	750,000	100%
9	2.5	750,000	100%
10	2.5	750,000	100%
11	2.5	650,000	100%
12	2	350,000	100%
13	2	350,000	200%
14	2	250,000	200%
15	2	250,000	200%
16	2	250,000	200%
17	2.5	500,000	200%
18	2.5	650,000	200%

NOTES

1. The "©" symbol indicates a calculated field.

Source: Hawthorne Communications, Inc.

Sample Pro Forma

Production Cost	$350,000
Beginning Air Date	June 1997
Multiple Payments (months)	2
% Converted to Single Payment	50%
Product Development Cost	$195,000

DIRECT SALES

Revenues

Retail Price/Unit		89.99
Shipping & Handling		9.95
Total Revenues		99.94

Expenses

Cost of Goods		9.50
Inventory Costs		0.00
Premiums		0.00
Returns & Bad Debt (%)	5.0%	
Returns & Bad Debt ($)		4.50
800 Service		2.00
Order Processing (incl. shipping)		6.00
Bank Card Fees/Check Processing	2.6%	
Credit Card Order %	90%	
Check/MO Order %	10%	
Bank Card Fees/Check Processing		2.60
Customer Service		1.50
Dub Cost		0.40
Royalties (5%)		4.50
Other Royalty		1.00
Total Expenses		32.00

Gross Margin/Unit **67.94**

Scenario ID:	32904.41869

Direct Sales Pro Forma Cash Flow

Month	Media Efficiency Ratio	Media Buy	Unit Sales	Gross Sales	Gross Receipts	Cash Flow*	Cumulative Cash Flow	Multiple Payment Receivables
June	0.0	$0	$0	$0	$0	$0	$0	0
July	2.0	40,000	800	80,000	60,000	34,386	34,386	20,000
August	2.0	150,000	3,002	300,000	245,000	148,949	183,335	75,000
September	2.0	250,000	5,003	500,000	450,000	289,914	473,249	125,000
October	2.5	350,000	8,755	875,000	781,250	501,100	974,349	218,000
November	2.5	500,000	12,508	1,250,000	1,156,250	756,036	1,730,385	312,500
December	2.5	650,000	16,260	1,625,000	1,531,250	1,010,971	2,741,356	406,250
January	2.5	750,000	18,761	1,875,000	1,812,500	1,212,178	3,953,534	468,750
February	2.5	750,000	18,761	1,875,000	1,875,000	1,274,678	5,228,213	468,750
March	2.5	750,000	18,761	1,625,000	1,875,000	1,274,678	6,502,891	468,750
April	2.5	650,000	16,260	700,000	1,687,500	1,167,221	7,670,113	406,250
May	2.0	350,000	7,004	700,000	931,250	707,130	8,377,242	175,000
June	2.0	350,000	7,004	700,000	700,000	475,880	8,853,122	175,000
July	2.0	250,000	5,003	500,000	550,000	389,914	9,243,037	125,000
August	2.0	250,000	5,003	500,000	500,000	339,914	9,582,951	125,000
September	2.0	250,000	5,003	500,000	500,000	339,914	9,922,865	125,000
October	2.5	500,000	12,508	1,250,000	1,062,500	662,286	10,585,151	312,500
November	2.5	650,000	16,260	1,625,000	1,531,250	1,010,971	11,596,122	406,250
TOTALS (Month 1–18)		7,440,000	176,656	17,655,000	17,248,750	11,596,122	11,596,122	406,250
TOTALS (Month 19 fwd.)		0	0	0	406,250	406,250	406,250	(406,250)
GRAND TOTALS (All Months)		7,440,000	176,656	17,655,000	17,655,000	12,002,372	12,002,372	0

*Note: Media, production, and product development costs are excluded.

Sample Pro Forma

Upsell Sales Pro Forma Cash Flow

Upsell Units/Direct Units Ratio		20%
Revenues		
Retail Price/Unit		24.99
Shipping & Handling		3.00
Total Revenues		27.99
Expenses		
Cost of Goods		12.00
Inventory Costs		0.00
Returns & Bad Debt (%)	5.0%	
Returns & Bad Debt ($)		1.25
Order Processing (incl. shipping)		2.00
Bank Card Fees/Check Processing	2.6%	
Credit Card Order %	90%	
Check/MO Order %	10%	
Credit Card Fees/Check Processing		0.73
800 Service		0.50
Other Royalty $2/Other (5%)		3.25
Total Expenses		19.73
Gross Margin/Unit		**8.26**
Scenrio ID:		32904.41869

Month	Unit Sales	Gross Sales	Cash Flow*	Cumulative Cash Flow*
June	0	$0	$0	$0
July	160	4,481	1,323	1,323
August	600	16,804	4,961	6,283
September	1,001	28,007	8,268	14,551
October	1,751	49,012	14,469	29,020
November	2,502	70,017	20,669	49,689
December	3,252	91,022	26,870	76,559
January	3,752	105,026	31,004	107,563
February	3,752	105,026	31,004	138,567
March	3,752	105,026	31,004	169,571
April	3,252	91,022	26,870	196,441
May	1,401	39,210	11,575	208,016
June	1,401	39,210	11,575	219,591
July	1,001	28,007	8,268	227,858
August	1,001	28,007	8,268	236,126
September	1,001	28,007	8,268	244,394
October	2,502	70,017	20,669	265,063
November	3,252	91,022	26,870	291,933
TOTALS	35,331	988,920	291,933	291,933

*NOTE: Media, production, and product development costs are excluded.

Sample Pro Forma

Outbound Sales Pro Forma Cash Flow

Production Cost	$350,000
Beginning Air Date	June 1997
Multiple Payments (months)	2
% Converted to Single Payment	50%
Product Development Cost	$195,000

Inquiry % of Total Inbound Calls	50%
Inquiry Conversion %	20%

Credit Card Decline %	4%
Credit Card Conversion %	75%

NOTE: The remaining input parameters are identical to those used in Retail Sales except for "Outbound Telemarketing" which is taken from the "Outbound Sales" section of the "Input Parameters" worksheet.

Revenues		
Retail Price/Unit		89.99
Shipping & Handling		9.95
Total Revenues		99.94
Expenses		
Cost of Goods		9.50
Inventory Costs		0.00
Premiums		0.00
Returns & Bad Debt (%)	5.0%	
Returns & Bad Debt ($)		4.50
Outbound Telemarketing		27.00
Order Processing (incl. shipping)		6.00
Bank Card Fees/Check Proc.	2.6%	
Credit Card Order %	90%	
Check/MO Order %	10%	
Bank Card Fees/Check Proc.		2.60
Customer Service		1.50
Dub Cost		0.40
Royalties (5%)		4.50
Other Royalty		1.00
Total Expenses		57.00
Gross Margin/Unit		**42.94**
Scenario ID:		32904.41869

Month	Inquiry Conversion Unit Sales	Credit Card Conversion Unit Sales	Total Unit Sales	Gross Sales	Gross Receipts	Cash Flow*	Cumulative Cash Flow*	Mulitple Payment Receivables
June	0	0	0	$0	$0	$0	$0	$0
July	160	23	183	18,250	13,688	3,279	3,279	4,563
August	600	84	685	68,438	55,891	16,859	20,138	12,547
September	1001	141	1,141	114,063	102,656	37,604	57,742	11,406
October	1751	246	1,997	199,609	178,223	64,381	122,123	21,387
November	2502	352	2,853	285,156	263,770	101,139	223,262	21,387
December	3252	457	3,709	370,703	349,316	137,896	361,159	21,387
January	3752	528	4,280	427,734	413,477	169,530	530,689	14,258
February	3752	528	4,280	427,734	427,734	183,788	714,477	0
March	3752	528	4,280	427,734	427,734	183,788	898,265	0
April	3252	457	3,709	370,703	384,961	173,541	1,071,806	(14,258)
May	1401	197	1,598	159,688	212,441	121,368	1,193,175	(52,754)
June	1401	197	1,598	159,688	159,688	68,614	1,261,789	0
July	1001	141	1,141	114,063	125,469	60,416	1,322,205	(11,406)
August	1001	141	1,141	114,063	114,063	49,010	1,371,215	0
September	1001	141	1,141	114,063	114,063	49,010	1,420,226	0
October	2502	352	2,853	285,156	242,383	79,752	1,499,978	42,773
November	3252	457	3,709	370,703	349,316	137,896	1,637,874	21,387
TOTALS (Month 1–18)	35331	4,968	40,300	4,027,547	3,934,871	1,637,874	1,637,874	92,676
TOTALS (Month 19 fwd.)	0	0	0	0	92,676	92,676	1,730,550	(92,676)
GRAND TOTALS (All Months)	35,331	4,968	40,300	4,027,547	4,027,547	1,730,550	1,730,550	0

NOTE: Media, production, and product development costs are excluded.

Sample Pro Forma

Retail Sales Pro Forma Cash Flow

RETAIL SALES

Revenues		
Wholesale Price/Unit		45.00
Total Revenues		45.00
Expenses		
Cost of Goods		9.50
Royalty Percentage	0%	
Royalty		2.25
Returns Bad Debt (%)	0%	
Returns & Bad Debt ($)		0.00
Order Processing (incl. shipping)		0.00
Inventory Cost		0.00
Other Royalty		1.00
Total Expenses		12.75
Gross Margin/Unit		**32.25**

Scenario ID: 32904.41869

Month	Retail/Direct Units Ratio	Unit Sales	Gross Sales	Cash Flow*	Cumulative Cash Flow*
June	0%	0	$0	$0	$0
July	0%	0	0	0	0
August	0%	0	0	0	0
September	0%	0	0	0	0
October	0%	0	0	0	0
November	0%	0	0	0	0
December	100%	16,260	731,689	524,377	524,377
January	100%	18,761	844,257	605,051	1,129,428
February	100%	18,761	844,257	605,051	1,734,478
March	100%	18,761	844,257	605,501	2,339,529
April	100%	16,260	731,689	524,377	2,863,906
May	100%	7,004	315,189	225,886	3,089,791
June	200%	14,008	630,378	451,771	3,541,562
July	200%	10,006	450,270	322,694	3,864,256
August	200%	10,006	450,270	322,694	4,186,950
September	200%	10,006	450,270	322,694	4,509,643
October	200%	25,015	1,125,675	806,734	5,316,377
November	200%	32,520	1,463,378	1,048,754	6,365,132
Totals		197,368	8,881,579	6,365,132	6,365,132

*NOTE: Media, production, and product development costs are excluded.

Sample Pro Forma

Combined Direct, Upsell, Outbound, and Retail Sales

Page 1 of 3

Product Development	$195,000
Production Cost	$350,000
Total Media Buy	$7,440,000

				Unit Sales						Gross Sales ($)					
1	2	3	4	5	6	7	8	9	10	11	12	13	14	15	16
Month	Media Efficiency Ratio	Media Buy	Retail/ Direct Units Ratio	Direct Sales (Units)	Upsell Sales (Units)	Outbound Sales (Units)	TOTAL TELE-MARKETING SALES (Units)	Retail Sales (Units)	TOTAL TELE-MARKETING & RETAIL SALES (Units)	Direct Gross Sales ($)	Upsell Gross Sales ($)	Outbound Gross Sales ($)	TOTAL TELE-MARKETING GROSS SALES ($)	Retail Gross Sales ($)	TOTAL TELE-MARKETING & RETAIL GROSS SALES ($)
June	0.0	$0	0%	0	0	0	0	0	0	$0	$0	$0	$0	$0	$0
July	2.0	40,000	0%	800	160	183	1,143	0	1,143	80,000	4,481	18,250	102,731	0	102,731
August	2.0	150,000	0%	3,002	600	685	4,287	0	4,287	300,000	16,804	68,438	385,242	0	385,242
September	2.0	250,000	0%	5,003	1,001	1,141	7,145	0	7,145	500,000	28,007	114,063	642,069	0	642,069
October	2.5	350,000	0%	8,755	1,751	1,997	12,504	0	12,504	875,000	49,012	199,609	1,123,621	0	1,123,621
November	2.5	500,000	0%	12,508	2,502	2,853	17,862	0	17,862	1,250,000	70,017	285,156	1,605,173	0	1,605,173
December	2.5	650,000	100%	16,260	3,252	3,709	23,221	16,260	39,481	1,625,000	91,022	370,703	2,086,725	731,689	2,818,414
January	2.5	750,000	100%	18,761	3,752	4,280	26,793	18,761	45,555	1,875,000	105,026	427,734	2,407,760	844,257	3,252,016
February	2.5	750,000	100%	18,761	3,752	4,280	26,793	18,761	45,555	1,875,000	105,026	427,734	2,407,760	844,257	3,252,016
March	2.5	750,000	100%	18,761	3,752	4,280	26,793	18,761	45,555	1,875,000	105,026	427,734	2,407,760	844,257	3,252,016
April	2.5	650,000	100%	16,260	3,252	3,709	23,221	16,260	39,481	1,625,000	91,022	370,703	2,086,725	731,689	2,818,414
May	2.0	350,000	100%	7,004	1,401	1,598	10,003	7,004	17,007	700,000	39,210	159,688	898,897	315,189	1,214,086
June	2.0	350,000	200%	7,004	1,401	1,598	10,003	14,008	24,011	700,000	39,210	159,688	898,897	630,378	1,529,275
July	2.0	250,000	200%	5,003	1,001	1,141	7,145	10,006	17,151	500,000	28,007	114,063	642,069	450,270	1,092,339
August	2.0	250,000	200%	5,003	1,001	1,141	7,145	10,006	17,151	500,000	28,007	114,063	642,069	450,270	1,092,339
September	2.0	250,000	200%	5,003	1,001	1,141	7,145	10,006	17,151	500,000	28,007	114,063	642,069	450,270	1,092,339
October	2.5	500,000	200%	12,508	2,502	2,853	17,862	25,015	42,877	1,250,000	70,017	285,156	1,605,173	1,125,675	2,730,849
November	2.5	650,000	200%	16,260	3,252	3,709	23,221	32,520	55,740	1,625,000	91,022	370,703	2,086,725	1,463,378	3,550,103
TOTALS (Month 1–18)		$7,440,000		176,656	35,331	40,300	252,287	197,368	449,655	$17,655,000	$988,920	$4,027,547	$22,671,467	$8,881,579	$31,553,046
TOTALS (Month 19 fwd.)		$0		0	0	0	0	0	0	0	0	0	0	0	0
GRAND TOTALS (All Months)		$7,440,000		176,656	35,331	40,300	252,287	197,368	449,655	$17,655,000	$988,920	$4,027,547	$22,671,467	$8,881,579	$31,553,046

Sample Pro Forma

Combined Direct, Upsell, Outbound, and Retail Sales
Page 2 of 3

Product Development	$195,000
Production Cost	$350,000
Total Media Buy	$7,440,000

				Sales Receipts*						Telemarketing Cash Flow**				
1	2	3	4	5	6	7	8	9	10	11	12	13	14	15
Month	Media Efficiency Ratio	Media Buy	Retail/ Direct Units Ratio	Direct Sales Receipts ($)	Upsell Sales Receipts ($)	Outbound Sales Receipts ($)	TOTAL TELE-MARKETING SALES RECEIPTS ($)	Retail Sales Receipts ($)	TOTAL TELE-MARKETING & RETAIL SALES RECEIPTS ($)	Direct Cash Flow	Upsell Cash Flow	Outbound Cash Flow	TOTAL TELE-MARKETING CASH FLOW	CUMULATIVE TELE-MARKETING CASH FLOW
June	0.0	$0	0%	$0	$0	$0	$0	$0	$0	$0	$0	$0	$0	$0
July	2.0	40,000	0%	60,000	4,481	13,688	78,169	0	78,169	34,386	1,323	3,279	38,988	38,988
August	2.0	150,000	0%	245,000	16,804	55,891	317,695	0	317,695	148,949	4,961	16,859	170,768	209,757
September	2.0	250,000	0%	450,000	28,007	102,656	580,663	0	580,663	289,914	8,268	37,604	335,786	545,543
October	2.5	350,000	0%	781,250	49,012	178,223	1,008,485	0	1,008,485	501,100	14,469	64,381	579,950	1,125,492
November	2.5	500,000	0%	1,156,250	70,017	263,770	1,490,037	0	1,490,037	756,036	20,669	101,139	877,844	2,003,336
December	2.5	650,000	100%	1,531,250	91,022	349,316	1,971,589	731,689	2,703,278	1,010,971	26,870	137,896	1,175,738	3,179,074
January	2.5	750,000	100%	1,812,500	105,026	413,477	2,331,002	844,257	3,175,259	1,212,178	31,004	169,530	1,412,713	4,591,786
February	2.5	750,000	100%	1,875,000	105,026	427,734	2,407,760	844,257	3,252,016	1,274,678	31,004	183,788	1,489,471	6,081,257
March	2.5	750,000	100%	1,875,000	105,026	427,734	2,407,760	844,257	3,252,016	1,274,678	31,004	183,788	1,489,471	7,570,728
April	2.5	650,000	100%	1,687,500	91,022	384,961	2,163,483	731,689	2,895,172	1,167,221	26,870	173,541	1,367,632	8,938,360
May	2.0	350,000	100%	931,250	39,210	212,441	1,182,901	315,189	1,498,090	707,130	11,575	121,368	840,073	9,778,433
June	2.0	350,000	200%	700,000	39,210	159,668	898,897	630,378	1,529,275	475,880	11,575	68,614	556,069	10,334,502
July	2.0	250,000	200%	550,000	28,007	125,469	703,476	450,270	1,153,746	389,914	8,268	60,416	458,598	10,793,100
August	2.0	250,000	200%	500,000	28,007	114,063	642,069	450,270	1,092,339	339,914	8,268	49,010	397,192	11,190,293
September	2.0	250,000	200%	500,000	28,007	114,063	642,069	450,270	1,092,339	339,914	8,268	49,010	397,192	11,587,485
October	2.5	500,000	200%	1,062,500	70,017	242,383	1,374,900	1,125,675	2,500,575	662,286	20,669	79,752	762,707	12,350,192
November	2.5	650,000	200%	1,531,250	91,022	349,316	1,971,589	1,463,378	3,434,967	1,010,971	26,870	137,896	1,175,738	$13,525,929
TOTALS (Month 1–18)		$7,440,000		$17,248,750	$988,920	$3,934,871	$22,172,541	$8,881,579	$31,054,120	$11,596,122	$291,933	########	$13,525,929	$13,525,929
TOTALS (Month 19 fwd.)		$0		$406,250	$0	$92,676	$498,926	$0	$498,926	$406,250	$0	$92,676	$498,926	$14,024,855
GRAND TOTALS (All Months)		$7,440,000		$17,655,000	$988,920	$4,027,547	$22,671,467	$8,881,579	$31,553,046	$12,002,372	$291,933	########	$14,024,855	$14,024,855

*NOTE: SALES RECEIPTS represent GROSS SALES distributed over more than one month for multiple payment programs. For single payment programs, the GROSS SALES and SALES RECEIPTS setions will be identical.

**Note: Product Development, Productions, and Media Buys are not yet deducted.

Sample Pro Forma

Combined Direct, Upsell, Outbound, and Retail Sales
Page 3 of 3

Product Development	$195,000
Production Cost	$350,000
Total Media Buy	$7,440,000

				Combined Cash Fow						
1	2	3	4	5	6	7	8	9	10	11
Month	Media Efficiency Ratio	Media Buy	Retail/ Direct Units Ratio	Total Product Development Creative, and Media Costs	TOTAL TELE-MARKETING NET CASH FLOW*	CUMULATIVE TELE-MARKETING NET CASH FLOW	Investment Capital (Product Development Creative & Media)	Retail Cash Flow	TOTAL TELE-MARKETING & RETAIL CASH FLOW	TOTAL CUMULATIVE NET CASH FLOW
June	0.0	$0	0%	$545,0000	($585,000)	($585,000)	$585,000	$0	($585,000)	($585,000)
July	2.0	40,000	0%	40,000	(111,012)	(696,012)	111,012	0	(111,012)	(696,012)
August	2.0	150,000	0%	150,000	(79,232)	(775,243)	79,232	0	(79,232)	(775,243)
September	2.0	250,000	0%	250,000	(14,214)	(789,457)	14,214	0	(14,214)	(789,457)
October	2.5	350,000	0%	350,000	79,950	(709,508)	0	0	79,950	(709,508)
November	2.5	500,000	0%	500,000	227,844	(481,664)	0	0	227,844	(481,664)
December	2.5	650,000	100%	650,000	425,738	(55,926)	0	524,377	950,115	468,451
January	2.5	750,000	100%	750,000	662,713	606,786	0	605,051	1,267,763	1,736,214
February	2.5	750,000	100%	750,000	739,471	1,346,257	0	605,051	1,344,521	3,080,735
March	2.5	750,000	100%	750,000	839,471	2,185,728	0	605,051	1,444,521	4,525,526
April	2.5	650,000	100%	650,000	1,017,623	3,203,360	0	524,377	1,542,009	6,067,266
May	2.0	350,000	100%	350,000	490,073	3,693,433	0	225,886	715,958	6,783,224
June	2.0	350,000	200%	350,000	306,069	3,999,502	0	451,771	757,840	7,541,064
July	2.0	250,000	200%	250,000	208,598	4,208,100	0	322,694	531,292	8,072,356
August	2.0	250,000	200%	250,000	147,192	4,355,293	0	322,694	469,886	8,542,242
September	2.0	250,000	200%	250,000	(102,808)	4,252,485	0	322,694	219,886	8,762,128
October	2.5	500,000	200%	500,000	112,707	4,365,192	0	806,734	919,441	9,681,569
November	2.5	650,000	200%	650,000	1,175,738	5,540,929	0	1,048,754	2,224,492	11,906,061

	Media Buy	Total Product Development Creative, and Media Costs	TOTAL TELE-MARKETING NET CASH FLOW*	CUMULATIVE TELE-MARKETING NET CASH FLOW	Investment Capital	Retail Cash Flow	TOTAL TELE-MARKETING & RETAIL CASH FLOW	TOTAL CUMULATIVE NET CASH FLOW
TOTALS (Month 1–18)	$7,440,000	$7,985,000	$5,540,929	$5,540,929	$789,457	$6,365,132	$11,906,061	$11,906,061
TOTALS (Month 19 fwd.)	$0	$0	$498,926	$6,039,855	$0	$0	$498,926	$12,404,987
GRAND TOTALS (All Months)	$7,440,000	$7,985,000	$6,039,855	$6,039,855	$789,457	$6,365,132	$12,404,987	$12,404,987

NOTE: Media costs are paid out during month prior to airing.

Sample Pro Forma

Combined Direct, Upsell, Outbound, and Retail Sales Summary

Product Development	$195,000
Production Cost	$350,000
Total Media Buy	$7,440,000

1	2	3	4	5	6	7	8	9	10	11	12	13	14	15	16	17
Month	Media Efficiency Ratio	Media Buy	Retail/ Direct Units Ratio	Direct Sales (Units)	Upsell Sales (Units)	Outbound Sales (Units)	Retail Sales (Units)	TOTAL SALES (Units)	Direct Sales ($)	Upsell Sales ($)	Outbound Sales ($)	Retail Sales ($)	TOTAL SALES ($)	TOTAL MONTHLY CASH FLOW	TOTAL CUMULATIVE CASH FLOW	Investment Capital (Prod. Dev., Creative Media)
June	0.0	$0	0%	0	0	0	0	0	$0	$0	$0	$0	$0	($585,000)	($585,000)	$585,000
July	2.0	40,000	0%	800	160	183	0	1,143	80,000	4,481	18,250	0	102,731	(111,012)	(696,012)	111,012
August	2.0	150,000	0%	3,002	600	685	0	4,287	300,000	16,804	68,438	0	385,242	(79,232)	(775,243)	79,214
September	2.0	250,000	0%	5,003	1,001	1,141	0	7,145	500,000	28,007	114,063	0	642,069	(14,214)	(789,457)	14,214
October	2.5	350,000	0%	8,755	1,751	1,997	0	12,504	875,000	49,012	199,609	0	1,123,621	79,250	(709,508)	0
November	2.5	500,000	0%	12,508	2,502	2,853	0	17,862	1,250,000	70,017	285,156	0	1,605,173	227,844	(481,664)	0
December	2.5	650,000	100%	16,260	3,252	3,709	16,260	39,481	1,625,000	91,022	370,703	731,689	2,818,414	950,115	468,451	0
January	2.5	750,000	100%	18,761	3,752	4,280	18,761	45,555	1,875,000	105,026	427,734	844,257	3,252,016	1,267,763	1,736,214	0
February	2.5	750,000	100%	18,761	3,752	4,280	18,761	45,555	1,875,000	105,026	427,734	844,257	3,252,016	1,344,521	3,080,735	0
March	2.5	750,000	100%	18,761	3,752	4,280	18,761	45,555	1,875,000	105,026	427,734	844,257	3,252,016	1,444,521	4,525,256	0
April	2.5	650,000	100%	16,260	3,252	3,709	16,260	39,481	1,625,000	91,022	370,703	731,689	2,818,414	1,542,009	6,067,266	0
May	2.0	350,000	100%	7,004	1,401	1,598	7,004	17,007	700,000	39,210	159,688	315,189	1,214,086	715,958	6,783,224	0
June	2.0	350,000	200%	7,004	1,401	1,598	14,008	24,011	700,000	39,210	159,688	630,378	1,529,275	757,840	7,541,064	0
July	2.0	250,000	200%	5,003	1,001	1,141	10,006	17,151	500,000	28,007	114,063	450,270	1,092,339	531,292	8,072,356	0
August	2.0	250,000	200%	5,003	1,001	1,141	10,006	17,151	500,000	28,007	114,063	450,270	1,092,339	469,886	8,542,242	0
September	2.0	250,000	200%	5,003	1,001	1,141	10,006	17,151	500,000	28,007	114,063	450,270	1,092,339	219,886	8,762,128	0
October	2.5	500,000	200%	12,508	2,502	2,853	25,015	42,877	1,250,000	70,017	285,156	1,125,675	2,730,849	919,441	9,681,569	0
November	2.5	650,000	200%	16,260	3,252	3,709	32,520	55,740	1,625,000	91,022	370,703	1,463,378	3,550,103	2,224,492	11,906,061	0
TOTALS (Month 1–18)		$7,440,000		176,656	35,331	40,300	197,368	449,655	$17,655,000	$988,920	$4,027,547	$8,881,579	$31,553,046	$11,906,061	$11,906,061	$789,457
TOTALS (Month 19 fwd.)		$0		0	0	0	0	0	0	0	0	0	0	$498,926	$12,404,987	$0
GRAND TOTALS (All Months)		$7,440,000		176,656	35,331	40,300	197,368	449,655	$17,655,000	$988,920	$4,027,547	$8,881,579	$31,553,046	$12,404,987	$12,404,987	$789,457

Sample Pro Forma

Pro Forma Overview

18 Month Campaign

Product Development	$195,000
Production Cost	$350,000
Total Media Buy	$7,440,000

Average Media Efficiency Ratio	Investment Capital	Direct Sales (Units)	Upsell Sales (Units)	Outbound Sales (Units)	Retail Sales (Units)	Gross Sales	Total Cash Flow
1:1	2,744,646	74,445	14,889	16,983	84,050	13,336,261	635,846
2:1	794,795	148,889	29,778	33,965	168,101	26,672,521	9,256,692
3:1	676,518	223,334	44,667	50,948	252,151	40,008,782	17,877,537
4:1	657,024	297,779	59,556	67,931	336,202	53,345,042	26,498,383
5:1	637,529	372,223	74,445	84,913	420,252	66,681,303	35,119,229
6:1	618,035	446,668	89,334	101,896	504,303	80,017,564	43,740,075
7:1	598,541	521,113	104,223	189,879	588,353	93,353,824	52,360,920
8:1	585,000	595,557	119,111	135,862	672,403	106,690,085	60,981,766

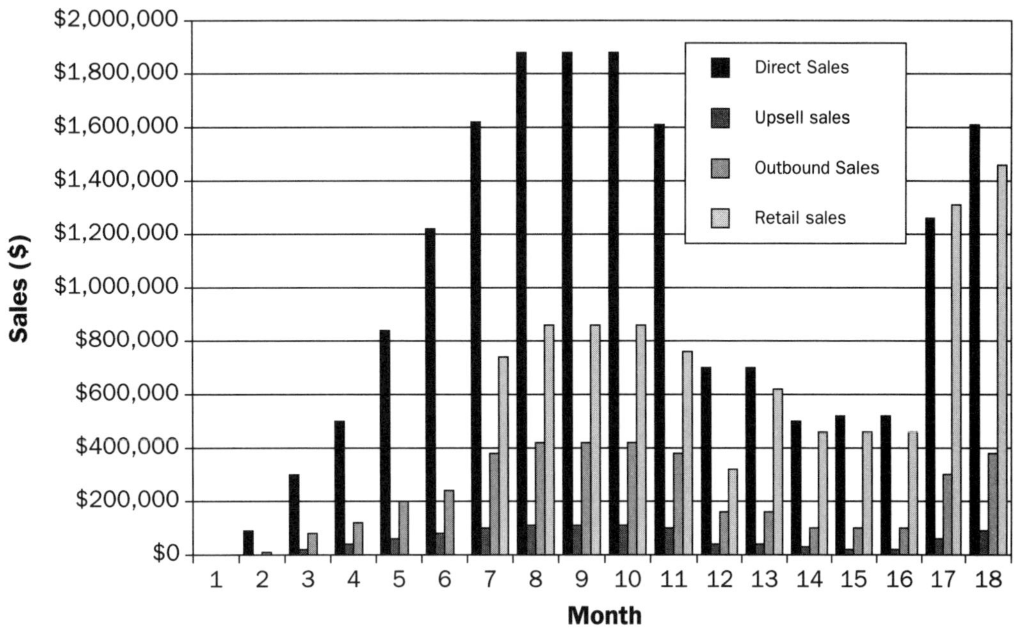
$2,000,000
$1,800,000
$1,600,000
$1,400,000
$1,200,000
$1,000,000
$800,000
$600,000
$400,000
$200,000
$0
Sales ($)
1 2 3 4 5 6 7 8 9 10 11 12 13 14 15 16 17 18
Month
Direct Sales
Upsell sales
Outbound Sales
Retail sales

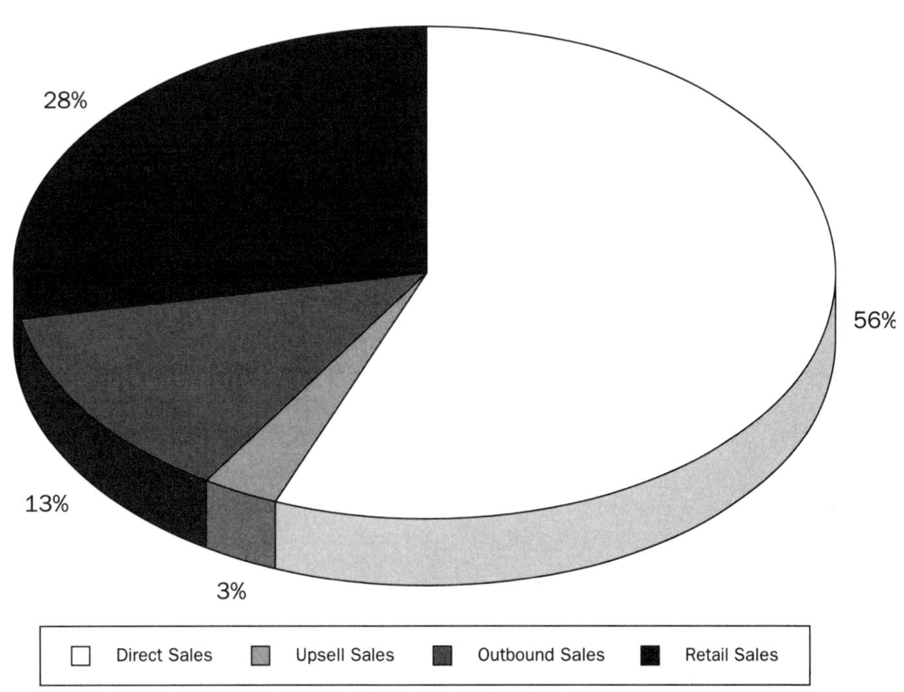
28%
56%
13%
3%
Direct Sales
Upsell Sales
Outbound Sales
Retail Sales

CHAPTER

Media Planning, Buying and Analysis

In this chapter, you'll find a range of background information and hints to help you make media buying decisions. Or, if you're using an ad agency, this chapter will help you work with your agency more effectively.

Media Buying for Image Spots vs. Infomercials

Infomercial media buying is highly specialized and miles apart from image spot buying or even short form (60, 90 and 120 second) DRTV spot buying.

Image spot campaigns usually have established media budgets. Infomercial media campaigns rarely have budgets (other than the initial $30,000 to $50,000 media test). As long as the media buys create profits, infomercial buyers will spend as much as they can.

Image spot campaigns buy media to obtain a pre-set amount of gross rating points (total viewer impressions). Infomercial buyers care very little about how many viewers watch. They concentrate on how many pick up the phone and order. Image spot buyers buy 6, 8, or 12 week campaign flights then take the commercial off the air. Infomercial campaigns can run continuously 52 weeks a year for 5 years or more. Spot buyers have difficulty reserving specific 30-second spot periods within any half hour. Infomercial buyers can secure 13-, 26- or 52-week contracts for specific half hours and essentially "own" the time.

Image spot media is planned, then purchased all at once, and then left alone to run its course. Infomercial media changes dramatically from week to week based on results and requires daily cancellation, rebuying, and renegotiation.

Image spot campaigns largely have no accountability measurements for success. Infomercial campaigns can measure success or failure within 24 hours of the media run. Image spot campaigns have no need for a historical media database. Infomercial media buyers rely on databases of thousands of previous telecasts and their revenue results to determine future strategy.

Media Buying for Short-Form DRTV Spots vs. Infomercials

Though infomercials are DRTV cousins to short form, the differences are striking. Short-form DRTV spot campaigns have never produced the revenue that a successful infomercial can. To my knowledge, there has yet to be a two-minute DRTV spot that generated $100 million plus in product sales in just one year as some successful infomercials have. And yet this is no reason to dismiss short-form DRTV.

In fact, short form often complements the infomercial campaign. Many infomercial clients cut 60-, 90- or 120-second commercials out of their infomercial and run a simultaneous short-form campaign. Normally, the short-form spots are not as profitable as the infomercial, but by reminding viewers of the product in short bursts throughout the day, they can create a synergy with the infomercial to boost profitability.

Some other drawbacks to short-form DRTV are that buyers are required to purchase groups of spots on a weekly rotation and measure success primarily on a station-by-station basis. Infomercial buyers can purchase one half hour, or many, on the same station and measure success for each individual half hour.

Also, short-form DRTV spots are run on a "remnant" basis—i.e., when and where the station chooses—and achieve on average a 50 percent clearance (the percentage of spots that run versus what you requested); infomercials time slots are set and secure for at least each upcoming quarter and clear 95 percent of the time.

Broadcast, Cable, Ratings, and Shares

Before jumping into the complex world of infomercial media planning and buying, it is probably a good idea to describe some of the media landscape and terminology.

In the United States, there are six commercial broadcast networks (ABC, CBS, NBC, FOX, UPN, WB), over 1,100 local broadcast TV stations, nearly 140 national cable networks, 43 regional cable networks and over 11,000 local cable systems. All of these are potential venues for running your infomercial.

Traditionally these media outlets have been advertiser supported; i.e. they make money selling that most perishable of commodities—time. For decades their primary business has been spot sales, peddling 60-, 30-, 15-, 10- and 5-second units of time, as much as 14 minutes per hour in aggregate. Every traditional media buyer knows what the value is of any spot time on a station or network. The rates are published fact. That value is called CPM—the "cost per thousand" viewers ($10 to $20 on average) who are watching the entertainment program within which your spot commercial runs. And the CPM is determined by knowing any program's rating.

Though infomercial media time is not purchased according to CPM, gross rating points, or GRPs, as is traditional 30 second spot media, understanding the basics is helpful.

First, A. C. Nielsen, the television rating company, has assigned all U.S. TV households (97 million) to a *Designated Market Area* (DMA), usually called a *market* (roughly whichever major city you live in or are closest to). Nielsen has designated there to be 212 such DMA markets in the U.S. Each market has multiple local broadcast stations and cable systems. Sprinkled among these markets, in carefully selected TV households, are nearly 5,000 electronic " people meters" which automatically measure TV viewing. Based on the viewing habits of these 5,000 "Nielsen families," TV networks get the good or bad news about their primetime program ratings.

What exactly is a *rating*? It is the percentage of total potential viewers watching a particular show. For example, "Seinfeld" averages a national rating of about 20, which means approximately 20 percent of 97 households—or 19 million households—watch Jerry, Elaine, George, and Kramer. The rating indicates the strength of a program relative to all programs aired at any time. "Seinfeld" usually ranks first or second in total number of viewers.

Nielsen also measures *households using television* (HUT). This is the percentage of total homes with a television that are actually watching it (or them) at any specific time (average HUT during primetime is 60.4 percent).

Another often reported number is a program's *share*. Share is the percentage of the HUT (actual households watching TV at any one time) who are watching a particular show. Share measures a program's relative strength against its immediate competition in a time period. If the HUT during "Seinfeld," for example, is 60 percent, then 57.5 million TV households are watching TV (any program) at 9 p.m. on Thursday. Now we can figure out the share by dividing 57.5 million into 19 million, which equals 33 percent meaning 33 percent of all people watching TV on Thursday at 9 p.m. are watching Jerry. Here's the formula to remember:

Rating = HUT (×) Share.

How many consumers might watch your infomercial? We need to discuss a few more numbers before we can calculate that.

Nielsen provides ratings for both national and local viewership. It's important to note this because most of your infomercial ratings will be local. For example, the Minneapolis/St. Paul market (DMA) has 1.8 million TV households. So if "Seinfeld" got a 20 rating in the Twin Cities, 360,000 TV households watched. If your infomercial got a 4 rating, that would be 4 percent of 1.8 million or 72,000 TV households.

Your agency might also report national cable network ratings. Note again, cable networks don't use a total universe of 95.8 million homes as the basis for their ratings. They use the total number of cable subscribers receiving their network. Of course, this can vary dramatically. If your infomercial got a 1 rating on USA Network, it's 1% of the number of TV households receiving USA; if you got a .5 rating on CNBC, it is .5 percent of the number of TV households that subscribe to CNBC.

How many individuals are watching the same TV program in the average TV household? In 1955, there was an average of 3.5 viewers per household (fewer TVs and bigger families). In 1994, that number dropped to 1.45 viewers (more TVs and smaller families). So if you want to calculate total viewers, not just households, as in the Minneapolis example, multiply 1.45 (×) 72,000 = 104,400.

Infomercials average from .1 to 1 ratings, although some name-brand infomercial ratings (Apple, Nissan, Microsoft) soar to 4, 5 even 7 with shares as high as 20. Ratings and total number of viewers, though critical to image spot buyers, are little more than ego strokes for infomercial media buyers. For one-step infomercial product marketers, the only number that counts is the weekly bank deposit.

Infomercials' Share of the Media Marketplace

In the U.S., approximately $35 billion is spent for all television TV ad time. Of that $12 billion goes toward the four major broadcast networks and about $15 billion to local broadcast stations. An additional $6 billion is spent on syndication and cable networks.

What portion does infomercial media have of this $35 billion pie? Barely 2 percent or $625 million. Through inflation and expansion, the domestic long-form media market may approach $1.2 billion within 10 years, still a fraction of the TV ad market. But this seemingly niche market is a boon to infomercial marketers. Quietly they continue to reap the windfall benefits of the best media investment in TV.

Media Planning and Testing

Before creating an infomercial, you or your infomercial ad agency should review your customer profile, market research, and historical sales results to determine demographic targeting and refine your campaign objectives. The following outline describes the strategies and considerations that should be used to structure the typical media test.

Determine the Purpose and Type of Your Ad Campaign

Which of the following do you want your show to achieve?

- Make a direct product sale (one step offer).

- Generate a lead (two step offer).
- Strengthen Customer Relationship: increase brand loyalty; develop one-on-one customer database.
- Influence purchase behavior: enhance product value, move excess inventory, create sales bump with seasonal or event promotion.
- Reach new prospects: encourage product trial and retention.
- Launch new product: rapid and inexpensive test marketing.
- Demonstrate additional product uses: deepen product understanding and education.
- Build brand awareness; clarify differentiation; enhance image.
- Sustain and build brand equity: communicate corporate good works; solve a PR problem
- Reposition brand: revive a mature product.
- Seasonal retail sales promotion
- Drive retail sales
- A mix of the above

The infomercial is profoundly capable of doing any of the above based on its half hour of product story telling time.

Set Target Test Date

Target a realistic start date for the media test, generally two to four weeks after production completion. This amount of time is required to finalize purchasing the best media avails and get station legal approval of the infomercial production. Remember, if production goes longer than expected, the test will be delayed and you may destroy months of valuable preparation. Keep the production on track at all costs.

Establish Media Test Budget and Duration

For one-step offers, it takes very few media dollars to determine infomercial success or failure. Unlike traditional spot campaigns that devote $2 to $30 million for media without learning the advertising's impact for months, infomercial marketers will know within 1 hour of the first major telecast. Nonetheless, I recommend a $30,000 to

$50,000 media test budget over a 10 to 14 day period, to get a clear understanding of the infomercials full potential.

If the infomercial is intended to drive retail, as in a name brand advertiser campaign, $150,000 to $250,000 of media should be tested over a 6 to 8 week period. The extra dollars and time are necessary to measure the delayed response that occurs with infomercials' impact on retail. It takes time for infomercial viewers to eventually get to a store.

Research the Best Broadcast and Cable Media Test Markets

Your media strategies should identify broadcast and cable markets for the test runs based upon the following parameters.

- Historical products sales results, if available
- Analysis of customer demographics, as provided by the client
- Product seasonality
- Your ad agency's knowledge of the U.S. markets/stations producing the best infomercial response overall
- Footprinting: research of previous successful infomercials with similar demographic appeal to determine daypart, station, market and telecast frequency

Calculate the Broadcast/Cable Media Mix

You will need a mix of cable networks and broadcast stations. We always recommend testing on two to four national cable networks (40 percent of test budget) and in 6 to 12 markets U.S. broadcast markets (60 percent of budget).

Calculate the Affiliate/Independent Station Mix

Network affiliates dominate the viewing in most TV broadcast markets. Independent stations (indies), which air mostly reruns, have a much smaller share of audience. This doesn't necessarily mean indy station infomercial time periods will be unprofitable. It does mean you will have fewer viewers and should pay less. When determining your affiliate/independent broadcast station mix, shoot for stations/markets with good direct response history. Strike a balance between affiliates and independent stations.

Ensure Regional Representation

Your infomercial campaign, if successful, will most likely be national in scope. With $50,000 in media test dollars, it's wise to test the program's response pull in five regions: East, South, Midwest, West and U.S./Canadian border. Try to select a market/station (and an alternate) in each region. U.S./Canadian border is considered a separate region because of its unique response characteristics. TV stations in markets like Buffalo, Seattle, Burlington, VT have thousands of loyal Canadian viewers. These markets have much higher response rates than other U.S. markets their size.

Select Dayparts

Generally, it's best to buy a spread of all dayparts (see Glossary). The infomercial product type, marketing strategy, target demographics and avails will influence daypart selection. In most cases, 50 percent of the test time slots will be Saturday/Sunday daytime, 25 percent in late fringe and 25 percent spread among all other dayparts.

Negotiate Test Media Costs

Media costs vary from quarter to quarter. They're highest during first and fourth quarters. Expect to pay about $.10 to $.30 per household for the time period, but be prepared for possible variations.

Prepare A/B Split Tests

Be advised to test two different offers, most likely with a high and low pricepoint. Then be sure your agency prepares a proper A/B split test, matching markets by region, DMA, or other criteria. Run the media simultaneously in the matched markets. Try not to run both versions in the same market. If you do have to run both versions at the same time, air the lower-priced version first.

Hold Test Media Time

Don't cancel test media time during the test phase—to do this is counterproductive. The intent of a media test is to "test" the sale potential of your product. To effectively fulfill this goal, let the test run as planned.

Some shows need viewers to watch the telecast several times before they are motivated to purchase. Again, this is the purpose of the media test. It gives you the variables inherent in your campaign that are necessary to create a successful venture.

If you have to cancel, most stations require two to four weeks advance notice.

Prepare your Inbound Telemarketing Service

Proper handling of your inbound telemarketing service (800 number and the recently launched 888 toll-free prefix) is one of the most important aspects of the entire test process. The 800/888 number call center/telemarketing service is responsible for the proper setup and processing of information transmission to you and your ad agency.

Setting up this process entails much work (see next chapter), from the beginning and throughout the test run. For example, the 800/888 service must be notified of the broadcast schedule with projected orders, in order to staff properly. The script for the 800/888 operators must be written cohesively and coherently to maximize sales and maintain a high level of quality communication. The entire campaign depends upon accurate information processing.

During the test phase and into roll-out, when 800/888 numbers are needed to place on the broadcast copies to be sent to stations, it is imperative that arrangements be made with the telemarketer to ensure accuracy and processing of toll-free numbers on a timely basis. Naturally, if your ad agency is managing the rollout, they will control and coordinate this process with the telemarketing call center.

Buying Infomercial Media

Buy Media Direct

Because agencies can "own" specific, highly profitable infomercial time slots for long periods of time, valuable long form media has become a hotly traded commodity. The marketplace has been rife with competition for 12 years. In this economic environment, the traditional buyer/seller relationship has been turned upside down. Media buyers do more selling (of themselves and the quality of their agencies and shows), than buying. And cable network sales staff and station national sales managers (NSM) are doing the "buying"—the picking and choosing of which agencies will get their best time slots.

It's advised not to let anyone interfere with this vital buyer/NSM relationship. Good media buyers purchase time slots directly from TV station and cable network sales departments, bypassing the TV sales rep firms. Simply put, the stations' NSM are the power people; they decide what to charge and what agency will get the infomercial time slots. TV rep firms must answer to them. Using rep companies can often put you too distant from the battle for hotly competed-for air time. Though some stations will not deal direct, preferring their sales rep company manage their infomercial time, your media agency still should be purchasing 85 percent of its time direct.

Because buyers deal mostly direct, their relationships with NSM's, both over the phone and in person, are of paramount importance. People like to do business with people they like. Media buyers often take nationwide "road trips" to visit and socialize with their station and cable network contacts whenever possible.

Evaluate Time Slots

One of the critical steps in buying infomercial media is evaluating a specific time slot's potential to produce profits. The system your agency uses can make all the difference between profit and loss. Today, most veteran infomercial media buying agencies have very sophisticated computer analysis programs that crunch numbers and probabilities. These programs are based on a basic process that can be (and used to be) done manually. Understanding this manual evaluating process will help you manage your media agency and their computer reports. Called the *Media Strategy Weighted Point System* (MSWPS), the evaluation uses a 200-point system to assess four categories:

1. Station (total possible points = 50)
    - market size (10)
    - strength in market (10)
    - past DRTV success (20)
    - relationship (10)
2. Time slot (total possible points = 85)
    - month (10)
    - day (10)
    - DRTV history (50)

- competition (10)
- demo appeal (5)

3. Cost per household for the considered time slot (total possible points = 45)
   - 5–10 cents/HH (25)
   - 11–20 cents/HH (15)
   - 21–30 cents/HH (5)
4. Lead-in/lead-out programs (total possible points = 20)
   - ratings (10)
   - demos (10)

Station Strength

When considering station strength using the MSWPS, give the highest values to the larger television markets because the potential to earn the greatest amount of money is in those markets. For example, New York City or Los Angeles would receive a 10 on a scale of 1 to 10.

Determine sign-on to sign-off strength based on the overall sign-on to sign-off market share for a specific station. As an example, WOR would receive a 5, while WNBC or WCBS would get a 10 on a scale of 1 to 10.

To determine the direct response strength, consider historical data for other products sold on the station in any time slot via direct response television. Project the suitability of the product to the market, as well. Use a scale of 1 to 20.

Evaluate the quality of your relationship with the station, along with the ability of the station to provide you with the avails (available time slots) and price levels that suit your needs. This factor is evaluated on a scale of 1 to 10.

The maximum sum of the subcategory points under the station category is 50 points. A score of 25 points or higher is acceptable.

Time Slot

Because the time slot is one of the most important factors for infomercial success, it carries a weight of 85 points. The month carries 1 to 10 points, the day carries 1 to 10 points.

DRTV history is the heaviest weighted category for this entire system, reflecting the importance of a specific half hour to consistently make money or not. The more history you have to review per time slot, the better your ability to predict success.

Competition is given points from 1 to 10 and evaluates the kind of programming on other channels in the market and their relative appeal. If you're competing against Seinfeld, give yourself 1 point. If you're up against old movies late at night, give yourself 10 points.

Demo appeal (5 points possible) measures how a time slot typically attracts your target demo. Women dominate daytime viewing while men dominate late night. If you run a product targeted for men during Tuesday daytime (and you rarely should), give yourself 1 point.

Cost per Household

As stated above, TV ratings and shares mean very little to infomercial media buyers (especially after the infomercial runs). The station and time slot DRTV history will always be the most important factor. But years ago we discovered a rough measurement that can be one more factor to consider: what was the rating for the time slot when it ran entertainment programming (such as *M*A*S*H* reruns)?

Determine the total number of households for *M*A*S*H*'s average rating then divide the households by the cost of the half hour. Simply stated, the lower the cost on a per household (HH) basis, the better the buy might be.

Lead-In, Lead-Out

Lead-in and lead-out programming can strongly influence the number of households you may be able to capture. This is because many viewers tend to continue watching the same channel after their preferred show, or tune into their preferred show early. The higher the rating for the lead-in/lead-out and the more parallel the demographics to your product's target, the more points you should give. For example, if you have a golf product infomercial and can buy the half hour immediately following The Masters on CBS, award all 20 points.

Total Points

Add the individual category subtotals. Total possible points is 200. Before you consider a time-buy at a given price, the point value per category should be at least one-half the maximum for the category. The total points should be at least 60 percent, or 120 points, of the total possible points.

The MSWPS is an important analytical tool that must be interpreted in the light of the time-buy manager's media experience. After all analyses, even if the points total is acceptable and meets all objective standards, the time-buy manager must make the final decision in the context of all other time-buys. This allows for a check of the buyer's work and allows other unforeseen criteria to influence the decision. Both objective criteria (MSWPS and historical data) and subjective criteria (discussion and gut level) should be used in the buying process, thereby ensuring that all known situations have been taken into account.

Make sure you understand how your agency's media software system takes all of the above factors into consideration.

Broadcast versus Cable

Broadcast TV media or cable network media. How much of which should your buyers be purchasing? There are over 1100 commercial television stations of which 90 percent accept infomercials. There are almost 140 cable networks right now, but only 44 of these that have any kind of penetration and accept infomercials.

Ninety -nine percent of all households have television, all of which receive broadcast TV stations. About 93 percent of all households have cable available to them, but only about 66 percent or 64 million homes, are paying to watch cable.

On average, cable subscribers tend to have higher incomes and are better direct response consumers because they have more disposable income, which is indicated by the fact that the household can spend $30 to $40 per month on cable TV service. People who have cable also tend to have more years of education, more children, and are younger.

Cable channels are more popular than broadcast channels among all cable subscribers. When asked to cite their favorite channels, in a recent survey, subscribers were far more likely to mention a basic cable channel (59 percent) than a broadcast network or independent channel (47 percent). Premium channels were mentioned as favorites by one-half (53 percent) of subscribers who get them. One in four (26 percent) subscribers refer to their favorite channels by position number.

With this as background, what mix of cable media vs. broadcast media would you recommend? You'd probably choose to purchase cable media exclusively. And you'd be wrong. First, the total number of half hours on those 44 cable networks is a fraction of what's available on nearly a 1000 broadcast stations—you'd severely limit your potential revenue. Second, the cost of many cable time slots has gone through the roof, making them profitable for only a handful of powerful infomercials. Third, infomercials tend to run on cable late at night. If you want to reach daytime viewers you need broadcast. Fourth, since seniors tend not to be cable subscribers, you'd be missing a rapidly growing segment of the population. And lastly, since cable is in only 66 percent of homes, you'd only be reaching two-thirds of your potential customers.

For these reasons, we typically recommend a media mix of 70 percent for broadcast TV stations and 30 percent for cable during rollout.

Understanding Infomercial Time Slot Value

Figuring what to pay for any long form time slot today is primarily a function of referencing an infomercial media agency's historical database and comparing how recent infomercials performed in that slot. But if the asking price for an avail is $1,000, how did the station ever arrive at that price? Is it 60 (×) their 30 second spot rate? Or is it 14 (×) the 30 second spot rate (the average number of 30 second spots sold in a half-hour entertainment program)? Could you simply refer to SRDS' published rates for the stations 30 second spots and do the multiplication? The answer is no.

Infomercial time slot value has been created by the pure capitalistic forces of supply and demand. That same $1000 time slot may have cost $200 10 years ago, but as the NSM continued to see the slot heatedly competed for, he/she raised the price, every quarter, until fewer and fewer agencies were willing to bid on it. The NSM finally reached a ceiling where the price sits today. And the only people who know what the absolute minimum the NSM will accept are those infomercial agencies who have it in their database.

Successful Infomercial Media Time Slots and Stations

The most successful infomercial media time slots are late fringe, late night, and Saturday/Sunday daytime. Why? Because the price is right and competing programming is minimal. 70 percent of your roll-out media will be on broadcast television stations but cable networks, especially The Discovery Channel, The Family Channel, Lifetime, CNBC, and TNN, deliver superior response. For years, though, some cable networks have been impossible to break into, such as CNN, MTV, A&E, American Movie Classics, ESPN, and TNT.

WTBS, which no longer runs infomercials, is probably the most profitable channel for short form commercials. But because of intense competition, it's almost impossible to get on with a new two-minute direct response commercial or infomercial. And the waiting list is intimidating.

Consult your infomercial agency for details on hot long form broadcast markets and stations.

Infomercial Campaign Duration

How long will your hit infomercial continue to make millions in profits? No one can say. We know the average life is 9 to 18 months. But many run longer and some run shorter. You will simply run your infomercial as long as the show sells your product and makes you money. Remember, the advantage of infomercials is immediate response measurement. You know exactly how well your show is doing every day by measuring the response to your infomercial. When your sales begin to dip, it's time to revive the campaign by restructuring the offer, reducing the price, redoing the creative, or testing new time slots. Try to think of, and apply, all strategies that a retailer would do to increase sales.

There have been programs on the air selling the same product with no productions changes for as long as two years or more. But, I recommended that a show be changed at least every 12 months. So count on additional production and tape duplication costs every year, and perhaps some changes or additions to your product in the form of new bonuses, premiums and price discounts.

What to Look for in Media Buying Agency

Experience. Period. Buying infomercial time is unlike any other media buying transaction. Find professionals who know the good cities to test, where and how to negotiate good prices, how to analyze results and, above all else, how to cancel unprofitable media immediately. Media buyers should be experts at determining the value of time and negotiating the best possible price. They have to be. Because if their clients are to continue buying media through them, the campaign must always be profitable, which directly depends on the cost of advertising.

And because infomercial time slots can be "owned" via long-term contracts, most of the prime media territory is already staked and claimed by the top half dozen infomercial media companies. They hold tens of millions of dollars of the most profitable time slots in "inventory" for their clients. For this reason, newcomers to long form buying will very likely waste your media dollars. They don't own good media time slots and because they have no historical database, they don't know the value of infomercial time they negotiate for. There are reports of some general ad agencies paying as much as five times the insider rate.

DRTV history is the most valuable asset infomercial agencies have. Huge databases of thousands of telecasts' results in all TV markets and countless time slots. There is no substitute for knowing a specific time slot's value—what to pay for it—based on how a dozen other infomercials performed in that slot previously. Without this historical database, how can a novice buyer possibly know what the time period's value possibly is? Believe me, the TV station or cable network ad sales person is not going to tell them what their last infomercial savvy client paid.

Also demand that your media agency be "full disclosure," meaning they will provide you with station affidavits detailing the exact amount the agency paid for a time slot. The "go-go" media market has been known to attract "non-disclosure" agencies and media brokers who shamelessly resell time slots with monumental mark-ups that are no-win investments.

And lastly, check out the experience and quality of the agency's all important media buyers, as professionals.

Media Buyer Qualifications

Infomercial media buyers are like small business owners. The best are great number crunchers and highly personable. Sometimes as young as their mid-twenties, they manage hundreds of thousands of dollars every week. They're heroes when the client is making money and bums when the campaign is running out of steam. It's a position that requires unique personal character.

First, they must be tough as nails negotiators. Media time is a commodity whose price is subject to supply and demand and whose price has been steadily climbing. Infomercial buyers need be highly trained in professional negotiating tactics that can often reduce prices as much as 50 percent to 60 percent from the initial rate card offer.

Second, buyers must be able to carry the burden of financial responsibility. Media buying mistakes, even the smallest, can have very large monetary repercussions. Buyers must be very detail-oriented, pay close attention to each individual telecast, and carefully execute the required follow-up. They need to be able to quickly compute net from gross buy, CPO's, ad allowables, MER's, profit dollars and how to allocate 13 percent of their media to Sunday morning, 8 A.M. to 10 A.M. time slots.

Third, buyers not only need strong business skills, but a deep understanding of the marketplace. They have to know who's watching television and what they're like. I require a good buyer to know general demographic facts, such as what percentage of the U.S. population is African-American? (12 percent) What percentage of the population is Hispanic? (9 percent) Asian? (2.9 percent) What percentage of the U.S. population has credit cards? (65 percent) What percentage of households has microwaves? (81 percent) Infomercial media buyers must know all these facts and many more.

But most important, a buyer must have personality. As mentioned above, they are constantly selling NSM's on why they, and not a competitor, should get a station's media. They need to establish a sincere relationship, nurture it and be memorable, so that when new media becomes available, the NSM calls him/her first.

In the world of all advertising media, there's not a more challenging job than that of an infomercial buyer.

Media Payments

Here again, the infomercial world is very different from traditional 30 second image spot buying. Spot buyers usually pay 30 to 60 days net. Long form buyers must pay cash up front, typically one to two weeks before air date. This stems from the infomercials' early days when the adage was, "religion and DRTV pay up front." It reflected the stations lack of confidence in these advertisers. Despite 12 years of successful payment history, stations and networks can still make the up-front payment demand. But now it's based on the tradition. There are some exceptions. The most reputable long form agencies can establish 30 day net payments with perhaps 30 percent of station and network contacts.

Agency Commissions

The standard media commission for an infomercial agency is 15 percent of the gross media cost. The agency pays the broadcast station or cable network the net (85 percent) and collects the difference as commission. Often clients will balk at this commission rate; it's uncommon today to pay a general ad agency 15 percent commissions. But once clients come face-to-face with the immense day-to-day management tasks involved, they understand 15 percent is what it takes for the infomercial agency to make a fair profit.

Media Roll-Out and Management

Media Roll-Out

The top infomercial agencies still control millions of dollars of quality time for their new clients to make significant profits from. I estimate there are approximately 500,000 hours per year available for long-form commercials on broadcast TV stations alone. This doesn't include the substantial number of hours coming available on many new cable TV networks sprouting up yearly.

Therefore, a strong infomercial program has lots of room for roll-out. A "homerun" infomercial can be telecast in over 200 television markets, 40 plus cable networks, and have as many as 600 broadcasts per week. At this level, a half-hour program would be spending $500,000 in media per week and bringing in two to three times that amount in gross revenues, resulting in $4 to $6 million in monthly sales.

Yes, there's plenty of good long form time available, but only for quality infomercials. There's lots of competition out there, and more can be expected. Many of the "cream" time slots on the major cable TV networks are locked up by some media agencies for a specific amount of time. To get a shot at these time slots, a program has to have legs. You literally have to stand in line in order to be rotated into the best cable time slots.

As an infomercial is marketed beyond its test phase, roll out media spending will vary, depending on how strong the MER is. Roll-out can be as gradual as adding 25 stations a week or as rapid as 100 to 150 per week. An additional cost to be aware of during rollout is dubs. Of course, every station or network that telecasts your infomercial needs a video copy. Depending on whether or not every tape needs special editing for a unique 800 number, these duplication costs can vary from $50 to $300 dollars per station. But remember, once a station has its tape, the successful show can run repeatedly for many, many months.

Within a few days of the initial media test broadcasts, you or your ad agency should evaluate the relative strength of the infomercial response and develop the rollout strategy accordingly.

The rollout occurs after your media test has proven successful. Now you'll purchase more media time on a continual basis in order to reap the benefits of direct response television.

From the media test you'll have determined that certain markets, regions, border markets and time slots are most profitable. This will help you determine which stations and dayparts to buy in the future for continued success.

In the months after your media test phase, you have to determine how much media time to buy for a successful campaign. Proper planning at this stage is very important for the smooth ramp-up of your campaign. You'll need to build adequate product inventory to meet the order volumes attendant upon the increased volume of media time.

In addition, it is important to implement the following:

- Determine the amount you desire to spend on media.
- Properly plan your expected cash flow.
- Have adequate cash reserves available at each stage for both your media budget and other cash needs.

I recommend a planned rollout over 60 to 90 days. Each distinct time slot becomes a profit center and not all new markets/stations and time periods chosen will be successful. After the test phase, cancel telecasts that aren't working. There will be multiple profit centers in each city that you'll have to coordinate and manage successfully. Guiding an infomercial media rollout campaign entails constant scrutiny of "working" (profitable) media and continued testing of new markets, stations and time slots.

A 3 to 6 month budget should be formulated for the rollout. When your budget is determined, establish media payments with your infomercial ad agency's accounting department. Payments to the stations running your show must be made two weeks in advance of each telecast. Therefore your agency should receive your payments a month in advance of each telecast airing. You'll also have to provide for dubbing if your ad agency isn't handling this service.

Your ad agency should be fully responsible for the daily management of the following media campaign functions:

- Buy test media
- Buy more working media
- Cancel non-working media
- Renegotiate marginal media
- Fax show schedule changes
- Allocate orders
- Allocate toll-free (800/888) numbers
- Verify and negotiate DNR's ("did not run")
- Adjust ad allowable
- Edit/ship/track dubs
- Obtain refunds
- Secure station legal approvals
- Telemarketing screen review
- Research and number crunching
- Client goal setting
- Receive affidavits
- Revise telecasts
- Reconcile fax/modem orders
- Improve vendor relationships
- Media payable checks
- Reconcile media accounts
- Adjust strategies
- Generate client reports
- Write inbound telemarketing scripts
- Manage inventory ordering
- Monitor customer complaints/service
- Complete client profile report

- Problem telecast resolution
- Receive 800/888 numbers
- Client contact
- Team account review
- Budget review and projection
- Letters and reports
- Match station affidavits to computer
- Solve affidavit discrepancies
- Forward affidavits to clients
- Invoice clients
- Contact stations for credit terms
- Contact stations for missing affidavits
- Trouble shooting

Infomercial time is becoming increasingly valuable. As more and more players join the infomercial ranks, stations are requiring more lead time for infomercial programming. The need for commitments on specific media has become more critical in recent times. This means that at periodic points in your campaign, there will be critical decisions to make regarding your upcoming media purchases.

Quality direct response media time doesn't grow on trees. In order to secure the "cream of the crop" media, you need to have your volume commitments by the dates when new avails are released by the stations for each upcoming quarter. The following quarterly deadlines apply:

Quarter	Commitment Date
1st Quarter	1st week of preceding November
2nd Quarter	1st week of preceding February
3rd Quarter	1st week of preceding May
4th Quarter	1st week of preceding August

Having your commitments by these dates gives you the best media selection. However, this doesn't mean you should rule out fire sales and one-time-only (OTO) opportunities. You and your agency should always be looking for good media buyers. However, the best way to establish and perpetuate the foundation of your campaign is to be able to strike while the iron is hot, which is to buy media time as soon as new avails are announced.

Media Analysis and Reporting

Media Analysis for Profitability

Within 24 hours of each telecast, you'll receive 75 percent to 95 percent of total orders and your media analysis for profitability can begin. This can be determined on a cost-per-order or cost-per-lead basis. If the telecast is profitable, buyers will go back to the station for more of the same or similar media time. Your media roll-out will be built on constantly testing new time periods, canceling those that lose money and keeping the money makers.

CPO's and Ad Allowables

In analyzing the results from a direct response television commercial, there are two important terms to understand: cost per order (CPO) and ad allowable. The CPO is determined by dividing the cost of media for a specific telecast by the number of orders generated by that telecast. For example, if you buy a half-hour telecast for $1,000 and generate 100 orders, your cost per order will be $10. But the question is, did you make a profit? The only way to know is to measure CPO against your product's ad allowable.

Ad allowable is the maximum amount you can afford to pay in media costs per unit sold (CPO) to achieve a minimum acceptable profit. The ad allowable is determined by taking the product's retail price and subtracting all direct costs such as cost of goods, royalties, toll-free 800/888 number service, fulfillment costs, shipping, etc., then subtracting a specific dollar amount for overhead (usually 15 percent) and minimum acceptable profit (usually 10 percent). The remaining dollar figure is the amount available to spend on advertising costs (media cost per unit sold).

The essence of making profits (and therefore your primary media strategy goal) in one-step offer infomercials is to keep the CPO at or below the ad allowable on as many telecasts as possible.

Obviously, the more powerful your product appeal, the greater number of orders you'll receive per telecast and the lower your cost per order, thus creating greater profit per product sold. Cost per order depends on many variables, including quality of the TV show, quality of the TV market and individual stations, seasonality, competition in the time-buying marketplace, cost per household of TV time, quality of television shows on competing stations during your time slot and, most importantly, the consumer appeal of your product.

And, of course, for any newly testing time slot, there's no guaranteed what the CPO will be. There are only educated guesses. The media test is critical to determine your infomercial's ability to produce response. And because every specific infomercial time slot on any television station or cable network is a unique profit center that needs profit/loss management after every telecast, infomercial media buying is a labor-intensive and highly specialized profession.

Calculating Your Ad Allowable

Here's an example using a product with a price of $99.95.

Revenue:	
Retail price/Unit	$99.95
Shipping & Handling	$7.95
Total Revenue	$107.90

Expenses:	
Cost of Goods	$9.50
Premiums	$1.40
Returns and Bad Debt (5%)	$5.00
800 Service	$2.50
Order Processing (incl. shipping)	$5.75
Bank Card Fees	$3.24

Dub Cost	$.25
Royalties (7.5%)	$7.50
Total Expenses	**$35.14**

Gross Margin/Unit	$72.76
Overhead (15%)	$10.91
Profit (10%)	$7.27
Ad Allowable *	**$54.58**

**The Ad Allowable denoted is calculated without contributions from upsell, retail, and outbound/aftermarket sales.*

As mentioned, the media buyer's goal is to create a profit on every telecast for the client by creating CPO's at or below the ad allowable. In the above example, the ad allowable is $54.58. If we paid $1000 for a half hour time slot that generated 30 orders, the CPO is $33.33 ($1000 divided by 30). The client has made a net profit per product sold (after all direct costs and overhead) of $21.25 ($54.58 minus $33.33) plus $7.27 (10 percent minimum profit figured into the ad allowable) for a total profit of $28.52 per unit sold. On this one $1000 telecast, the client has made a total net profit of $855.60. An 85 percent return virtually overnight on a media investment of $1000. When you can make profits like these so quickly, is it any wonder why infomercial marketing is as hot as a pistol?

The ad allowable amount directly corresponds to the gross profit margin. For some products whose COG are very low, the gross margin can be so great that the ad allowable can be 70 percent or more of the retail price. Typically, the ad allowable runs about 35 percent to 55 percent of retail.

Higher ad allowables are also possible in cases where the goal of the infomercial is primarily to drive retail store product sales. Any direct sales received from the infomercial can then be considered to be reductions of the cost of this highly effective image advertising. Ad allowables in retail driving infomercials can be as high as 75 percent to 150 percent of the product price.

For every telecast (hundreds per week), media buyers will compare the telecast's CPO to the ad allowable to determine whether it's profitable and worthy of another purchase. Of course, the beauty of television direct response advertising is that these results can be calculated within 24 hours of the telecast. A successful media test can then prompt a rollout strategy that can ramp up sales very quickly.

Cost of Goods Sold

In calculating the ad allowable, COG is defined as the cost of product development, raw materials, manufacturing and packaging attributed on a per unit basis.

Mark-up

Many product owners new to infomercial marketing question why products need such a high mark-up (5 to 1) in order to have a chance at success. (Mark-up = retail price divided by the cost of goods.) The answer rests with media buying and media prices.

In 1984, the average infomercial product's mark-up was three to one. Back then you could have an infomercial hit if, for every product sale, costs would be one-third for COG and one-third for media time expenditures, leaving one third for overhead costs and profit.

But rising television media prices have gobbled up more and more of a product's gross margin. In 1996, media costs averaged between 50 percent to 75 percent of a product's gross sales, thus requiring product markups of five to one or greater.

Once an infomercial has tested, much more accurate projections can be input into your financial pro formas (as outlined in Chapter 8), so that you can better prepare for cash flow and inventory requirements.

Computer Media Analysis

Professional media management companies rely on a variety of sophisticated technologies and mechanisms to carry out the complex media analysis and reporting process. To organize and properly manage the large volume of media and results data, for example, Hawthorne Communications developed a proprietary, half million dollar media analysis and reporting software program called TimeTrack™.

TimeTrack™ allows buyers and analysts to make immediate decisions to maximize profits. By providing the necessary information in seconds, media staff is able to spot key trends, buy more time, renegotiate better rates, cancel nonworking telecasts quickly, and increase the success rate in every time slot.

Sophisticated agencies maintain a database containing the details of the purchase and results of every individual telecast for every client for whom the agency has ever purchased media. This historical information enables the media buyer to know what kinds of shows have been successful in which markets on which stations. It also gives trends of rates for different quarters, years, and specific time periods. It allows media staff to do comparative research and generates all of the reports that help to make the judgment calls needed to adjust the media strategy.

These kinds of sophisticated systems help micromanage media campaigns to get the most value out of infomercial advertisers' media dollars. Media buyers use this tool to determine whether they need to buy more of, or cancel a particular daypart. Account managers use it to analyze and create new strategies and then know whether or not overall budgets are being met and thus whether or not media dollars are being fully utilized. It also gives the management team a vantage point to review each buyer's activity and ensure that they are doing the best possible job in the markets they manage.

The major telemarketing companies are tied into TimeTrack by modem so that all orders go directly into the agency system every hour. This creates a very fast turnaround of information. This kind of system also generates accounting information, payments, invoices, etc., and allows the agency to accurately manage the finances of each infomercial campaign.

Following are some examples of the kind of TimeTrack reports used to manage media campaigns:

- Weekly overview
- Media analysis by daypart
- Market history
- Broadcast schedule
- Broadcast change report
- Broadcast history
- Monthly campaign analysis overview

These and other reports enable the media staff to adhere to, and adjust when necessary, media strategies; maintain budget parameters, determine a successful mix of cable, border and broadcast media; carefully target markets, stations and dayparts; perform a weekly review of the overall campaign for strategy adjustments and profit trends.

Client Reports

Following are brief explanations of standard client media reports provided by infomercial agencies.

Media Strategy

A media strategy is a report that tells the buyers what changes to make in their media buying and canceling activities to improve the results of the campaign. This is a manually created report that is prepared after review and analysis of many of the other reports. This is an internal infomercial agency report, but is available upon request.

The sample media strategy report included here illustrates an advanced stage of a particular campaign. One can see at a glance that the strategy can become involved and detailed as the campaign matures based on analysis of results produced from the original and evolving strategies (client specific information has been removed to honor client confidentiality).

Weekly Overview

Faxed weekly, the weekly overview shows a campaign's progress week by week. Included is a weekly and cumulative CPO, spending, orders and number of telecasts with credit card and upsell percentages.

Weekly Overview/Market Segmentation

Faxed weekly, the weekly overview/market segmentation report details the same information as the weekly overview, but broken out by market segments: cable, border, U.S. broadcast stations (USBC).

EXHIBIT 9.1 Sample Media Time Table

Date Due	Item	Action
Week 1	Media test strategy	• Client approval of media test (markets, telecasts, and budgets per market) • Agency media buyers incorporate client's test needs into fourth quarter planning
Week 3	Rollout strategy	• Agency presents rollout strategy • Client approval • Agency buyers incorporate client's rollout needs into fourth quarter planning
Week 4	Media deposit invoice	• Agency sends media deposit letter • Media test deposit due
Week 5	Media purchase	• Infomercial sent to cable networks and stations • Complete media test purchases • Ship program dubs to cable networks and stations
Week 9	Program airs	• Evaluate results • Make rollout decisions and refine media strategy • Begin media purchases for rollout
Week 12	Rollout	• Negotiate and purchase media • Analyze results • Refine media strategy

Media Analysis by Daypart. The media analysis by daypart is an internal infomercial agency tool for the account management team, and is also available to the client upon request. It is used to target which dayparts are working and to identify trends. It is broken down by the Nielsen dayparts. It gives CPOs, number of telecasts, and how much has been spent in the selected dayparts for the selected time period, i.e., a weekend or the entire campaign.

Market History. Sent monthly or at a greater frequency, if required, the market history report helps in analyzing order impact in specific markets. It gives all telecasts, spending totals, and market/station CPOs.

Broadcast Schedule. Faxed weekly on Thursday, the broadcast schedule shows all media assigned to the client's account starting with the upcoming Monday. The number of weeks out can vary depending on the client's needs.

Broadcast History by Market Groups. The broadcast history by market groups report shows the client's weekly results, telecast by telecast, in the border, cable, and USBC categories (Monday through Sunday of the previous broadcast week). A cover sheet summarizes all the data for the week. This report is faxed Tuesday and Friday or upon demand. During the test phase, reports may be sent on Monday afternoon for the first and second weekend of the testing.

Monthly Campaign Analysis Overview. An overview showing a campaign's progress month by month is generally faxed monthly. Exhibit 9.2 shows a typical media strategy update.

Common Infomercial Media Questions and Answers

Following are answers to some common questions about infomercial media.

- How many people will see my program during the test? The number of people who will see your program depends on your product, customer profile, past history in the market, and other factors. With a $50,000 media buy, you could probably get on 15 broadcast

EXHIBIT 9.2 Sample Strategy Update

ACCOUNT MANAGER: ______________________ DATE: __________

SHOW TITLE:

SHOW CODE: (offer–$299 single payment or four payment option)

CLIENT:

SHOW CHANGE: WOW! Keep up the great work—the client is very happy. We can go over the March budget either with the original or new dayparts. (This weekend is too light March 13–20.)

STRATEGY GUIDELINES:

AD ALLOWABLE: $100

BUDGET: March = $300,000 April = $650,000

BUY GUIDELINES:

- 2x tests for telecasts ≤ $1,000
- 1x tests for telecasts $1,000+
- Buy continuing media regardless of dayparts
- Frequency—2x per month per telecast. If you think your station can sustain more frequency—talk to me.
- Do not book against the "Final Four" in March. (See your Sports Schedule.)

MEDIA BUY APPROVALS: If you have any questions see me!

- I want to approve buys ≥ $3,000.

DAYPARTS TO BUY:

Sat/Sun	7:30A–12:30P	Mon–Fri & Sun	6:30P–11:59P
Sat/Sun	4:00P–6:00P	Mon–Fri	12:00A–5:59P
		Fri	7:30A–9:00A

ADDITIONAL DAYPARTS TO BUY:

- Make sure we get media in these markets before April 1:

Boston, MA	Long Island, NY	Peoria, IL
Champaign, IL	Milwaukee, WI	Richmond, VA
Chicago, IL	Minnesota all markets	Seattle WA
Dallas, TX	Nashville, TN	Spokane, WA
Hartford, CT	New York, NY	St. Louis, MO

EXHIBIT 9.2 Sample Strategy Update (Continued)

DAYPARTS TO AVOID:	All the rest	
MARKET INFORMATION:	Do not buy media in the following markets:	
	<u>Arizona</u>	<u>Florida</u>
	Phoenix	Orlando
	Tucson	West Palm Beach
	Yuma	Jacksonville
		Ft. Myers
		Tallahassee
		Gainesville
		Panama City
		Tampa
		Miami
	• The client is interested in more East coast media.	
GENERAL INFORMATION:		
	• CPO improves with frequency. • Favor Sunday telecasts over Saturday where possible.	

Source: Hawthorne Communications Inc.

stations and two to three cable networks. If you bought two times on each station that would be a total of 30 telecasts on broadcast and six telecasts on cable.

One telecast on broadcast would probably pull 10,000 households per showing, so 30 telecasts × 10,000 is 300,000 households × 1.45 persons per household = 435,000 people. Cable, on average, has 320,000 viewing households. Therefore, the potential audience size is 6 telecasts × 320,000 households = 1,920,000 households × 1.45 persons per household = 2,784,000 potential viewers.

- What times should I be airing my infomercial and why? You should air two telecasts per each station. A two times test gives you a flavor of the true success or failure, whereas one telecast could be an aberration, not to be relied on.

- How many markets should I be in and why? You should air in 6 to 10 broadcast markets and on two to three cable networks. Ten broadcast markets will allow you to test your product in every region of the United States. Cable is all-pervasive and gives you a flavor of your performance nationwide.

- After the test phase is completed, how soon can I buy more time? You can buy time immediately after the test phase is completed.
- How long will it be before I get on the air once the station has given approval? Usually it can take anywhere from two to four weeks, depending on programming and availability of time, which is always changing.
- How quickly can I roll out? Once you are on a station, you can roll out immediately, depending on your strategy to buy time, availability, and budget. The more decisions and approvals have been made up front, the more quickly you can react.
- How late can I cancel? Cancellations usually require four weeks' advance notice.
- How do I determine the initial strategy and the ongoing strategy? Your initial strategy depends on your product, customer profile, past history, and budget, as well as on what days, dayparts, and markets are likely to result in the best sales. All of these factors should be weighed against each other to determine a test strategy.

  The ongoing strategy should be based on the results of the rollout. Buy more success and cut failures. Make your campaign grow around your successes. This is the obvious basic strategy. You can also use more sophisticated approaches based on your profit, closure, and loss equations.
- How quickly can changes in media strategy be implemented? The speed of implementing changes in media strategy is dictated by the cancellation lead times of the stations. Because these lead times are typically two to four weeks, strategy changes usually don't begin to show up at the telecast level for a minimum of two to three weeks.

Dubbing and Trafficking

Once the stations have been selected, you or your ad agency should send each station a VHS copy of your show for approval. It is standard in the industry for each television station to approve every show that is requested to air on television. The program is generally reviewed by the station's standards and practices office.

Dub Masters and Toll-Free Numbers

Dubbing is the process in which your completed show is transferred from the on-line master tape to a tape that will be used for broadcast. This dub will have a specific 800/888 number for each TV station.

Each time a new 800/888 number is created, a dub master must be made. Because editing is required, a dub master is more expensive to create than a dub. From the dub master, a dub must be generated for each station on which the infomercial is to be aired. Each cable station will need to have its own exclusive 800 or 888 number. Many broadcast stations, depending on the size and geographic location of the test, will be able to share a toll-free number. Thus, dub prices are higher for cable than for broadcast because cable stations require a special edit, while the same dub master can be used to produce dubs for broadcast stations throughout the country.

Broadcast Dub Production and Trafficking Services

Your ad agency may offer its media clients in-house dub production and trafficking to provide a full spectrum of coordinated media campaign services. These services generally include the following:

- Produce dub masters and dubs to client specifications using the most cost-effective methods, while maintaining the highest levels of quality.
- Ship dubs in the most timely, secure, and cost-efficient manner.
- Ensure that all booked telecasts have the proper dub in hand to meet station clearance and telecast requirements.
- Provide immediate dub production and shipping to take advantage of last-minute, deeply discounted media purchases.
- Effectively control multiple dub situations at single stations by assigning systematic program codes and titles and recalling outdated copies of programs. This action minimizes occurrences of airing an incorrect version of the infomercial.

Typical Dubbing and Editing Costs

Exhibit 9.3 lists average rates for videotape dubbing services as of 1996. These rates typically include tape stock and box, but not shipping charges. Exhibit 9.4 lists average rates for commercial and program editing as of 1996.

EXHIBIT 9.3 Typical Dubbing Costs

	30-Minute Programs	One- to-Two-Minute Spots
1/2" VHS Demo	$15	$10
3/4" Demo—Recycled Tape	$26	N/A
3/4" Broadcast Dub	$40	$24
1" Broadcast Dub	$80	$20

Note: There can be an additional charge per tape for 24-hour turnaround.

EXHIBIT 9.4 Typical Editing Costs

	30-Minute Programs	One- to-Two-Minute Spots
800/888 # Master*	$300 and up	$36
Special Edit**	$300 and up	N/A

**800/888 number masters are created each time a new toll-free number is used.*
***Special edits are required for changes in show length (as specified by certain cable networks), product price changes, inserting special keys and crawls into the body of the show, voice or music change, graphic tag change, and so on.*

Media Invoicing, Payments, Adjustments, and Timing

Expect your agency to send an invoice to you four weeks in advance of the telecasts of your infomercial. This is because the agency must disburse funds to the various stations and cable networks within the time frame that they require payment, usually two weeks in advance. Media buys are usually invoiced weekly, typically by fax, to save time.

Common Infomercial Media Accounting Questions and Answers

Following are answers to some common questions about media accounting.

- When there has been a cancellation or strategy change and I know that a broadcast listed on an agency invoice is not going to be aired, can I make an adjustment to that invoice?

Yes. Because these kinds of changes are so common, a useful procedure is to issue an adjustment invoice monthly that captures all of the changes and credits. This keeps things simple, and it seems to work out best for everyone to have all of the adjustments for a given month made at once.

- Why don't lists of projected telecasts and the invoices match up?

  Your projected telecasts could change within a few days or even within hours of an invoice being sent to you. This can lead to apparent discrepancies. There is still a need to have funds for media available well ahead of scheduled air dates, so you will commonly receive updated telecast schedules after invoices have been sent to you.

- What happens if, at the end of my campaign, there is still a credit in my media account with my ad agency?

  You should receive a courteous and prompt refund of any remaining credit in your account with your ad agency at the end of your campaign. Contact your agency immediately if you don't.

Increasing Acceptance of Infomercials by Broadcasters

Broadcasters no longer look down their noses at infomercials, according to a survey done by the BJK&E Media Group. In fact, nine out of ten TV stations air infomercials. Of the 709 television stations that responded to the survey, 91.5 percent said they air infomercials. About half (49.1 percent) of the respondents said that they air more infomercials now than they did in 1990. The survey also showed that infomercials are being aired at a wide variety of times. More than 14 percent of the stations responding said they air infomercials during prime time hours, while 25 percent said they air infomercial programs during the daytime. Other survey findings include:

- Eleven percent of stations are willing to work with advertisers on a per-inquiry basis.
- More than 33 percent of stations said they required cash in advance for infomercial payments.
- Infomercials are prescreened by 28.9 percent of stations.

- Infomercials that use 900 telephone numbers are rejected by 7.2 percent of stations.

CHECKLIST

- ✔ The earning power of infomercials will be reflected in the amount of media dollars you spend on your show.
- ✔ Your infomercial ad agency should provide a full spectrum of coordinated media campaign services.
- ✔ Infomercial product position self-determines the viewer/prospect demographic.
- ✔ Media expenditures (during rollout) run from $50,000 to $500,000 per week. A $1,000,000 media expenditure yields 10,000,000 viewing households.
- ✔ The goal of your infomercial media agency should be to maximize your sales and profits.
- ✔ The media test helps establish budget, determine winning markets and time slots, determine impact at retail, and evaluate strengths and weaknesses of the program.
- ✔ Consider market price fluctuations regarding seasons and holidays, special programming considerations, and local market events.
- ✔ By the time your campaign rolls out, you should have developed (and perhaps adjusted) your strategy; established budgets; nailed down your cable/broadcast mix and target markets, and have in hand campaign-to-date reviews as needed.
- ✔ Infomercial agency professionals have established relationships with cable networks and television stations, which are essential to obtaining optimum media placement and prices.
- ✔ Evaluate cost-per-order (CPO) and ad allowables.
- ✔ Buy media that works, cancel what doesn't.
- ✔ Infomercial media buying is a specialty service requiring daily management, accountability, and a historical database.

- ✔ Software systems such as Hawthorne's TimeTrack™ Media Management System are designed to maximize profits, minimize losses, and provide safety and clarity. They incorporate years of experience in media buying, analysis, and programming. Overviews and summaries are provided quickly and efficiently.
- ✔ Your media management should be chosen according to experience, reputation, contacts and relationships, and appropriate skills needed to get the best media at lowest cost.
- ✔ Your infomercial media agency should have a minimum of five years infomercial experience, $10 million annual infomercial media buy, excellent reputation and contacts, own multiple media time blocks, and purchase a minimum of 85 percent of media buys direct from stations and cable networks rather than reps.

CHAPTER

Inbound Telemarketing

With new entrepreneurs continuing to flood the market and increasing numbers of new corporate advertisers joining the infomercial ranks, the need for quality inbound telemarketing services is immense. Since their inception in 1967, 800-prefix numbers have given businesses of all types the ability to allow their customers to call them at no charge. In fact, toll-free 800 lines have proven to be so lucrative that telephone companies have run out of new numbers. Recently, the Federal Communications Commission (FCC) began allocation of a new toll-free prefix, 888, with the same function as the 800 prefix. Some 491,430 of the 7.9 million 888-prefix numbers were available for use, as of mid-February 1996, according to NIMA International, citing Database Services Management, the national entity that administers toll-free numbers. Approximately 100,000 more 888 numbers have already been reserved. Within a year the FCC is expected to again have to initiate action to meet the ever-increasing demand for new toll-free numbers.

Today's infomercial profit streams flow well beyond the initial program's airing, with various aftermarketing efforts often generating up to four times the up-front infomercial sales volume. A substantial portion of this is done by outbound telemarketing of continuity programs and cross-selling related products. However, the first add-on revenues are often generated at the inbound call center through upsells.

Upselling and cross-selling are delicate operations. Unless the telemarketer has the knack and a really strong offer, you risk offending your prospect with an overly aggressive sales pitch, perhaps even losing the order. Still, carefully crafted and monitored upsell and cross-sell programs can add 20 to 30 percent to your campaign sales.

When Customers "Call Now!"

When we think of 800/888 numbers, we generally envision businesses, large and small, getting customers to call them for free so someone can sell them something. A retail business, for example, may have one or two 800 lines and any staff member is qualified to pick up the calls, answer questions, and take orders. Larger businesses may have more 800/888 lines going, and will therefore hire specialized staff to handle the calls in-house.

With direct response television, we're talking much, much bigger call volumes and intensities. Infomercials running at all hours all across the country are flashing their toll-free numbers again and again, because the advertisers know that customers are more likely to call if the call is free. Thousands of calls may come in all at once in response to an enticing offer. A typically successful one-step infomercial with a $50 product offer might be spending as much as $250,000 in media per week, generating $500,000 to $750,000 in sales. *For the inbound telemarketer, that means 10,000 to 20,000 calls per week generated by just one infomercial.* (See Exhibit 10.1.)

Front-end domestic infomercial sales volume will probably increase an average of 5 percent to 10 percent per year for the next five years. Within five years, today's 15 percent of lead-generating infomercials will increase to 50 percent. The reason? Major corporations in the automotive and financial fields, for example, will use infomercials regularly to qualify consumer prospects at a low cost per lead (CPL). CPLs will range from $5 to $30, which means a $250,000 weekly media budget could generate as many as 50,000 calls for more information.

Therefore, infomercial marketers must depend on experienced DRTV telemarketing centers to efficiently handle the huge volume of calls their programs bring in. For each infomercial or short-form DRTV program their client is running, the telemarketing centers must make their operators familiar with the details of the product

EXHIBIT 10.1

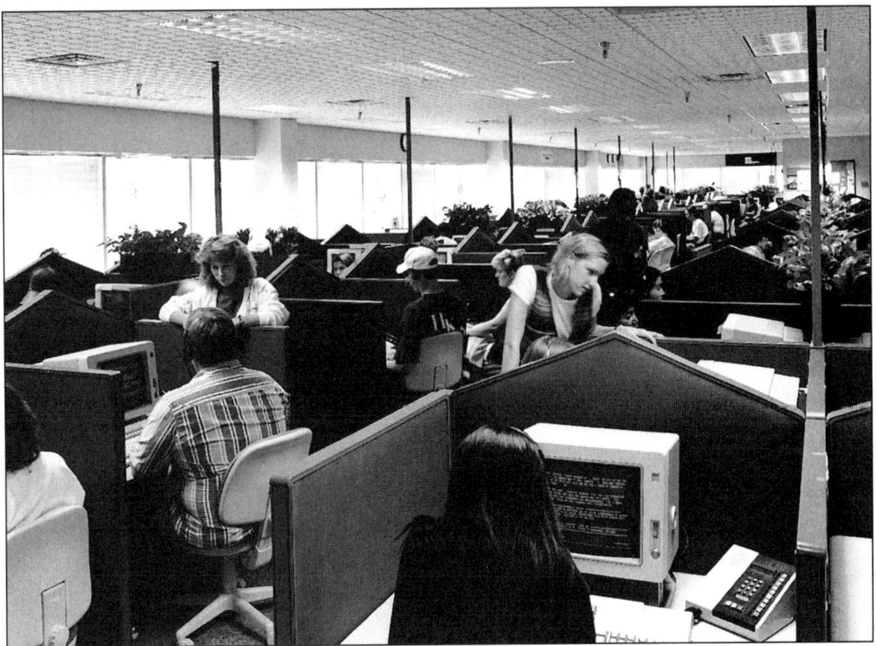

MATRIXX Marketing, which serves many infomercial and DRTV clients among others, has allocated 1,400 stations and 4,000 operators, 24 hours a day in its Ogden, Utah facility for its inbound business alone.

offer, the company, charges, shipping information, upsells, cross-sells, and more.

Since many consumers calling an 800/888 number to order a product through an infomercial program are under the assumption that they are talking directly to someone who works for the company sponsoring the show, it is critical that every customer be treated courteously and professionally. In addition, the call-handler must have in-depth knowledge of the product(s) advertised. The importance of finding the right telemarketing company to handle the calls generated by your infomercial cannot be stressed enough.

Telemarketer Shopper's Guide

Right now, there are perhaps only a half dozen major companies involved in infomercial telemarketing. These veterans have learned their service lessons the hard way, through years of trial and error.

Here are some guidelines to help you avoid potential obstacles in a typical telemarketing center shopping expedition:

Beware of telemarketers new to infomercials and DRTV. Like every element of infomercial marketing, it takes highly specialized knowledge to do the job properly. The telemarketing service representatives must be experts in infomercials, and able to make shrewd recommendations to you based on experience. Infomercial ad agencies, DRTV marketers, producers, directors, and fulfillment houses can assist you in finding the ideal telemarketer. Your agency will also help create an irresistible telemarketing script and make changes as necessary. Your specialized infomercial vendors know their stuff. Listen to them.

Carefully scrutinize any telemarketing firm that claims to specialize in both inbound and outbound call handling. The industry does need more high quality, integrated inbound/outbound companies to institute more synergistic campaigns. At present, there are few telemarketing companies that have demonstrated that they can do both well. (For more information on outbound telemarketing, see Chapter 11.)

Finally, go surfing! Spend a Saturday night surfing your cable channels. Watch the infomercials to see how their offers and 800/888 numbers are presented. Ninety percent of the shows you'll see are money makers—they're using techniques that lead to success. You might even order a product or two. See how the telemarketers lead you through the order and evaluate how they make you feel—like a valued customer dealing with a professional, or like someone trying to order a product from an alien being.

What to Expect from Your Inbound Telemarketer

Low Percentage of Inquiry Calls

The goal of infomercials is typically to generate orders for your product, not to invite viewers to call in and merely ask questions. It's acceptable if your telemarketer receives up to 50 percent inquiry calls. But if they're getting more than that, there's probably something about your infomercial that needs changing. Good inbound telemarketers will spot this problem immediately, and you and your infomercial agency will be advised to make changes. Be proactive! Some possible solutions include the following: the price and payment plan needs to be better showcased; the address for viewers to send checks needs to be on the screen longer; the charge for shipping and handling needs to be graphically enlarged; the commercial needs to explain in more detail exactly what product the viewer is getting for his or her money.

Low Blockage Rates

Blockage rates (percentage of calls getting a busy signal) reflect a telemarketer's inability to keep up with "call spikes" that occur at the times the show is running. Your infomercial media-buying agency can help by giving the inbound call handlers weekly media reports listing air dates/times and estimated call volumes, allowing them to gear up for the onslaught of simultaneous calls.

Prompt/Accurate Order Reports

On the day of an infomercial's first run (usually a Friday night or Saturday morning), ask your telemarketing service representative to call you with the results within 30 minutes of the broadcast. One telecast may not mean much to a giant telemarketing center, but you've probably been waiting 6 to 18 months for these initial results. Then make sure your order allocation system is top notch. Each product order placed is matched to the 800/888 number given to the TV station where the order originated. It is considered acceptable if three percent or less of orders are unmatched to a specific telecast.

Prompt Fulfillment Coordination

Find out which infomercial fulfillment houses are the best and learn about their information gathering/processing systems. Who are their key personnel? What do they need from you and your agency to eliminate customer service problems? The telemarketer, working with your infomercial agency, will help you choose the fulfillment house that will best suit your products and marketing goals.

Competent Handling of Complaints

Many new infomercial marketers come from the manufacturing/wholesale sector that until now, rarely interacted directly with consumers. Consider building your own in-house customer service department dedicated to your infomercial customers only—that can be patched through from your telemarketer's operators to your operators, if possible, or an accurate 800/888 number referral. Don't botch this. One major mishandle and you could lose the business generated from your infomercial.

High Upsell Percentage

Your telemarketing agency can work with your ad agency to structure your upsell strategy. They've seen what works and can recommend product, price, and positioning. If your inbound telemarketers close 25 percent or more of your upsell offers, you should be happy. A well-versed, professional telemarketer can elicit orders that surpass the original television offer. Exhibit 10.2 is just one example of an inbound telemarketing script designed to convert a multipayment purchase into a fully paid transaction using a "free bonus incentive." Many different upsell programs are possible, designed to accomplish any number of marketing goals.

EXHIBIT 10.2 Sample Upsell Script

Free Bonus Incentive Payment Plan Upsell Conversion

Telemarketing service representative (TSR):

You may order your (product) with one payment of $ ________ plus shipping and handling and sales tax, and receive our beautiful signature Travel Case valued at $40 absolutely free as our special gift to you. Would you prefer the convenience of our one-payment plan and receive this free gift?

Results:

- Products costing less than $60, conversion rate to full pay is 65 percent to 80 percent.
- Products costing more than $60 but less than $100, conversion rate to full pay is between 60 percent and 75 percent.
- Products more than $100 but less than $150, conversion rate to full pay is between 50 percent and 70 percent.
- With products costing more than $150, conversion rate to full pay is between 50 percent and 60 percent.

Source: Sample script provided by World Class Marketing, Inc.

Other upsell strategies include: Free delivery for conversion to one-payment from multipayment plan; upsell two or more products; one-half the original product's price; two for the price of one; send another to a loved one as a gift for half price. (See Chapter 11.)

Script Effectiveness

Changing an infomercial offer already running on television is expensive; changing your inbound script isn't. Your infomercial agency and telemarketing specialists should test various upsells, multiple payments/bill-me options, and so on. Successful inbound scripting can add 10 to 20 percent to your bottom line. With discount upsell offers that include 50 percent discounts, conversions can range from 25 to 50 percent.

Recommend Aftermarketing Programs

The telemarketer, working with your infomercial agency, will teach you ways to increase your profits through aftermarketing programs, and help you choose the aftermarketing specialist that will best suit your needs and goals. (See Chapter 11.)

Willing to Know Your Product and Offer

As an infomercial customer, you pay more to telemarketers than do many of their other customers, including short-form DRTV. For best results, offer all the help you can to the telephone reps who are handling your calls. Have your product(s) and infomercial on display. Give away free product samples. Make sure your operators are walked through the inbound script.

Automatic Call Response

Automated call response systems—rarely used by infomercials today—will increasingly be in demand to handle the high volume of calls prompted by infomercials designed for lead generation. For example, a Buick infomercial broadcast on a Sunday morning on WNBC in New York could generate as many as 10,000 to 20,000 calls for free information. The telemarketer would then provide these leads to the prospect's closest Buick dealer for follow-up.

How Your Infomercial Ad Agency Fits into the Phone Loop

A good infomercial agency will recommend basic program elements that will help eliminate potential problems at the inbound telemarketing level. "Call-to-action" expertise is an essential part of your infomercial program. Keep in mind the following call-to-action strategies that have proven to reap positive results.

- Leave the 800/888 number up on the screen a minimum of 45 seconds each time the offer appears.
- Don't disguise or bury the price—leave it on the screen a minimum of 30 seconds.
- Don't place 800/888 number on the screen until the price has been mentioned.
- Find out which infomercial fulfillment houses are the best and learn about their information gathering/processing systems.
- The "send-check address" should remain on the screen a minimum of 20 seconds during each call to action.
- The voice-over announcer should state the 800/888 number and address twice during each call to action.
- Specify "Sorry, no C.O.D.s."
- Have a "Call Now!" motivating premium on screen.
- Your company/advertiser name/address and full shipping and handling costs must be on screen during each call to action.

Inbound Management

The best infomercial ad agencies will execute a proactive inbound-management program designed to achieve and maintain the highest quality telemarketing service for you. Make sure you can count on them to carry through on the following:

- Submit a request for proposal to traditional inbound telemarketers.
- Review the proposals and make recommendations for the ideal telemarketers.

- Create scripts to maximize sales and leads. Make adjustments to the scripts as necessary and provide changes to the 800/888 service centers.
- Supply VHS tape copies of your program to 800/888 service centers as a training aid.
- Supervise the 800/888 operators' training to properly educate the operators about the product and offer.
- Perform accuracy monitoring on the operators to ensure they are accurate, friendly, and selling your product.
- Make test calls at all hours.
- Design special report forms which the 800/888 service must provide to monitor results. (See Exhibit 10.3.)
- Coordinate with the 800/888 service the assignment of 800/888 numbers to stations to ensure that the assigned 800/888 numbers provide for accurate tracking of orders or leads.
- Monitor call blockage at the 800/888 service centers by making test calls during expected peak response times. When necessary, work with the 800/888 service centers to lower call blockage.
- Audit the 800/888 service invoices for accuracy. Perform necessary corrective action.
- Coordinate multiple 800/888 services if necessary.
- Verify the accuracy of reported orders, investigate discrepancies, and correct counts if necessary.
- Provide the 800/888 service with broadcast schedules and provide projected calls per telecast to ensure that adequate operator staffing is provided.
- Ensure timeliness of reports from the 800/888 service.
- Work with the 800/888 service to resolve procedural problems in order taking.
- Coordinate optional services offered by the 800/888 service—i.e., credit card authorization and label generation.
- Coordinate 800/888 service operators focus groups and incentive programs.

EXHIBIT 10.3 Telemarketing Call Report

West Telemarketing

ICSC6010 Ver. 01 (Source Code Hour Report) ORDER DATE: 05/05/96
RUN DATE: 05/06/96 PAGE: 1

CLIENT NUMBER -
PRODUCT ID - PRODUCT DESCRIPTION -

SOURCE CODE	0000	0100	0200	0300	0400	0500	0600	0700	0800	0900	1000	1100	1200	1300	1400	1500	1600	1700	1800	1900	2000	2100	2200	2300	TOTAL
ACTS*			772-5777																						
ORD CNT	0	0	0	0	0	3	2	0	0	0	0	0	0	0	0	0	0	0	1	0	0	0	0	0	6
UPS1YES	0	0	0	0	0	0	1	0	0	0	0	0	0	0	0	0	0	0	0	0	0	0	0	0	1
BL ORDS	0	0	0	0	0	0	0	0	0	0	0	0	0	0	0	0	0	0	0	0	0	0	0	0	0
CC CNT	0	0	0	0	0	1	0	0	0	0	0	0	0	0	0	0	0	0	1	0	0	0	0	0	2
CHK DEB	0	0	0	0	0	0	1	0	0	0	0	0	0	0	0	0	0	0	0	0	0	0	0	0	1
CK UP Y	0	0	0	0	0	0	1	0	0	0	0	0	0	0	0	0	0	0	0	0	0	0	0	0	1
COD'S	0	0	0	0	0	2	1	0	0	0	0	0	0	0	0	0	0	0	0	0	0	0	0	0	3
ACTV			314-8989																						
ORD CNT	0	0	0	0	0	3	0	0	0	2	0	0	0	0	2	0	0	2	0	0	0	0	0	0	9
UPS1YES	0	0	0	0	0	1	0	0	0	0	0	0	0	0	0	0	0	1	0	0	0	0	0	0	2
BL ORDS	0	0	0	0	0	0	0	0	0	0	0	0	0	0	0	0	0	0	0	0	0	0	0	0	0
CC CNT	0	0	0	0	0	2	0	0	0	2	0	0	0	0	2	0	0	2	0	0	0	0	0	0	8
CHK DEB	0	0	0	0	0	0	0	0	0	0	0	0	0	0	0	0	0	0	0	0	0	0	0	0	0
CK UP Y	0	0	0	0	0	0	0	0	0	0	0	0	0	0	0	0	0	0	0	0	0	0	0	0	0
COD'S	0	0	0	0	0	1	0	0	0	0	0	0	0	0	0	0	0	0	0	0	0	0	0	0	1
BRAV			843-0606																						
ORD CNT	0	0	0	0	0	0	0	0	14	6	1	1	0	1	0	0	0	1	0	2	0	0	0	0	26
UPS1YES	0	0	0	0	0	0	0	0	3	0	0	1	0	0	0	0	0	0	0	1	0	0	0	0	5
BL ORDS	0	0	0	0	0	0	0	0	0	0	0	0	0	0	0	0	0	0	0	0	0	0	0	0	0
CC CNT	0	0	0	0	0	0	0	0	14	6	1	1	0	1	0	0	0	1	0	2	0	0	0	0	26
CHK DEB	0	0	0	0	0	0	0	0	0	0	0	0	0	0	0	0	0	0	0	0	0	0	0	0	0
CK UP Y	0	0	0	0	0	0	0	0	0	0	0	0	0	0	0	0	0	0	0	0	0	0	0	0	0
COD'S	0	0	0	0	0	0	0	0	0	0	0	0	0	0	0	0	0	0	0	0	0	0	0	0	0
CAM			214-5511																						
ORD CNT	0	0	0	0	0	0	0	0	0	0	0	0	0	0	0	0	0	0	0	0	0	0	0	0	0
UPS1YES	0	0	0	0	0	0	0	0	0	0	0	0	0	0	0	0	0	0	0	0	0	0	0	0	0
BL ORDS	0	0	0	0	0	0	0	0	0	0	0	0	0	0	0	0	0	0	0	0	0	0	0	0	0
CC CNT	0	0	0	0	0	0	0	0	0	0	0	0	0	0	0	0	0	0	0	0	0	0	0	0	0
CHK DEB	0	0	0	0	0	0	0	0	0	0	0	0	0	0	0	0	0	0	0	0	0	0	0	0	0
CK UP Y	0	0	0	0	0	0	0	0	0	0	0	0	0	0	0	0	0	0	0	0	0	0	0	0	0
COD'S	0	0	0	0	0	0	0	0	0	0	0	0	0	0	0	0	0	0	0	0	0	0	0	0	0
CBN *			714-3200																						
ORD CNT	1	0	54	0	0	2	0	0	0	0	1	0	2	1	4	1	1	1	1	0	1	0	1	0	71
UPS1YES	0	0	10	0	0	0	0	0	0	0	0	0	1	0	1	0	0	1	0	0	0	0	0	0	13
BL ORDS	0	0	0	0	0	0	0	0	0	0	0	0	0	0	0	0	0	0	0	0	0	0	0	0	0
CC CNT	1	0	45	0	0	2	0	0	0	0	1	0	2	1	3	1	1	1	1	0	1	0	1	0	61
CHK DEB	0	0	1	0	0	0	0	0	0	0	0	0	0	0	0	0	0	0	0	0	0	0	0	0	1
CK UP Y	0	0	0	0	0	0	0	0	0	0	0	0	0	0	0	0	0	0	0	0	0	0	0	0	0
COD'S	0	0	8	0	0	0	0	0	0	0	0	0	0	0	1	0	0	0	0	0	0	0	0	0	9
INSP			NC 895-9966																						
ORD CNT	0	0	0	0	0	0	0	0	0	0	0	0	0	0	0	0	0	0	0	0	0	0	0	0	0
UPS1YES	0	0	0	0	0	0	0	0	0	0	0	0	0	0	0	0	0	0	0	0	0	0	0	0	0
BL ORDS	0	0	0	0	0	0	0	0	0	0	0	0	0	0	0	0	0	0	0	0	0	0	0	0	0
CC CNT	0	0	0	0	0	0	0	0	0	0	0	0	0	0	0	0	0	0	0	0	0	0	0	0	0
CHK DEB	0	0	0	0	0	0	0	0	0	0	0	0	0	0	0	0	0	0	0	0	0	0	0	0	0
CK UP Y	0	0	0	0	0	0	0	0	0	0	0	0	0	0	0	0	0	0	0	0	0	0	0	0	0

Source: West Telemarketing Corporation

Telemarketing call reports are used to track response. Thorough reports, like this one, reflect quantity, origin, hour of the day or night, and result of the inbound calls generated by each infomercial airing.

Questions and Answers Regarding Toll-Free Number Services

Following are answers to some common questions about 800/888 inbound telemarketing services.

- What 800/888 telemarketing service should I use?

  The best 800/888 number service is one that can provide you with what you need for the best possible price. Keep in mind that the ability to meet expanding needs may also be very important.

- Should I use more than one 800/888 telemarketing service?

  If you believe that your call volume will exceed 1,000 calls per hour, then having an additional 800/888 number service and splitting the calls between them will be prudent.

- Should I use more than one 800/888 number?

  Yes. For accurate tracking of results, multiple 800/888 numbers will have to be used. This information allows the media buying department to make correct media analysis and buying decisions.

So often, telemarketers are the unsung heroes of direct marketing—infomercials included. But there is much more to their job than simply taking orders. They are increasingly involved in creative input and expanding telemarketing services specifically for the growing infomercial marketplace. Within the call-handling business, this means the competition for your business is heating up—always a good thing for prospective clients. Still, even though more telemarketing companies are becoming proficient in anticipating and answering the specific needs of infomercial clients, most have not reached the stage of proficiency you need. Again, heed the advice of experienced infomercial agencies and marketers.

CHECKLIST

- ✔ Infomercial marketers must depend on experienced DRTV telemarketing centers to efficiently handle the huge volume of calls their programs bring in.
- ✔ Since consumers who call 800/888 numbers to order infomercial products think they are speaking to your company, make sure your telemarketing center treats every customer courteously and professionally.
- ✔ Beware of telemarketers new to infomercials and DRTV. Like every element of infomercial marketing, it takes highly specialized knowledge to do the job right.
- ✔ If your inbound center is receiving too many inquiry calls, chances are there's a problem with your infomercial.
- ✔ Find out which infomercial fulfillment houses are the best and learn about their information gathering/processing systems.
- ✔ On the day of an infomercial's first run, ask your telemarketing service representative to call you with the results within 30 minutes of the broadcast.
- ✔ Your telemarketing agency can work with your ad agency to structure your upsell strategy.
- ✔ For best results, offer all the help, sample products, and background information you can to the telephone reps who are handling your calls.
- ✔ A good infomercial ad agency will recommend basic program elements that will help eliminate potential problems at the inbound telemarketing level.

CHAPTER

Aftermarketing: Extending Your Infomercial Profits

In retailing, aftermarketing is a standard marketing strategy. Sell the razor, then sell the razor blades. Sell the automobile, then sell rust protection.

But in the infomercial world, this kind of marketing was ignored for years. During the 1980s, direct-over-TV sales were so profitable that all marketing efforts focused on creating the next mega-hit program.

As the industry matured and profits got squeezed by escalating media prices, aftermarket gurus like Jeff Glickman rescued many potential infomercial flops by "working the backend"—by aftermarketing.

Today, a majority of on-air infomercials rely on a complex set of aftermarket tools for significant profits. Chief among them:

1. Outbound telemarketing: call back infomercial customers for cross-selling (offer a different but complementary product) and upselling (offer the "deluxe" version of the basic product).

2. Continuity programs: tie customers into an ongoing stream of products in an extensive product line or periodically replenish the original product purchase.

3. Drive retail: capitalize on the infomercial's brand and awareness-building impact to introduce the product at retail or dramatically lift sales of product already at retail.
4. Catalogs: "As Seen On TV" products in catalogs are hot sellers.
5. Inserts: in credit card bills and packages.
6. List management: infomercial customers are proven buyers of direct marketing offers. List rentals make money.
7. Online sales: the latest, fastest growing backend marketplace—with the greatest potential for future sales.
8. International: it's a booming market on six continents as television viewers get introduced to infomercials' unique personality and products.

Outbound Telemarketing

Outbound telemarketing requires different skills than inbound, and thus far, few call-handling centers can handle both inbound and outbound telemarketing well. Outbound companies can help convert inquiries to sales, resell canceled or returned orders, reactivate old customers, convert one-time buyers to continuity programs, upsell and cross-sell. These programs can add 15 to 50 percent to your revenue.

Testing and Refining Programs

To maximize sales revenues, it's often appropriate to test, develop and implement the following programs through an outbound telemarketing firm.

Cross-Sell Programs. You can use a cross-sell program to test the telemarketing of other products within the product category to which the customer has already responded. Another approach has the telemarketer courteously advising a prospect about a new, special discounted introductory offer on a related product, which will be available for a very limited time. The customer says yes, and you have yet another successful back-end cross-sell program delivering the goods.

Customer Surveys. Outbound telemarketers can effectively use customer surveys to help determine consumer attitudes, address inquiry call concerns, and help decide if adjustments to the infomercial or to the offer could enhance orders. The sample outbound telemarketing survey script in Exhibit 11.1 is one example of how this marketing tool can work.

EXHIBIT 11.1 Sample Inquiry Survey Program Script

Telephone service representative (TSR): Hello. May I speak to Mr./Ms._______, please? (Get response)

If (customer) asks: "Who's calling?" or "What's this about?"

This is (TSR name) with (Sample) Company. I'm calling with a short survey designed to better understand the needs of our customers. Is he/she available?

If not:

- I'll be glad to check back later. When is the best time to call back?

If yes:

- Hello, Mr./Ms._______, I'm calling on behalf of (Sample) Company. You saw our infomercial on television and I'm calling to ask you a few questions as part of our national customer survey designed to better understand our customers' needs. It will just take a few minutes, okay? (Get response)

1. Great! Mr./Ms._______ First of all, when you called, had you watched the program before?

   Yes/No

   If yes:

   - How many times?

   Once/Twice/Three or more times.

2. Mr./Ms. _______, after watching our infomercial program, what is the major reason you called our (800/888) number? Was it for more information or to place an order?

   More information/Order

   If more information:

   - Did you receive the information you requested?

   Yes/No/Received call

   - Did you order from us after you received this information?

   Yes/No

EXHIBIT 11.1 Sample Inquiry Survey Program Script (Continued)

If no:

- What is the major factor that made you decide not to order? (Get response, open-ended. If they need help, then use one of the following answers):

  Too expensive/Must ask spouse/Could buy elsewhere/Already using another product/Other.

3. Mr./Ms._______ , before you saw our program, had you heard about (Product X) before? (Get response.)

   If yes:

   - Where? (Get response) Other/Store/Print
   - Have you taken it before? Yes/No

4. Mr./Ms._______ , Do you presently use any supplements such as vitamins, bee pollen, calcium? (Get response)

   Yes/No

   If yes:

   - Which type? (Note individual vitamins, etc.)

5. Mr./Ms._______ , where do you usually purchase your (product indicated above)?

   Drug store/grocery/discount/health food store/catalog/magazine

6. Mr./Ms._______ , have you ever purchased from television before?

   Yes/No

   If yes:

   - What type of product(s) have you previously purchased from television?

7. Mr./Ms. _______, which of the following categories best represents your present income:

   Less than $25,000
   $25 to $50,000
   $50 to $75,000
   Over $75,000

8. Mr./Ms._______ , what is your present occupation? (Get general category response.)

   Sales, manager, retired, manufacturing, service, other

9. Mr./Ms._______ , we are in the process of creating an audio health series, with information pertaining to different aspects of nutrition. Would this type of program interest you? (Get response.)

EXHIBIT 11.1 Sample Inquiry Survey Program Script (Continued)

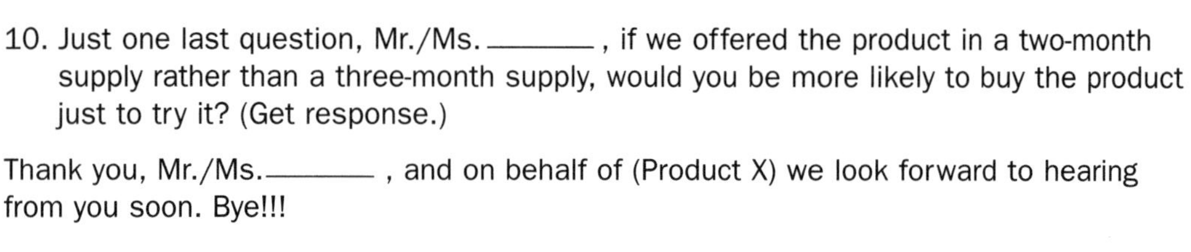

10. Just one last question, Mr./Ms. ______, if we offered the product in a two-month supply rather than a three-month supply, would you be more likely to buy the product just to try it? (Get response.)

Thank you, Mr./Ms. ______, and on behalf of (Product X) we look forward to hearing from you soon. Bye!!!

Source: Sample script furnished by World Class Marketing, Inc.

Inquiry Conversions. You can facilitate inquiry conversions by sending inquirers a mailing piece describing the features, benefits, and pricing of specific products and following up with a phone call to secure the order. The effectiveness of these mailers can be tested and rolled out, based upon conversion rates.

Credit Card Upsell Programs. One of the greatest potential sources of immediate revenue is credit card upsell programs, where a customer who promised to send a check is called back and encouraged to place the order on his/her credit card.

Additional Call-Backs. A first-time customer can often be turned into an ongoing customer by using additional call-backs. This entails the telemarketer calling again to check on the customer's satisfaction and offer an additional product(s). Aftermarket telephone programs can also support your brand name at retail and help consumers locate their local retailers.

Decline Programs. Outbound telemarketing can be used to implement decline programs directed to those consumers who have returned their order for a refund, or whose credit card account declined to initially take the charge.

Your infomercial ad agency or direct marketer will need to implement the following functions to successfully manage an infomercial's outbound campaign:

- Submit a request for a proposal to the outbound telemarketing centers.
- Review the proposal and make recommendations for the ideal outbound telemarketer.

- Create scripts to maximize sales. Make adjustments to the scripts as necessary and provide changes to the outbound telemarketer.
- Supply VHS tape copies of your program to the outbound telemarketer for a training aid.
- Supervise the outbound telemarketing sales representative (TSR) training to properly educate the operators about the product and offer.
- Perform accuracy monitoring on the TSRs to ensure they are being precise, friendly, and selling your product to callers.
- Design special reports which the outbound telemarketer must fill in to monitor results.
- Audit outbound telemarketer's invoices for accuracy. Perform necessary corrective action.
- Coordinate multiple outbound telemarketers, if necessary.
- Verify the accuracy of reported orders, investigate discrepancies, and correct counts if necessary.
- Ensure timeliness of reports from the outbound telemarketer.
- Work with the outbound telemarketer to resolve procedural problems resulting in TSRs not closing sales.
- Coordinate optional services offered by the outbound telemarketer.
- Coordinate outbound telemarketer TSR focus groups and incentive programs.
- Supervise the computer link between the 800 service center, the fulfillment house, and the outbound telemarketer.

Many new companies (Fortune 500 companies, in particular) will be introduced to the infomercial format in the next few years. Infomercial producers and ad agencies will depend heavily on their inbound and outbound telemarketing firms to keep these new companies happy. Several infomercial companies such as Matrixx Marketing, West Telemarketing, and InfoCision have a substantial presence already.

Continuity Programs

Before launching a continuity program, it's a good idea to gather information about your target audience, their buying habits, preferences, and possible interest in related products. For example, Victoria Principal had successfully established her skin care program through infomercials and was considering a line of hair care products. Before proceeding, her skin care customers were surveyed to ascertain their receptiveness to this new offering. Her "Principal Secret" skin care customers responded favorably and the hair care line was developed and offered to those customers through inserts and outbound telemarketing. Eventually her hair products were sold on their own as well as through continuity programs.

An extensive product line makes for a great continuity program. Infomercial customers will often join the continuity program while placing their first order. Music and book clubs are classic continuity programs. Other products, such as Victoria Jackson's color cosmetics line, are prime examples of consumable products that must be reordered and provide exceptionally strong back-end revenues. Another example might be a manufacturer of skin care products who advertises a sample-sized product package through an infomercial. When calls come in, the telemarketer uses the opportunity to advise the customer about additional continuity programs. Of course, unknown new products are not good candidates for continuity programs; after the product becomes recognizable and a proven success, its continuity opportunities open up.

The outbound telemarketing continuity script (Exhibit 11.2) is just one small sampling of the many outbound continuity offers that can be made. (All product, company, and individuals' names are fictitious.)

Drive Retail

Many Fortune 500 marketers are averse to the typical hard-sell techniques formerly associated with infomercials. But if you want to make money with a soft-sell infomercial advertising campaign, incorporating retail strategies is essential.

Indeed, retail sales can skyrocket by inspiring consumers who may be reluctant to purchase products directly from television. Retail

EXHIBIT 11.2 Sample Continuity Offer Script

JOY'S AMAZING SKIN CARE PRODUCT

TSR: Hello, May I speak to Mr./Ms. _______, please? (Get response.)

This is (TSR name) calling on behalf of "Amazing Skin," with new information on Joy's Skin Care Program for Mr./Ms. _______. Is he/she available? (Get response.)

If no:

- When would be the best time to reach him/her? (Note time.)

Hello, Mr./Ms. _______, this is (TSR) calling in regard to Joy's Amazing Skin Care Program. How are you today? (Get response.) Great! Mr./Ms. _______, I'm calling to give you new information on Joy's Complete Skin Care System and to answer any questions you may have about our program, but first, have you received your order yet? (Get response.)

If no:

- Mr./Ms. _______, you should receive your complete deluxe program any time now, but just to make sure that we have all your delivery information down correctly, let me confirm your address. Mr./Ms. _______, I will call you back within the next week to confirm that you have received your order, okay? (Get response.)

If yes, continue presentation here:

Great! Have you started using Joy's Amazing Skin Care System yet? (Get response.)

If no:

- Well, Mr./Ms. _______, Joy's System is unique because it is effective, simple and easy to use, yet it incorporates the latest in skin care technology. You'll really see and feel the difference once you start using the program. Would you mind if I called you in a couple of weeks to discuss your progress with the program? (Get response.)

If yes:

Well, first I'd like to ask you how you feel about the system and how well it's working for you. Mr./Ms. _______, your complete skin care system is specifically designed for your skin type and is available for the first time at use at home. As you saw on the infomercial, we have spent more than 30 years perfecting the system to help you achieve a flawless face. This is the only complete skin care system that specifically addresses the problems we have that are caused by today's environment. Let me ask you this, you ordered the (kit name/type), is that correct? (Get response.)

As you know, Mr./Ms. _______, we have created three complete kits, each containing

EXHIBIT 11.2 Sample Continuity Offer Script (Continued)

four unique products. Based on your skin profile, I would recommend . . . (go to customer's selection):

Package One: The Premium Beauty & Revitalizing Program (give details)
Package Two: Deluxe Skin Care System (give details)
Package Three: Regular Skin Care System (give details)

Mr./Ms. ______ , Joy knows exactly what you want and need. Many people have gained increased confidence and improved their self-esteem just by using and seeing the results of this incredible system. By following the easy, step-by-step directions, you will have smooth, even-toned and radiant skin. Have you noticed the effect of the (particular item within package choice)?

Mr./Ms. ______, what is the most significant effect you've seen so far with this system?

Yes, it is so effective because it incorporates more than 30 years of advancements in skin care technology.

This beauty routine should be performed twice a day, both in the morning and again in the evening before you go to sleep. Are you taking the time to follow the schedule? (Get response.)

Well, great! Mr./Ms. ______, the overall effect of the system is to give you the effective, time-saving skin care system that works for your type of skin and will leave your face looking and feeling younger and naturally beautiful. The more often you apply the regime, the faster you will see the results and that's what you want, right? Results?

I'm happy you are experiencing the tremendous results that we know are important to anyone wanting the best for their skin.

Mr./Ms. ______, because we know how important it is to maintain your skin care program without interruption, Joy has asked me to tell you about our convenient new program. Normally, the (customer's selected product) skin care program is sold for (choose one: Premium $79.95; Deluxe $69.95; Regular $59.95), but as a special offer to our customers, we've developed an automatic delivery program that I'm sure you will appreciate. For a limited time, you can enroll in our automatic delivery program and receive a special bonus—a $40.00 value—free with your order, today.

(CLOSE)

Mr./Ms. ______, so you can stay on the program without a break, you will automatically be shipped a 60-day supply of the (customer's selected package) program, including the (list package components), every two months for only (Premium $59.95; Deluxe $49.95; Regular $39.95) (plus $6.00 shipping and handling and sales tax). That's a savings of more than $20! One of the best things about this program is that, as your needs change,

EXHIBIT 11.2 Sample Continuity Offer Script (Continued)

you can easily change your choice of system. Of course, the complete system is backed by our 60-day money-back guarantee. How does that sound? (Get response.)

All I need to get your next shipment of (name selected package) skin care system out to you right away for the special price of only $______ (plus S&H and sales tax) is confirm your address as (give customer's address). Is that correct? (Get response.) Great! Will you be using your VISA, MasterCard or Discover card? (Get response.) (Get complete credit card information along with expiration date.)

It's been great talking to you. Thanks for your time and order. You won't regret it! Bye!

Source: Sample script furnished by World Class Marketing, Inc.

sales driven by your infomercial can be anywhere from one to five times your infomercial sales. Dollar for dollar, infomercials can be a more effective retail sales promotion technique than many print campaigns.

Today, one-step-offer infomercials for products unable to get retail shelf space are used primarily to attain retail distribution. Infomercial marketers can tell a retailer that more than a million consumers ordered their product directly from television and thousands of others called for more information. These kinds of figures grab the attention of a good many retailers, who then purchase and showcase infomercial products realizing that "as seen on TV" are big sellers at retail.

In some cases, infomercials can succeed in driving retail beyond your wildest dreams. For example, a major housewares and personal care products retailer needed to revive lagging retail sales of a specific product. The resultant infomercial paid for itself and increased retail sales twofold in just six months.

Retail sales of infomercial products are so significant that your revenue/profit projections (see Sample Pro Forma, Chapter 8 Appendix) should factor in an infomercial retail multiple (IRM), which can be anything from one to five. Use it to multiply your infomercial units sold to predict your retail sales.

Today products that previously were sold at retail exclusively—from automobiles to kitchen appliances—are featured in infomercials to enhance retail sales, build brand awareness, add additional direct television sales, generate leads, and capture consumer information for a variety of future selling opportunities. The future of infomercials is strongly tied to their ability to drive retail.

Catalogs

Traditionally, catalogs have been used by infomercial marketers to extend their back-end profits. The successful HealthRider infomercial is augmented by the product's availability in catalogs such as *Hammacher Schlemmer* and *The Sharper Image.* Cataloger Hanover House claims that the "as seen on TV" tag increases sales. With the emergence of online and CD-ROM catalogs, this back-end revenue stream will undoubtedly rise dramatically.

Inserts

Many infomercial marketers have followed the lead of the traditional direct marketers and catalogers by issuing product line inserts for infomercial products in credit card statements, bank statements, and newspapers. The rising costs of printing and postage may seem prohibitive, but those who have used the insert system successfully swear by it as extra profit center. An example may be a $500 fitness product purchased through an infomercial. In the product shipment, among the packing peanuts, the customer will find a hefty brochure of related products and accessories. The marketers of HealthRider have found this tactic profitable, along with the many other back-end strategies they employ.

List Management and Rentals

Don't underestimate the value of all those names of callers who responded to your infomercial. Even callers who didn't place orders can be valuable. Develop an outbound telemarketing program that will track both buyers' and nonbuyers' responses. The time will come when you have another product that may be lower priced or improved in some way, and both previous buyers and nonbuyers may turn into active customers. The information added through outbound telemarketing to your caller list can be invaluable in plotting your future infomercial marketing course.

After consulting a list broker, you might also consider renting your lists; 50,000 names for $20 per thousand, rented repeatedly, can become a welcomed source of extra income—pure profit. Don't worry. You maintain control of your customer names because this is a *rental* process. Your attorney can help you with list security issues that may arise when your customers buy from the company that rented your list.

On-line Sales

The new frontier of computer on-line services is opening up an area of potential profits that is, at this point, hard to fathom. The beauty of on-line sales is that they are synergistic with infomercial marketing in many ways. According to on-line expert and media personality Kim Komando, the keys to successful on-line marketing are closely related to those of infomercials. You have a great product, present it in an appealing setting, promote it, have a dynamite call to action, and offer immediate feedback and gratification. Thus, many of the components in your effective infomercial can be transferred to the on-line arena, where your prospective customer base numbers in the millions. With this commercial world just beginning, the potential for all businesses, including those who market via infomercials, is incredibly exciting. Many infomercial marketers already have joined the multitudes of businesses that are using on-line Web sites and other on-line shopping avenues to sell products. Infomercial marketers are extremely fortunate in that their format is easily transferrable to on-line avenues.

International

You've heard how the international box office is booming for Hollywood exports; for the past three years, the same has been true for infomercials. From London to Istanbul, Bombay to Hong Kong, Sydney to Rio to Johannesburg, infomercials have more than tripled their overseas revenues since 1992.

Pioneered by U.S. infomercial direct marketing power houses like National Media, Guthy Renker, and HSN Direct, hundreds of international terrestrial TV stations and satellite networks are making room for infomercials. It's expected that, by the year 2000, the international market may surpass the North American market in total infomercial revenues, if not sooner. Even today, you can sit in your hotel room in Tokyo or Moscow and delight to Mike Levey pitching Auri car wax in Japanese and Russian.

And international audiences love it. The response to infomercials is huge. It's a new, fun, entertaining, and convenient way to shop. And, after exhausting themselves in North America, many infomercials find a new lease on profitability—one that can provide revenues for years.

How do you tap into this growing megamarket? Your infomercial agency will already have relationships with both domestic and overseas distributors (see Appendix D). They should facilitate contractual agreements with distributors that provide the right to telecast your program for a specific territory and purchase your product at wholesale.

Then get ready for a hectic time of repackaging your product in languages from Kurdish to Swahili.

CHECKLIST

- ✔ The first add-on revenues are often generated at the inbound call center through upsells.
- ✔ Infomercial leads generated for electronics, autos, insurance, vacation packages, skin care and health products, lawn and garden goods, computers, records, books, investment opportunities, and many others will require creative, cost-effective outbound selling.
- ✔ Outbound companies can help convert inquiries to sales, resell canceled or returned orders, reactivate old customers, convert one-time buyers to continuity programs, upsell, and cross-sell.
- ✔ If you want to make money with a soft-sell infomercial advertising campaign, incorporating retail strategies is essential.
- ✔ Information gathered through outbound telemarketing surveys can be invaluable in plotting your future infomercial marketing course.
- ✔ Inquiry conversions can be facilitated by a mailing piece describing the features, benefits, and pricing of specific products, followed up with a phone call.
- ✔ Before launching a continuity program, gather information about your target audience, their buying habits, preferences, and possible interest in related products.
- ✔ Cross-sell related products.
- ✔ Keep mailing and calling your customer database with new product offers and preferred client opportunities.

✔ Many of the components in your effective infomercial can be transferred to the on-line arena, where your prospective customer base numbers in the millions.

CHAPTER

Fulfillment and Packaging

Order fulfillment is one of those unglamorous areas of marketing that seem so easy to take care of that many people are inclined to ignore it or give it short shrift. But if you do that, you do so at your peril. Because unless your orders are packaged, handled, and shipped in a timely and professional manner, your entire infomercial effort—both in time and money—will have been a colossal waste.

From lead generation to back-end selling and follow-up, selecting a professional fulfillment house can be one of the most important investments you make in your entire program. Several full-service companies specialize in meeting the needs of infomercials marketers. They can provide everything from warehousing to custom packaging, reports, and customer service. The Appendices to this chapter give guidelines to the uses of fulfillment houses and to selecting the right one for your needs.

Warehousing

No small facilities are these fulfillment houses. They must have adequate warehousing area to store large quantities of products so they can be shipped as soon as the orders roll in. The facilities must have controlled temperatures to accommodate such popular infomercial products as cosmetics, skin care products, and audio or video packages. In addition, an extensive security system should be in place to protect your inventory.

Inventory control and reporting must also be well in hand. Inventory control programs log each product as it comes in, record its location in the warehouse, track each shipment's progress to the consumer and returns when necessary.

Packaging

Your fulfillment house can be one of your best assets when it comes to product packaging. Their experience with postal regulations and shipping can save you megabucks, and maintain an attractive package design. Many fulfillment centers will assemble your product kits and provide automated wrapping and sealing services; some also have creative designers that will work with you on attractive—and cost-effective—packaging. Years of fulfillment experience give the best centers a razor-sharp edge when it comes to selecting the best package design for your method of shipment.

Shipping

You can expect a good fulfillment house to ship your product within two to four days. They'll generate a shipping manifest for UPS, USPS or an overnight delivery service, and help you choose the most cost-efficient mode of delivery.

Special offers, such as free gifts, and multi-item or multi-step programs can be powerful selling tools. But they directly affect the fulfillment house's work load. Custom packing services that answer the needs of "customer's choice" multi-item infomercials can add significantly to costs.

Upsells, as they affect fulfillment, will complicate the picture further, according to World Class Marketing CEO Jeffrey Glickman, who furnished the following sample incentive program and script:

Free Bonus Gift, Plus Delivery Incentive
(payment plan upsell conversion)

> "You may order your ' ' with one payment of $, plus S&H, and receive a beautiful travel case, valued at $40 free as our special gift to you. Plus, you'll receive a priority delivery. Would you prefer the convenience of our one-payment plan and receive these special bonuses?"

Obviously, your fulfillment house must stay on its toes with order variables like these built into infomercial campaigns.

Order Processing

Fulfillment centers handle order processing to different degrees. Some will simply ship the products after the credit cards have been processed; others receive electronic orders directly from your inbound telemarketing company.

EXHIBIT 12.1

Some fulfillment companies like Fosdick (shown here) house U.S. Postal Service Centers to expedite customer shipments, plus offer a variety of other shipping methods. Full packaging services are a necessity for cost-effective, high-quality infomercial product fulfillment.

Others will process all orders and set up payment systems. According to an article in *ResponseTV* magazine, companies such as Tylie Jones & Associates, also will process non-credit card options, which includes setting up a post office box, manual order entry, and banking deposit services for checks, money orders, and CODs.

Credit Card Authorizations

Computerized systems have brought together fulfillment services with credit card processors, making these transactions extremely efficient. In addition, big fulfillment centers also handle chargebacks for marketers, and some also offer monthly account debiting for continuity or installment pay programs.

Customer Service and Reports

The status of any product ordered should be online with your fulfillment center and easily accessible to you or your customers. Part of their service is also to procure product information upon request, so the companies strive to learn all they can about your product and company. Reputable fulfillment houses will also provide a variety of reports, including inventory, status of sales, returns and customer complaints. Efficient order and shipment tracking is a key element in the fulfillment service package.

A strong MIS department is essential to the fulfillment process. Computer tracking of products, orders and payments is the fulfillment service that enables infomercial marketers to get a good night's sleep after a goodly quantity of program airings. Some companies, such as Fusion Fulfillment, also offer merchandising projections or advertising return reports to assist you with your future media buys.

Returns

How returned products are handled is extremely important. No matter how good your product, program and systems, expect from 3 to 10 percent of your products to come back. A fulfillment house will generally process returns on a daily basis, return undamaged merchandise to stock, and salvage and repackage products whenever possible.

Extras

Your fulfillment house can also help you build extra profits. Once the basics are covered, having your fulfillment company maintain your database, generate mailings to targeted buyers, and even add bounce-back cards with each order are some of the "extras" infomercial marketers appreciate most.

Your infomercial ad agency will oversee the fulfillment process. The traditional tasks of a fulfillment center are to assemble kits, ship products, manage inventory and perform customer service functions related to order status inquiries, UPS tracers, product information, reorders and selling additional products. A comprehensive fulfillment management program will ensure that your bases are covered at this all-important stage of your campaign. Make sure your infomercial ad agency will follow through on the functions listed on the following checklist in this chapter.

CHECKLIST

- ✔ Submit request for proposal to fulfillment centers in the United States and Canada.
- ✔ Recommend the best fulfillment center for you.
- ✔ Set up a fulfillment house with a designated telemarketer (including electronic transmission, hard copy of orders and layout of your program).
- ✔ Relay all client information to the fulfillment house (product price, upsells, shipping method(s), payment method(s), lock-box address).
- ✔ Work with the fulfillment center on merchant account set up for credit card authorizations.
- ✔ Send your infomercial to the fulfillment house to familiarize them with the product and offer.
- ✔ Train the fulfillment customer service operators to receive calls for checking on orders, adding to orders, reordering, cancelling orders or obtaining more information on the product.

- ✔ Set up all labels, grief letters and information packages with the fulfillment house.
- ✔ Set up all reports for your specific management needs.
- ✔ Perform test calls on the fulfillment house customer service telephone service representatives (TSR) to insure that they know the product and can help the consumer with questions.
- ✔ Audit the fulfillment house invoices for accuracy. Make necessary corrections.
- ✔ Verify the accuracy of all reports.
- ✔ Insure timeliness of reports.
- ✔ Work with the fulfillment house account manager to resolve any problems as soon as they arise.

APPENDIX A

How Fulfillment Impacts Lead Generation

Your fulfillment company plays a big part in the success of your lead-generation program, affecting everything from company image to profitability.

Just as properly handling orders and customer service calls are vital to product success, so is handling the would-be client at the information stage. "If products are shipped in a timely way, then those consumers are happy and their names become much more valuable," says Michael Medico, president of E&M Advertising in New York. The same goes for leads. After just one week, the value attached to the names of infomercial respondents can be diminished significantly. "If the reporting (from your fulfillment house) is accurate and timely, then management can use it as a tool to accurately monitor the profitability of those names and follow up effectively," says Medico. "If no, you can lose valuable leads in generating future sales."

Medico relies heavily on fulfillment house reporting to determine which lead-generation programs are going to be profitable for clients. "We have to determine what media is working best," he says. "Are sufficient names being generated from lead marketing to justify the cost of the lead-generation approach?" Names that are converted into sales are tracked and formulas are applied to estimate "actual dollar amounts that will be generated by those names in the future," says Medico. The ability of the fulfillment house to provide needed reports promptly on any given set of indicators is paramount to the success of their clients.

For this reason, E&M selects a handful of fulfillment companies, which he depends on to serve his clients well. "We give them two or three fulfillment houses to choose from, based on their needs and what stage of the process they are at," he says. To get the E&M seal of approval, "We look at a few things. First of all, are the fulfillment houses used to working with the direct response industry—do they do their own caging? Are they hooked up with the various processing centers? Are they able to handle the thousands of orders that may pour in after an airing? Second, we look at their reporting system—how thorough the reports are, how quickly they are turned around. Third, customer service. This is absolutely crucial."

According to Tylie Jones, president of Tylie Jones Fulfillment Group in Burbank, California, fulfillment companies familiar with the direct response industry know only too well that there are a limited number of customers out there. "Our [infomercial/DRTV marketing] clients need to build a lifetime value with their customers," she says. "For us, that means having effective database management for their customer development. We need to know why they've called, what questions they've asked, if they've ordered, why they've ordered and what their needs are. And we need to get our clients that information quickly."

In addition, fulfillment companies can add special touches to lead-generation marketing. "When a person asks for information, but doesn't order, we sent them a letter thanking them for the inquiry and telling them more about the product and that an order has been reserved in their name if they decide they would like to order in the future," says Jack Gersh, president and CEO of Comar in Valencia, California. "When they do order, we send pre-bills thanking them for the order and reminding them of credit card options if they want them. We set the stage for future orders."

Some companies have even begun offering design and development services to make their operation more appealing to the "one-stop" shoppers. But both Medico and Penny Boatright, supervisor of telemarketing and fulfillment for Hawthorne Communications in Fairfield, Iowa, say that their lead-generation clients do not look to fulfillment companies for these services. "Reporting capabilities are what's vital, as is the ability to effectively refer callers to local stores for purchases," says Boatright, whose clients, like Apple Computers, rely on lead-generation marketing for sales.

Source: *ResponseTV,* April 1996

APPENDIX B

How to Select the Right Fulfillment Vendor

The fulfillment process is a complex one, so choosing the right company to handle it for you is paramount. The accompanying list of questions are designed to guide you and your infomercial ad agency in selecting the fulfillment company that is right for your campaign. Not all the questions will apply, but they will prompt you to think about your options.

Begin the search early in the process, not only to make sure these vital functions are in place, but to avoid costly mistakes in packaging or unnecessary outsourcing to other vendors. Remember, too, your fulfillment company may be your best link to a network of other critical services, such as manufacturers, inbound call centers, direct response/infomercial ad agencies and print syndicates that understand the DRTV business. Here's what else to look for:

- What is the company's history? Founders? Financial stability? Longevity?
- Has it ever executed a similar project (e.g. shipping a video or cosmetic)?
- When are its customer service hours? If your customer calls at 2 a.m.—when your infomercial airs—will the call be answered?

- Are there bilingual order processors and customer service agents available to field calls from Spanish-speaking markets?
- Can it process bounce-back orders?
- Does it bill for continuity or installment pay programs?
- Can it prebill or invoice with order?
- Will it handle mail orders, including deposit of receipts? What about CODs?
- Does it have computerized inventory control?
- Can it interface electronically with your telemarketer to receive orders?
- Can it interface electronically with your credit card processor?
- Does it accept orders via magnetic tape, disc or cassette?
- Will it custom assemble kits or variations on your basic package?
- Can it pick and pack for reorders?
- What is the turnaround time for shipping?
- How does it handle peak demand?
- What shipping methods are offered? Is drop shipping available?
- How large is the warehouse? Is it clean and temperature-controlled?
- What security mechanisms are in place?
- Can it ship products to Canada or other countries?
- Does it offer chargeback management services?
- Does it offer lettershop services?
- Does it manage your database for back-end marketing?
- How does it process and analyze returns?
- What are the monthly/weekly minimums?

Source: *ResponseTV,* May 1994

CHAPTER

Five Ways to Avoid Committing Infomercial Suicide

If you've been considering doing an infomercial, be sure to check out the failures first. Some very expensive, highly creative Fortune 500 long-form commercials are in the infomercial morgue because their producers pulled the trigger without knowing how to aim.

And because they've read the obits for program-length ads such as Bell Atlantic's "The Ringers," many corporate marketers and traditional ad agencies embarking on an infomercial advertising campaign feel like they're entering a Stephen King novel—menacing goblins are everywhere. What do we sell? What's it going to look like? Who knows how to do this? My goodness, we're going to be held *accountable* for the sales results!

And how about interactive advertising in the year 2001? Same questions, same goblins. Since infomercials are a basic form of interactive media, the lessons learned in recent long-form advertising are a primer for the coming age of interactive marketing. Now is the time for advertisers and agencies alike to test potential infomercial strategies without increasing the failure count.

Here are the five infomercial-suicide traps most major advertisers and agencies are prone to fall into . . . and strategies that will help you avoid them.

Don't Sell Toothpaste!

Too many marketing directors have been hoodwinked by the hype of "gadget" infomercials. They are somehow led to believe they can sell standard brands using direct response television advertising and the standard one-step offer, "Call now and give us your credit card number!" Yes, it's possible, but don't expect a profit on the front end.

Successful one-step-offer infomercial products have always been an elite group characterized by uniqueness (Flowbee Haircutter), ability to demonstrate (juicers), mass appeal (get-rich-quick schemes), vanity appeal (cosmetics, diets, exercise) and high margins (minimum 5-to-1, retail price to cost of goods). Very few products meet these criteria and virtually no major brands do.

Although many standard products can be sold over television home shopping channels such as QVC and HSN (clothing, jewelry, furniture, packaged goods, etc.), and will be a staple of interactive home shopping of the future, they can't be sold via infomercials today for one simple reason: The cost of media is too high.

Because of this obstacle, infomercial newcomers must understand that long-form advertising can fulfill many functions beyond the traditional one-step, direct sell offer. Lead generation, key outlet promotions, product promotions, brand and image enhancement, marketplace differentiation, and driving retail sales are all popular alternative infomercial strategies for Fortune 1000 companies. Any one of these may be just right, depending on the brand manager's marketing goal.

The easiest way to hit an infomercial bull's-eye with a major brand is to produce a retail-driving infomercial with minimal or no direct television sales accountability. The product offer can be crafted to ask for a direct television sale, generate leads, or direct viewers to specific retail outlets. No matter. Each of these offers will drive retail sales significantly. In fact, for every product sold direct over television, one to five products will be sold at retail. This is what we call the *infomercial retail multiple (IRM)*. Using infomercials to drive retail sales is the preferred strategy used by major advertisers today.

Don't Do a Sitcommercial!

Do yourself a favor: Remind your creative director at the outset that this is a commercial, not Hollywood. It's marketing, not entertainment. Although your infomercial should be interesting to watch, your goal is to sell, not get ratings.

Your creative concept should be driven first by the product offer. Documercial, storymercial, talk show, whatever you choose as a format, let it fit the product naturally. Don't develop theme and concept until you understand the details of the product offer, benefits, and features. Your half-hour, no matter what the creative concept, must promote the product constantly.

This is a classic suicide attempt by major brand marketers. By attempting to create a soft-sell infomercial, they don't sell at all. They waste the infomercial's key asset: time. So, instead of talking about their product creatively for 30 minutes, they talk about a related, seemingly more entertaining topic for 24 minutes and throw in three 120-second product commercials. They might as well have sponsored "Meet the Press."

Don't Sell Three or Four Products!

It's now in print; you'll have no excuse when you blow it. Don't sell more than one product in your infomercial. It won't work.

Although it may seem logical that you can adequately explain several products in six to eight minutes each, 12 years of failed multiple-product infomercial tests have proven otherwise.

Why? Give consumers multiple choices or multiple sales messages and, one—the impact of each message is weakened plus, two—response drops dramatically. (Of course, 30-second-spot clutter has created the same problem for years.)

You'll get sales from a multiple-product infomercial; you just won't get as many direct television sales per minute. This again demonstrates the power of time. For every minute you spend selling the same product in an infomercial, your response rates rise exponentially, not arithmetically.

There are exceptions. If your strategy is to drive retail sales and direct television sales are less important, a multiple-product infomercial could be the most economical decision.

Don't Lower the Budget to Reduce Risk!

How can you possibly maintain major brand-image equity for 30 minutes for the same cost as launching a 30-second commercial? It's insane! Yet many marketing VPs are walking the plank by producing their infomercial for the cost of a 30-second spot.

This isn't another in-house sales training video! It can take up to six months to do an infomercial. You should have $250,000 to $750,000 to commit for production or forget it. You'd be wasting time and money.

As for risk? How much riskier can an infomercial be than spending millions of media dollars on a 30-second image television campaign and then not know for as long as *six to twelve months* whether or not you've even increased sales, profits, or market share?

After a $50,000 to $100,000 media expenditure on the infomercial test, you'll know within *two to six weeks* whether your marketing research and creative instincts were right. Your infomercial expenditures will be immediately measurable.

Don't Have a Traditional Ad Agency Do the Infomercial

Unless your agency has a creative director with at least five infomercials under his or her belt, and is doing a minimum of $10 million per year of infomercial media buying, having a traditional agency do your infomercial is a big mistake. Listen: Infomercial marketing isn't rocket science, but it *is* an advertising specialty. Would you have your TV-spot scriptwriter compose a six-page direct mail letter? Would you have your 30-second spot media buyer purchase billboards and magazine space? Only if you want him or her to learn a new business at your expense.

Infomercial offer structure, creative positioning, formatting, and scripting are not learned in a day. Quality infomercial media time is mostly owned at the best rates by the seasoned infomercial agencies and direct marketers, who buy it in bulk quantities months in advance. Remember, this is highly developed 12-year-old marketing industry that only recently was discovered by Madison Avenue.

Pride goeth before a fall. Do it right the first time and hire an experienced infomercial agency to team with your traditional agency. Such infomercial agency alliances are working successfully for a half-dozen major advertisers even now.

Infomercials are here to stay. Because they're long-form, nonintrusive, and elicit a response, they are the forerunners to the interactive advertising avenues that will be firmly entrenched by the 21st century. It's time for all major advertisers to close the Stephen King book and take a *safe* plunge into infomercials.

CHECKLIST

- ✔ Be realistic about what can be sold direct over television. Drive retail sales.
- ✔ The infomercial creative goal is to sell all the time, not to outpull the hottest sitcom of the day.
- ✔ Never do a multiple-product infomercial unless you're driving retail sales.
- ✔ Don't pinch the infomercial budget.
- ✔ Hire the experts.

CHAPTER

NIMA International and Regulatory Issues

In response to investigations of consumer complaints about early infomercials by the Federal Trade Commission (FTC), the United States Postal Service, the Federal Communications Commission (FCC), House subcommittees, and the U.S. Congress, the National Infomercial Marketing Association (NIMA) was formed in July 1990.

NIMA was incorporated as a not-for-profit corporation in the District of Columbia by Attorney Jeffrey Knowles of the law firm of Venable, Baetjer, Howard and Civiletti and lead counsel for NIMA International. NIMA's nine directors, representing various facets of the infomercial industry, set out to establish industry-wide guidelines, which all members would be required to meet. By establishing the Marketing Guidelines and Self-Certification program soon after, the association demonstrated that the industry was serious about policing itself. NIMA International (renamed to reflect a more diverse membership) has subsequently experienced enormous institutional and membership growth and enhanced the quality and quantity of services to its members. NIMA International's guidelines for the production of a television commercial are self-regulatory.

The following sections highlight key NIMA International guidelines, which are printed in full in NIMA International publications and can be found at NIMA's Web site, *www.nima.org*.

Mission of NIMA International

NIMA International promotes infomercial and related industries in the best interests of the public and the association's membership. NIMA International works to maintain and further the development of a commercial environment in which the consumer can make an informed choice, based upon the information offered through the industry's unique forms of programming.

NIMA International advocates industry interests before state and federal government entities and maintains enforceable program content and advertising policies and guidelines which all members must follow. NIMA International acts as an informational resource for consumers, the media, and other interested parties, and conducts educational activities that provide opportunities for discussion and analyses of timely industry issues.

Membership

NIMA International membership entitles companies to participate in the Self-Certification Program, use the NIMA International logo in company advertising, receive discounts on certain member services, and vote for the prestigious NIMA International awards.

Most importantly, NIMA International continually monitors legislative developments at the state and federal levels that may affect the infomercial industry and other electronic media participants. When appropriate, NIMA International advocates its members' interests before these same government entities with a view to fostering the development of direct marketing through infomercial programs.

NIMA International sponsors an annual conference and trade exhibition, as well as educational meetings. NIMA International has a vast and growing library of publications including a comprehensive monthly newsletter, a weekly fax newsletter, an annual membership directory, educational booklets, and periodic regulatory updates.

Purpose of Marketing Guidelines

NIMA International's Marketing Guidelines provide individuals and companies involved in producing and distributing infomercials with a set of principles of ethical business conduct that are consistent with existing laws and regulations governing advertising. The marketing guidelines also serve to help the owners and operators of video media judge the acceptability of programming submitted to them by NIMA International members. Programs produced or distributed by NIMA International members are required to comply with the marketing guidelines.

Self-Certification Program

NIMA International's member program for self-certification of compliance with the NIMA International Marketing Guidelines and the corresponding enforcement program represent a credible and balanced effort to enforce standards in the infomercial industry. NIMA International members in good standing are expected to certify to broadcasters and cablecasters that the programs being supplied comply with NIMA International's Marketing Guidelines.

Summary of Marketing Guidelines

It is the policy of NIMA International that all programs produced by its members contain truthful information and comply with all existing laws and regulations. NIMA International supports the freedom of its members to exercise their first amendment rights by providing information to consumers. Because NIMA International's policy is to foster public confidence in the accuracy and reliability of infomercial programming, its guidelines address the following issues:

- Sponsorship and identification
- Program production
- Product claims substantiation
- Testimonials and endorsements
- Ordering, prices, warranties, guarantees, and refunds

- Monitoring enforcement of guidelines
- Guidelines for continuity programs

Below is an example of NIMA's specific guidelines for continuity programs:

- Consumers must have a clear understanding of their rights and obligations before they enter into a continuity program.
- The terms and conditions of the continuity program must be disclosed to the consumer in a specific manner.
- Program members should receive a separate written statement that repeats the terms and conditions of the program.
- Program members must be provided with a means to cancel their participation in the continuity program with each shipment.
- Once the consumer notifies the marketer of his or her cancellation, the marketer must cease shipment and billing immediately.

Guidelines for Marketing Children's Products

Manufacturers and distributors of products designed for children have discovered the benefits of infomercials. Not only can infomercials provide marketers with the time necessary to explain the educational and developmental qualities of their products, but they can also promote education, family values, and other concepts important to teachers and parents.

For quite some time, however, advertising for children's products has been subject to the scrutiny of Congress and the FCC as well as the criticism of many nonprofit watch-dog organizations. Understanding that marketing products in this area requires special care, NIMA International has developed the following Guidelines for Marketing Children's Products in order to safeguard the interests of children, broadcasters (including cable operators) and marketers.

- The Children's Television Act of 1990 limits advertising during children's programming.
- Infomercials marketing children's products are permitted provided they are designed to appeal to adults or families.
- The FCC will analyze the producer's intent and other factors in determining whether the infomercial is geared primarily to children.

- Not all products are appropriate for infomercials.
- The risk remains that the television station, which faces a fine or license renewal difficulties, may not air an infomercial for a children's product.
- Producers and marketers face possible negative public relations consequences.

For the complete text of NIMA International Guidelines, membership, information on the association's expanding services, conferences, and other resources, please contact the association.

NIMA International
12251 New York Avenue, NW, Suite 1200
Washington, DC 20005
phone: 800-987-NIMA
202-289-6462
fax: 202-682-0603
e-mail: www.nima.org

NIMA International (London)
Acre House
69–76 Long Acre
London WCZE 9JH
England
phone: 44-171-395-1322
fax: 44-171-497-5538

CHECKLIST

✔ To ensure that your infomercial campaign meets all legal and regulatory requirements, work with an infomercial agency or direct marketing company that is a member of NIMA International.

✔ Contact NIMA International regarding any concerns you may have about the industry or questionable infomercials you may have viewed on television.

- ✔ For information about attending its established industry trade exhibitions, seminars, conferences, educational programs, and other networking opportunities, call NIMA International.
- ✔ If you have questions about international distribution of your infomercial, contact NIMA International.

CHAPTER

The Future of Infomercials

Where are infomercials headed? Definitely down the fast lane of the information superhighway. When consumers have complete control of their viewing, they won't choose to watch a 30-second spot for Clorox. As the Internet and interactive TV invade more TV homes, the days of intrusive advertising and the short-form commercial may soon be numbered.

Advertisers in the interactive online age will soon be creating informative long-form commercials that are designed to attract viewers who have a choice. Prospective electronic marketing consumers will be invited to preview "chapters" of information of specific products. The goal of the advertiser will be the same as the goal of the infomercial producer today: Get the viewer to spend time with the product—interacting, asking questions, requesting more information as much as possible.

The days when infomercials were either ignored or ridiculed by mainstream marketers and advertisers are just about over. Ironically, it's the infomercial producers, directors, and writers who will be leading the way in 21st century interactive and online selling. They are the ones who have known for years that the more you tell, the more you sell, and they have honed these skills.

Forerunners to Online and Interactive Advertising

Infomercials are a kind of first-generation interactive shopping. An infomercial marketer doesn't depend on viewers who actually plan to sit down and watch their program. Viewers stumble onto long-form ads as they surf the channels with their remote controls. A viewer's interest must be captured in two to ten seconds, or the channel zapping will continue. If viewers stay with an infomercial, they'll be asked to interact—to respond—to pick up the phone and order. Every year millions of Americans do just that.

Infomercials are natural advertising formats to make the transition to online selling. The elements of presentation, price points, service, and call to action are virtually the same. Now is a great time to use your infomercial productivity and apply it to online sales opportunities as well.

Infomercials are also the forerunners to interactive television. This revolution in how advertising will be delivered and viewed will make the 30-second copy writer obsolete. For 60 years, television advertising has been based on intrusion—interrupting viewers glued to "Jeopardy" and "Home Improvement" to present a commercial message. Twenty years ago, the television audience had little choice when an ad intruded upon them: They could either watch it dumbly or head for kitchen or bathroom. The 1980s gave the viewer another choice—to zap commercials with their remote controls. Forty-nine percent of viewers now zap spot commercials, consistently.

The Internet and interactive television present a more serious threat to advertisers than does the remote control. When home viewers can watch anything they want at any moment, how will we get them to watch our product message? Given the choice, will anyone choose to watch a commercial for Dove, Crest, Tide, Coke, or McDonalds? Not likely. Unless you give them an incentive! Television advertising is moving from the age of intrusion to the age of attraction. Viewers will elect to watch commercial messages for two basic reasons: First, they will be compensated by advertisers for their attention through product discounts, coupons, contests, or Internet/cable TV subscription discounts. This category of products will be low-involvement, low-ticket items, such as food and packaged goods. Second, viewers will decide on their own that they want information because they're in the market to buy what will probably be high-involvement, high-ticket items such as electronics, large appliances, and autos.

Regardless of the product, advertising messages will need to be highly enticing. Otherwise, the consumer will move abruptly to one of the 49,000 other viewing options available. Ability to attract viewers through program quality is exactly what infomercials must possess even today. Audiences watch infomercials not because they have to, but because they want to. Long-form ads never intrude; viewers choose to watch them because they appeal to their desire for product information—information presented over a 30-minute period in an entertaining way.

In the age of the Internet and interactive television; commercials won't be 30 seconds or 30 minutes long. In all likelihood, a product will have six to ten chapters of information available to screen, each two to eight minutes long. The goal of 21st century advertisers will be the same: Keep viewers watching as long as possible; keep them moving from one information chapter to the next; keep them engaged, asking questions until they are finally sold. Advertisers should learn the art of infomercial creative today, because tomorrow's advertising will follow closely in its footsteps.

A New Breed of Infomercial

There is a new breed of infomercial—where an authentic brand image is created, right along with the selling mechanics of direct response television—where a lead or a sale is generated in combination with an arresting creative level reflecting high brand identity. We call this hybrid long-form a *brandmercial*. In this evolutionary venue, DRTV mechanics are combined with high creative and production imagery to create sales along with a powerful brand position. Especially attractive is the flexibility of this kind of commercial. Any format can be used—as long as it fits the product—to achieve the brand-building objective.

Apple Computer's and Nissan's breakthrough long-form campaigns are examples of this new breed of 30-minute brandmercial. In both of these programs, the show body is beautifully produced, yet structured with a wealth of product information and benefits. And the call-to-action commercials (designed to generate leads and drive retail) are crafted to portray an elegant image while enticing a huge audience to respond via the 800 number. Both campaigns have produced dramatic results, including measurable qualified leads, ultimate sales, and the enhancement of brand imagery (see Exhibit 15.1).

Nissan's Brandmercial

When Hawthorne ran Apple's "The Martinetti's Bring Home a Computer" infomercial (media managed by Hawthorne), it was, for Nancy Edwards, Senior Manager, Marketing Initiatives and Research, Nissan Motor Corporation, U.S.A., a "trigger" for the Nissan Altima "The Art of Buying a Car" infomercial that ultimately would evolve. "My department is all about trying things that haven't been done before," Edwards reflected recently. "We don't rely on traditional benchmark marketing."

She had been working on an initiative for marketing to women and considering how to use television as part of an integrated marketing mix:

> Our research showed that women weren't comfortable with the car-buying process. We needed to explain the whole process in an entertaining and informative way. There was no way that could be accomplished in a traditional 30-second commercial. Apple's infomercial legitimized the effectiveness of the long format for a high-priced and high-profile consumer product.

In the Nissan corporate environment, it was necessary for Edwards to come up with compelling evidence of the effectiveness and value of this marketing venue before moving ahead. Like many high-profile Fortune 500 companies, there were preconceptions and thus apprehension that an infomercial format might harm, rather than build, Nissan's high-quality brand image.

Edwards continued: "I set out to make sure this was the right strategy for Nissan—that meant lots of research. Our first step was to ask our target consumer (women) if the medium itself was appropriate and to find out if they would even watch a Nissan infomercial."

Edwards used many of the qualifying formulas and techniques outlined in this book to thoroughly research what Nissan could achieve through an infomercial in today's media environment.

Nissan's "The Art of Buying a Car" tested in Dallas and Phoenix,

EXHIBIT 15.1

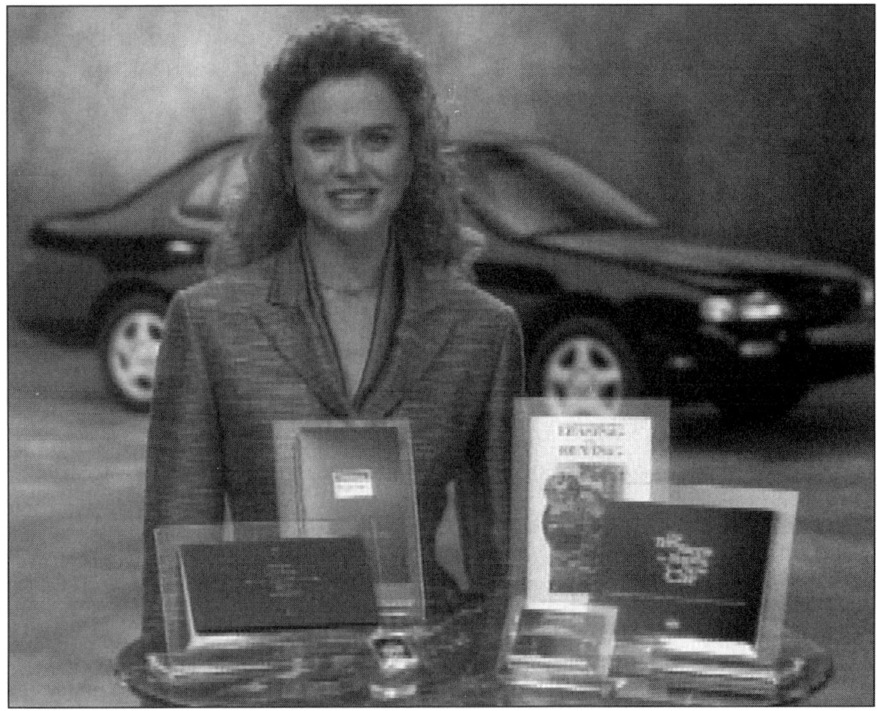

Nissan's "The Art of Buying a Car" show, produced by Hawthorne Communications in asociation with Harmony Media, has won numerous awards for excellence and has produced excellent leads and results—the quintessential brandmercial at its best.

June through September 1995. Edwards said that, at the end of the initial test period, classic direct marketing measurement methodology showed that the infomercial run had done "okay." Yet, traffic at the dealer level had shot up dramatically. What was going on?

Puzzled, Edwards conducted additional research by contacting substantial numbers of new Altima buyers to ask what made them go into their Nissan dealerships and ultimately purchase a new car. Over and over again, they were told how the infomercial had influenced their purchasing decisions.

And, there was an interesting twist to Nissan's successful storymercial, according to Edwards:

> We used a research technique I had seen for political speeches. We ran the infomercial for an audience in a room where each person held a response mechanism and would

> turn the dial to the right or left, depending upon how they were feeling throughout the show. It actually graphs their reaction minute by minute. We tested the show on both men and women to ensure that while it did appeal to women, it would not offend men.

The show generated responses from an equal number of men and women, which meant that the information was valuable regardless of gender.

As one of the pioneering forces in the Fortune 500's trend toward marketing via infomercials, Edwards recommends "Research, research and more research" before embarking on a program. "Make sure you don't only rely on traditional benchmarks, because these infomercials can do more. We have seen our storymercial drive retail directly and help send more "qualified" leads to dealerships. In fact, our dealers in the two test cities converted infomercial leads at a rate three times higher than they did for any other program during that period. We definitely proved to the company that (the infomercial) was a highly efficient, productive, and effective marketing tool."

But there's more to the payback with the brandmercial format. Research shows that a traditional infomercial (for products such as exercise and kitchen gadgets) will attract an audience for an average of 7 to 13 minutes. Yet, the Apple and Nissan brandmercials have succeeded in attracting their audiences for more than 25 minutes of viewing time. This is big news because it spells big results: The selling opportunity, along with the heightened brand image, is doubled.

21st Century Electronic Marketing

Live home shopping and pretaped infomercials will be among the dominant video-viewing categories of the 21st century. Electronic marketing sales will probably grow from $5 billion to more than $20 billion in the next ten years alone.

Will some infomercials in the year 2010 still look like the Juiceman's slicer-dicer program and Victoria Jackson's cosmetics talk show? Undoubtedly. As long as there are noninteractive television homes, the basic half-hour infomercial we see today will endure. Fully interactive, fiber-optic television is expected to penetrate perhaps only 30 percent of homes by the year 2010. Although increasingly dominated by major advertisers such as General Motors, IBM, AT&T, and

Sony, traditional 30-minute infomercials will continue to be a mainstay in old-style analog TV homes.

Consumer Control of Advertising

The reason that infomercials can generate a billion dollars in orders are road signs for television creative techniques of tomorrow. A few of those reasons are following.

First, there has been a general increase in the need for consumer product information for making buying decisions. This increase probably stems from changes in lifestyles (less time, more choices), a growing distrust for institutions and advertising in general, and a growing awareness about consumption and concern about product quality, ingredients, and value.

Second, the number of new products in the marketplace has increased exponentially. The real challenge lies in turning new products into new brands. And infomercials can be key. As information about product benefits and features increases in a long-form advertising message, new brands can be born. The reason Victoria Jackson, a complete unknown just a few years ago, could create a $250 million cosmetic empire in just two years is that she had time—30 minutes of time—to emphasize over and over again her products' benefits and features.

Third, consumers in general—and viewers in particular—want more control. A recent Yankelovich research study indicated consumers do want more information about products—when they choose to watch. With the remote control in hand, the infomercial viewer of the nineties chooses whether he or she will spend 10 minutes, 30 minutes, or 30 seconds with an infomercial. In essence the viewer is in control.

Addressing Consumer Control

Consumer control of advertising impressions will be the hallmark of interactive television in 2010. The primary challenge to the new age of advertisers will be how to compensate for this loss of control when their messages are delivered. We need to make plans now to regain some of that control. Whether the commercial message is short or long form, following are some possible strategies:

1. Reward the Viewer's Attention. Give the viewer something concrete for the time they spend viewing your commercial. Offer a product discount, two-for-one packages, a sample offer, limited time offers, or viewing points that can be accumulated for product discounts as frequent flier points are. In an interactive environment, if a customer prospect takes the time to view an advertiser's message, the advertiser will need to respond with concrete favors.

2. Target Consumers Individually. Digital TV and data storage capabilities will allow advertisers to target viewers individually. Advertisers will know the viewer's age, income, and lifestyle preferences. Short- and long-form commercials will eventually be transmitted and stored in the target prospect's communications center for later viewing. A media director with a top ten agency recently complained: What are we doing? Chasing the consumers one at a time? Yes, that's exactly what's going to happen—and marketing and sales efficiency will increase dramatically!

3. Trade on Interactivity. Lastly, the ability to be interactive will become a traded commodity. Time is money. Having prospective customers spend time viewing an advertiser's message will be valuable indeed. In 2010, if a consumer agrees to view a certain number of commercial messages before, during, or after selecting favorite entertainment programs, perhaps his or her monthly cable fee will be lowered. Of if the consumer chooses to limit or eliminate intrusive commercial messages, he or she might agree to pay a higher monthly cable fee.

Future Creative for Infomercials

In the past few years, infomercials have emerged as a mandatory marketing technique for major corporations scrambling to enter the interactive age of the information superhighway. In the brave new world where viewers control what they watch on television, some new creative fundamentals are required for effective infomercials.

Advertising in general must provide more abundant information. The creative will feature more reality and less fantasy. Sure, there will always be beauty shots, dream images, and fictional slice-of-life vignettes. But as advertisers tell their product story, they'll need to establish a connection with the television viewers' real world. The need to justify—in practical terms—a viewer's purchasing decision is more important in a long-form commercial message. Even in a fiction-based storymercial, it will be important to have a real-life, on-camera host who speaks directly to the audience regarding the basic offer, costs, availability, and the like.

Advertisers will create their product story in modules or chapters, each probably two to eight minutes long. The Ford Explorer infomercial, for example, would be divided into "chapters" such as safety features, options and accessories, four-wheel-drive capabilities, and luxury and comfort benefits. Viewers will essentially become their own programmers, selecting their own personal path for discovering the benefits and features of the advertised product. Viewers may spend 2 to 30 minutes with an infomercial, depending on their interest in the product and the advertiser's ability to keep their attention. In this interactive selling environment of the future, advertisers will have a very important new creative goal: To keep the viewer walking the product's path of discovery and interacting with the product as long as possible.

The Entertainment Show Packed with Products

How will advertisers keep viewers' attention for as long as possible? This is the primary goal of infomercial producers even today. Some of the creative formulas they practice now will be basic keys in 2010.

On-screen celebrities or product presenters will need to do more than be engaging and charismatic. More than ever, they must truly believe in the product. The talent you choose must be someone with whom viewers want to relate, making them want to spend more time watching your program.

Infomercials of the future must create a sense that there's something of value to be had at the end of the viewing experience. They must be leading, enticing, stimulating viewers into participating in the viewing journey until the goal is achieved. It could be something as basic as a surprise discount or free offer that can only be accessed after time has been spent viewing the infomercial. Or, the infomercial might be crafted around a fictional story with a beginning, middle, and end. A story that requires, through conflict and the desire to see it resolved, a long period of time to be spent in relationship with the advertiser's product.

Advertisers need to learn how to create interactivity. Infomercials must engage all the viewers' senses. A cruise ship infomercial may require the viewer to push the asterisk button, for example, to view the most posh onboard suites (which are now available at half price during the off-season!). In other words, advertisers will no longer present a flashy one-way monologue. They'll create the desire in viewers to watch and perform some action to achieve the full dialogue experience.

The reason? The more involved the prospective customer is in the selling dialogue, the greater the chances of converting a prospect to a consumer. There's an old Chinese proverb that goes: "I hear and I forget; I see and I remember; I do and I understand." Advertisers' creative designs will no longer simply be for display. They must create interactivity that will hold the viewers' attention for the longest amount of time possible and boost response. Infomercials will, in 2010, be the preferred advertising mode.

Predictions

Infomercial Costs

The infomercial is here to stay. Infomercial media time will expand on both broadcast stations and cable. The cost of media will continue to rise. By the year 2000, the average broadcast will cost $2,050—eight times what it was in 1985. The cost and quality of productions will also continue to rise.

Increase in Corporate Infomercials

Fortune 1000 companies will continue to push the infomercial industry from the era of one-shot hard-goods marketing to lead generation and 30-minute retail-driving advertising. By 2000, only 20 percent of all infomercials will be selling hard goods in one step and infomercials will be an accepted part of most major corporations' media/marketing mix. Auto manufacturers, insurance companies, top ten retailers, electronics and computer manufacturers, magazines, book and newsletter publishers, cruise companies, entertainment parks, distressed companies, and many more will be using infomercials. (See Exhibit 15.2.) Because of the influx of new strategic corporate infomercials, other quality product infomercials probably won't succeed—programs on how to overcome drinking and drug addiction, how to get a better job, or personal financial planning courses will probably be bumped from the advertising line-up.

EXHIBIT 15.2

Braun Corporation and Black & Decker were among the first retail brand-names to use the infomercial format. Shown here is the Braun Handblender.

Consolidation of the infomercial Industry

Faced with rising media costs and a shortage of high markup items, by 2000 50 percent of today's half-dozen major infomercial direct marketers will go out of business, be acquired, or be forced to adapt. The consolidation of the industry has already begun. The major infomercial advertising agencies are all considered targets for acquisition by major infomercial direct marketers or traditional Madison Avenue ad agencies. These industry acquisitions may help ease the kind of competitive pressure that has forced up media prices for so long.

Increase in Multiproduct Infomercials

Multiproduct infomercials will take hold in the marketplace. Marketers will take two or three or more related products with the

EXHIBIT 15.3

Sony Electronics' recent storymercial for its "Instant Surroundsound Speaker System," produced by TYEE, represents the new age of high quality, image-enhancing programs.

same demographic appeal such as self-development and financial products, and produce a multiproduct infomercial with product segments running 10 to 15 minutes each. This is the equivalent of the 10- or 15-second spot versus the 30-second spot. But since stations don't currently sell 10- and 15-minute blocks, marketers will buy 30 minutes and create 10- and 15-minute blocks inside of it. This strategy should bloom in the future.

Image Infomercials

In the future many major advertisers will supplement their traditional marketing efforts with infomercials. In addition, as infomercials become increasingly "respectable" (i.e., they continue to demonstrate their effectiveness), they will move into the mainstream of marketing, in the "lead" position as well as a supplemental tool. Their interactive quality in particular—as a vehicle for providing information and for providing incentives to buy now—lends them to increased use in the future.

Infomercials are ideal for use in traditional marketing programs, namely, to introduce new products, reposition existing products, and extend existing lines.

For instance, more and more marketers are taking advantage of the infomercial's 30-minute time periods to explain and demonstrate the benefits of new products. In some cases, these programs are used as add-on tactics, in others, as the leading marketing tactic. This trend is likely to continue. Similarly, infomercials are a powerful vehicle for repositioning or extending existing product lines to reach potential buyers missed by other marketing media.

This brief list shows how infomercials can be the ideal vehicle for delivering traditional buying incentives:

1. Offer a sample package—single or multiple product samples for a minimum introductory price.
2. Package the retail product with unique premiums and bonuses, driving the television selling price higher than the solo product's price at retail.
3. Offer free inspection/test drive offers for high-ticket items, or discounts, cash back, etc.
4. Go for straight lead generation, call for more information, mail-back print and video promotion materials, follow up with outbound telemarketing and direct mail.
5. Offer coupons with money-back packages designed to drive consumers to retail.

The future of infomercials is especially bright when considered in relation to the rise of interactive media. Marketers who have experimented with interactive media have found them to be the most useful as a public relations medium—delivering information to consumers and thereby building and enhancing brand image. The perfect role for infomercials! Consumers want more product information, and infomercials are the ideal way to provide it.

This trend toward a new age of infomercials reflects two fundamental, enduring truths about marketing:

1. The longer you keep a potential customer's attention on your product's benefits, the greater the chance he or she will buy. (Or, as I have said throughout this book: the more you tell, the more you sell.)
2. As consumer cynicism becomes the cultural norm, a customer/or prospect will demand more information before making a decision to purchase.

In one sense the future will be less a matter of a "new age" of infomercials than simply a matter of the time when they take their rightful place in mainstream marketing.

CHECKLIST

- ✔ Start preparing now for the future of online interactive infomercials, using two- to eight-minute chapters to keep viewers interacting/watching as long as possible.
- ✔ Learn the selling skills now to use for infomercials and on-line sales. Infomercial marketers are putting up home pages on the Internet now, which will allow interested parties to access information on the company and its products, learn how to use products, as well as place orders.
- ✔ Remember this is charted territory. The history of television advertising is based on an entertainment medium supported by commercials.
- ✔ Nowhere in the theory of persuasion does it say that brevity in communication is most effective. The truth is just the opposite: the more you tell, the more you sell. This is true for all sales, infomercials as well as on-line sales and the coming era of interactive television.
- ✔ Television viewership in the year 2010 will consist of 30 percent interactive television-owning households and 70 percent linear/analog television households.
- ✔ Get ready for the "interactive media center" (the "telecomp")—a combination of television, computer, telephone, fax, and radio, with fiber optic–fed, digital storage. The much-heralded 500 cable channel concept is linear and obsolete.

APPENDIX A

Contributors

Our heartfelt appreciation to the following companies and individuals who contributed their insights and time for all the readers who will benefit from their up-to-date knowledge and unique perspectives on the infomercial industry and how it works. In addition, a special thank you to those who allowed us to reprint photographs, special reports, portions of their books, surveys, and articles.

Comar
25060 Avenue Tibbitts
Valencia, CA 91355
805-294-2700
805-294-2717 fax
800-49-COMAR
Jack Gersh, President

Concepts Video Productions
170 Changebridge Rd., Ste. B2
Montville, NJ 07045
201-808-5646
201-808-5823 fax

E&M Advertising
60 Madison Ave.
New York, NY 10010
212-481-3663
212-481-4265 fax
Michael L. Medico, President

Edelman Public Relations Worldwide
200 E. Randolph Dr., 63rd floor
Chicago, IL 60601
312-240-3000
312-240-2900
Nancy Gohring

Electronic Retailing Magazine
Creative Age Publications, Inc.
7628 Densmore Avenue
Van Nuys, CA 91406-2088
818-782-7328
818-782-7450 fax
Eretailing@aol.com

Fosdick Corporation
10 Alexander Dr.
Wallingford, CT 06492
800-759-5558/203-269-0211
203-265-1697
Steve Constantino
VP Sales & Marketing

Infomercial Marketing Report
11533 Thurston Circle
Los Angeles, CA 90049
310-472-5253
310-472-6004 fax
Steve Dworman

Infomercial Monitoring Service
810 Parkway, Satellite 2
Broomall, PA 19008
610-328-6902
610-328-6791 fax

Inphomation Communications, Inc.
23–25 Walker Ave.
Baltimore, MD 21208-9708
410-653-6211
410-484-7620 fax

Jordan Whitney, Inc.
17300 17th St., Ste. J-111
Tustin, CA 92680
714-832-2432
714-832-3053

Kent & Spiegel
6133 Bristol Parkway
Culver City, CA 90230
310-337-1010
310-342-5498
Laura Fox

Komando Corporation
4332 N. Wells Fargo Ave., Ste. 200
Scottsdale, AZ 85251-3408
602 970-1207
602 970-1207
Kim Komando

KRPR
163 N. Arnaz Dr., #4
Beverly Hills, CA 90211
310-289-7900
310-289-7976 fax
Kim Rahilly

MarComm Associates
504 Kingman Circle
Fairfield, IA 52556
515-469-3144
515-469-3237
Maggie Argiro

MATRIXX Marketing
One Matrixx Plaza
1400 W. 4400 S.
Ogden, UT 84405
800-MATRIXX/800-543-6423
801-629-6272 fax
Clifton R. Critchlow

MicroMall
c/o Microware Systems
1900 NW 114th St.
Des Moines, IA 50325
515-224-9655
515-224-9620
Chuck Spong
President

MIT Consulting
26 Shrewsbury Ave.
East Sheen SW14 8JZ
London, UK
http://ourworld.compuserve.com/homepages/budd margolis
Budd Margolis

NIMA International
12251 New York Avenue, NW
Suite 1200
Washington, DC 20005
800-987-NIMA
202-289-6462
202-682-0603 fax
www.nima.org

Nissan Motor Corporation U.S.A.
Corporate Office
18501 South Figueroa St.
Gardena, CA 90248-4500

Periscope Communications
921 Washington Ave. S.
Minneapolis, MN 55415
612-399-0585
612-339-1700 fax
Craig Evans
cevans@qm.ps-mpls.com

***ResponseTV* Magazine**
Advanstar Communications, Inc.
210 E. Sandpointe, Ste. 600
Santa Ana, CA 92707-5761
800-854-3112
714-513-8400
David Nagel, Editor

Script to Screen
200 N. Tustin Ave., Ste. 100
Santa Ana, CA 92705
714-558-3971
714-558-1759 fax
Tony Kerry

SSA Public Relations
16027 Ventura Blvd., Ste. 206
Encino, CA 91436
818-501-0700
818-501-7216 fax
Theresa Ward

TeleMark
7303 SE Lake Road
Portland, Oregon 97267
800 783-6000

TYEE
513 NW 13th Ave., 5th floor
Portland, OR 97209
503-228-5555
503-228-0560 fax

Tylie Jones & Associates, Inc.
Fulfillment Services-California/New Jersey
Corporate office: 3519 W. Pacific Ave.
Burbank, CA 91505
800-922-0662
818-955-8542
Tylie Jones, President

Venable, Baether, Howard & Civiletti
1201 New York Ave. NW, Ste. 1000
Washington, D.C. 20005
202-962-4800
202-962-8300 fax
Jeffrey Knowles, Esq.

West Telemarketing Corporation
9910 Maple St.
Omaha, NE 68134
800-542-1000
402-571-9864 fax
Jan Kruse
Corporate Marketing Manager

World Class Marketing, Inc.
33 Orchard St.
Greenwich, CT 06807
203-861-1879
203-861-6791 fax
Jeffrey A. Glickman
President/CEO

APPENDIX B

Networks

Broadcast Networks

CBS
NBC
ABC
FOX
UPN
WB
PBS

Cable Networks

Action Pay Per View
A&E Television Network
All News Channel
AMC (American Movie Classics)
America's Talking
ANA Television
Asian American Satellite TV
BET (Black Entertainment Television)
The Box
Bravo Cable Network
Cable Health Club
Cable Video Store
Canal de Noticias NBC

Canal Sur
Cartoon Network
Catalog 1
Channel America Television Network
CineLatino
Cinemax
Classic Arts Showcase
CMT: Country Music Television
CMT
CNBC
c/net: The Computer Network
CNN (Cable News Network)
CNNI (CNN International)
Comedy Central
Consumer Resource Network (CRN)
Courtroom Television Network (Court TV)
The Crime Channel
C-Span (Cable Satellite Public Affairs Network)
C-SPAN 2
Deep Dish TV
The Discovery Channel
The Disney Channel
E! Entertainment Television
ENCORE
ENCORE Thematic Multiplex Services
STARZ!-encore 8
ESPN
ESPN2
EWTN: The Catholic Cable Network
Faith & Values Channel
The Family Channel
The Filipino Channel
Flix
FoxNet
fx
fxM: Movies from Fox
Galavisión
Game Show Network
GEMS International Television
The Golf Channel
HBO: Home Box Office
Headline News
The History Channel
Home & Garden Television
Home Shopping Networks I and II
The Idea Channel
The Independent Film Channel
The Inspirational Network (INSP)
International Channel
Jewish Television Network
Jones Computer Network (JCN)
Kaleidoscope: America's Disability Channel
KTLA/UV
Ladbroke Racing Channel
The Learning Channel
Lifetime Television
Mind Extension University (ME/U):
The Education Network
MOR Music TV
The Movie Channel (TMC)
MTV: Music Television
MTV Latino
Muchmusic USA
NASA Television
NET—Political NewsTalk Network
Network One
NewsTalk Television
Newsworld International
Nickelodeon/Nick at Nite
The '90s Channel
Nostalgia Television

Playboy TV
Prime SportsChannel Networks
Product Information Network (PIN)
QVC
Q2
Request Television
Sci-Fi Channel
Scola
Shop at Home
Showtime
SingleVision
Spice
Adam & Eve
TBS
Telemundo
Television Food Network (TVFN)
TNN: The Nashville Network
TNT (Turner Network Television)
The Travel Channel
Trinity Broadcasting Network
Trio
Turner Classic Movies (TCM)
TV Asia
TV-Japan
U Network
Univision
USA Network
Valuevision
VH1 (Video Hits One)
Via TV Network
Video Catalog Channel
Viewer's Choice
Continuous Hits 1, 2, 3
Hot Choice
Viva Television Network
The Weather Channel
WGN/UV
The Worship Network
WPIX/UV
WSBK
WWOR/EMI Service
Z Music

Note: For contact information for any of the cable networks listed please call or write:
The National Cable Television Association
1724 Massachusetts Ave. NW
Washington, DC 20036-1969
(202) 775-3550

APPENDIX C

Related Agencies and Industry Associations

Academy of Television Arts & Sciences
5220 Lankershim Blvd.
N. Hollywood, CA 91601
818-754-2800
818-781-ATAS fax

American Marketing Association (AMA)
250 S. Wacker Dr., Ste. 200
Chicago, IL 60606-5819
312-648-0536
312-993-7542 fax

Association of National Advertisers (ANA)
155 East 44th St.
New York, NY 10017
212-697-5950
212-661-8057 fax

Cabletelevision Advertising Bureau (CAB)
757 Third Ave.
New York, NY 10017
212-751-7770
212-832-3268 fax

Direct Marketing Association (DMA)
1120 Avenue of the Americas
New York, NY 10036-6700
212-768-7277
212-768-4546 fax

Federal Communications Commission (FCC)
1919 M St. NW
Washington, DC 20554
202-418-0200
202-418-2809 fax

Federal Trade Commission (FTC)
Sixth Street and Pennsylvania Ave. NW
Washington, DC 20580
202-326-2000
202-326-2050 fax

International Interactive Communications Society (IICS)
11242 Waples Mill Rd., Ste. 200
Fairfax, VA 22030-6079
703-273-7200
703-278-8082 fax

Interactive Television Association (ITA)
1019 19th St., 10th floor
Washington, DC 20036
202-408-0008
202-408-0111 fax
officeita@aol.com

National Association of Broadcasters (NAB)
1771 N St., NW
Washington, DC 20036-2891
202-429-5300
202-429-7427 fax

National Association of Television Programming Executives (NATPE)
2425 Olympic Blvd., Ste. 550 E
Santa Monica, CA 90404
310-453-4440
310-453-5258 fax

National Cable TV Association (NCTA)
1724 Massachusetts Ave., NW
Washington, DC 20036-1969
202-775-3550

NIMA International
12251 New York Avenue, NW Suite 1200
Washington, DC 20005
800-987-NIMA/202-289-6462
202-682-0603 fax
www.nima.org

APPENDIX D

Global Infomercial Marketing Resources

The following information will help you locate companies that can extend the global reach of your infomercials.

AFRICA

Egypt

Tamima-Teleseen
Contact: Hany Fathy
Phone: 011-202-375-1375
Fax: 011-202-351-3656

South Africa

Verimark Holdings (Pty) Ltd.
Contact: Michael van Straaten
Phone: 011-2711-883-5050
Fax: 011-2711-883-5055

AUSTRALASIA

Australia

Data Dial Pty Ltd.
Contact: Matt Ainscough
Phone: 011-61-2-299-7377
Fax: 011-61-2-299-7818

Editel Pty Ltd.
Contact: Colin Mullins
Phone: 011-61-9-388-1544
Fax: 011-61-9-388-1541

Homeware Innovations (Aust) Pty.
Contact: Carl Crane
Phone: 011-612-3193196
Fax: 011-612-3193179

Hong Kong

Epic Group Ltd.
Contact: Mark Presser
Phone: 011-852-2857-2560
Fax: 011-852-2549-1367

Lawsons Marketing Services Ltd.
Contact: Barry Chan
Phone: 011-852-811-5022
Fax: 011-852-505-0080

Star/Wamaco
Contact: Eddie Wang
Yu-Chang
Phone: 011-852-2621-9696
Fax: 011-852-2621-9698

TV Media International Ltd.
Contact: Newson Tan Y.S.
Phone: 011-852-2515-7979
Fax: 011-852-2505-4947

India

United Teleshopping Ltd.
Contact: Ronnie Screwvala
Phone: 011-91-493-0336

Indonesia

PT & Sarana Mail Indonesia
Contact: Jasin Halim
Phone: 011-62-21-893-4605
Fax: 011-62-21-893-4607

Japan

Oak Lawn Marketing, Inc.
Contact: Robert Roche
Phone: 011-81-52-950-1124
Fax: 011-81-52-950-1524

Prime Network Inc.
Contact: Kazuhira Tabata
Phone: 011-81-52-934-2301
Fax: 011-81-52-934-2308

Malaysia

Ambang anika SDN BHD
Contact: Azman Othman
Phone: 011-603-284-4003
Fax: 011-603-284-5004

New Zealand

L.V. Martin & Son Ltd.
Contact: Neil Martin
Phone: 011-644-472-4356
Fax: 011-644-478-1611

Prestige Marketing Ltd.
Phone: 011-649-525-7700
Fax: 011-649-525-7710

Philippines

Basic Advertising
Contact: Concepcion Balmaceda
Phone: 011-632-815-0871
Fax: 011-632-815-4332

Quartermaster International, Inc.
Contact: Jose Gerardo Castro
Phone: 011-632-810-3003
Fax: 011-632-815-3970

Russia

Russian State Television and Radio (RTR)
Phone: 011-7-095-213-7090
Fax: 011-7-095-213-7170

Singapore

M.O.G Group
Contact: Anthony Yeo
Phone: 011-65-748-4321
Fax: 011-65-744-9961

Pacific Market Concepts
Phone: 011-65-323-0997
Fax: 011-65-323-0937

TV Media PTE Ltd.
Contact: Bob Robertson
Phone: 011-65-292-3422
Fax: 011-65-295-8355

EUROPE

Finland

MTV 3ÑFinland
Phone: 011-358-0-15-001
Fax: 011-358-0-1500-690

France

Canal
Contact: Paul-Herve Vintrou
Phone: 011-331-4425-1465
Fax: 011-331-4425-1733

Direct TV
Phone: 011-331-4235-8002
Fax: 011-331-4829-2234

Euro-RSCG Infomercials
Contact: Mondher Abdennadher
Phone: 011-331-4134-3255
Fax: 011-331-4134-4104

Matrixx Marketing Europe S.A.
Contact: R. J. Ashcroft
Phone: 011-331-53-606060
Fax: 011-331-53-606064

Mediashop
Contact: Katia Destro
Phone: 011-331-44-29-1305
Fax: 011-331-44-29-1301

Telesys
Contact: Phillippe Fau
Phone: 011-33-1-4246-0810

TV Mission
Contact: Daniel Saada
Phone: 011-331-44-43-7979
Fax: 011-331-44-430-7980

Germany

DomoStar Vertriebsqes, mbH
Contact: Kerstin Wichers
Phone: 011-4989-462-3230
Fax: 011-4989-462-32346

European Institute for the Media
Phone: 011-49-211-901-040
Fax: 011-49-211-901-0456

H.O.T.-Home Order Television
Contact: Dr. Buchelhofer
Phone: 011-49-89-9507-3100
Fax: 011-49-89-9507-3110

Medox Median GMBH
Contact: Horst Putz
Phone: 011-49-211-986-850
Fax: 011-49-211-986-8555

Greece

Telemarketing SA
Contact: Manos Markakis
Phone: 011-301-6125-000
Fax: 011-301-6127-389

Iceland

The Icelandic Homeshopping Market
Contact: Vidar Gardarsson
Phone: 011-354-562-2070
Fax: 011-354-515-8181

Ireland

RMR Ltd.
Phone: 011-35-3-915-6691
Fax: 011-35-3-915-66907

Italy

Costa Crociere SpA
Contact: Lorenzo Pellicioli
Phone: 011-39-10-548-3210
Fax: 011-39-10-548-3314

Daniels SpA
Contact: Alessandro Doria
Phone: 011-39-2-9036-1233
Fax: 011-39-2-9036-1122

Media Partners SRL
Contact: Enrico Barozzi
Phone: 011-392-77-1121
Fax: 011-392

Mercator SpA
Phone: 011-39-2-4836-6727
Fax: 011-39-2-4836-6700

Promotions Italia SpA
Contact: Gianni Riscassi
Phone: 011-39-2-581-851
Fax: 011-2-894-06534

Shopping Club SRL
Phone: 011-39-2-242021
Fax: 011-392-24202

Netherlands

CO-Matics BV
Phone: 011-31-20-607-7152
Fax: 011-31-20-607-7200

European Teleshopping Services
Contact: Robert Monas
Phone: 011-31-20-675-8461
Fax: 011-31-20-675-8676

Hulsink Direct Marketing
Contact: Frits Hulsink
Phone: 011-31-54-904-3434
Fax: 011-31-546-543-466

PTT Post International
Phone: 011-31-23-567-5175
Fax: 011-31-23-562-1267

Squeeper
Contact: Charl Coetzee
Phone: 011-318350-223334
Fax: 011-318350-210135

Tel Sell
Contact: L. A. Mulder
Phone: 011-31-36-5-358-355
Fax: 011-31-36-5-362-122

Norway

TV TORGET AS
Phone: 011-47-2282-8470
Fax: 011-47-2233-9921

Portugal

Forum International
Contact: Steve Swanbeck
Phone: 011-351-1-487-0056
Fax: 011-31-36-5-362-122

Rep. of Croatia

ELDA
Contact: Darlo Marenic
Phone: 011-385-35-361-361
Fax: 011-385-35-362-362

Slovenia

Studio Moderna
Contact: Branimir Brkjac
Phone: 011-386-61-1327-082
Fax: 011-386-61-1327-082

Spain

A3Z Sumum Films S.A.
Contact: Luis Velo Pulg-Duran
Phone: 011-341-663-9000
Fax: 011-341-663-6347

AsociacionEspanola De Marketing Directo
Contact: Elena Gomez
Phone: 011-34-3-414-5272
Fax: 011-34-3-201-2988

European Home Shopping
Contact: Alexander Chacon
Phone: 011-341-420-1853
Fax: 011-341-429-7022

Industex, S.L.
Contact: Philip Bouldstridge
Phone: 011-343-418-8788
Fax: 011-343-212-7111

Movierecord Line
Phone: 011-559-12-28-2805
Fax: 011-559-247-25-61

Venta Catalogo S.A.
Contact: Jacques Knapougel
Phone: 011-343-814-4000
Fax: 011-343-814-2069

Sweden

Film & TV Media
Contact: Magnus Hansson
Phone: 011-46-40-490-610
Fax: 011-46-40-28-6959

TV-Shop Group
Contact: Jorgen Hansen
Phone: 011-46-40-601-6000
Fax: 011-46-40-28-6959

Turkey

Evpa Pazarlama A.S.
Phone: 011-901-544-5511
Fax: 011-901-544-5510

United Kingdom

Best Direct (International) Ltd.
Contact: Simon Woodcock
Phone: 011-441-81-868-4355
Fax: 011-441-81-429-3668

Channel Four Television
Phone: 011-44-71-396-4444

Enterprise
Contact: Ingrid Pires
Phone: 011-44-181-941-7968
Fax: 011-44-181-941-8190

Hammond Companies
Contact: Peter Hammon
Phone: 011-44-171-235-2432
Fax: 011-44-171-235-6140

International Marketing Campaign
Phone: 011-447-182-31714
Fax: 011-447-182-31001

MIT
Contact: Budd Margolis
Phone: 011-44-181-876-0359
Fax: 011-44-181-878-2993

New Media Sales
Phone: 011-071-418-9400
Fax: 011-071-418-9401

NIMA International (London)
Phone: 011-071-630-9977
Fax: 011-630-9806

Olwen
Phone: 011-440-181-688-7999
Fax: 011-440-181-688-1211

Quantum International Limited
Contact: David Carmen
Phone: 011-44-171465-1234
Fax: 011-44-171-465-8084

Regal Shop International
Contact: Hayley Benson
Phone: 011-44-171-434-0567
Fax: 011-44-171-434-0796

Time Warner Enterprises Ltd.
Contact: Chris Kirby
Phone: 011-44-171-487-2500
Fax: 011-44-171-487-2517

TV Shop (Distribution) Ltd.
Contact: Simon Willis
Phone: 011-441-273-728222
Fax: 011-441-273-776277

Worldwide Licensing Ltd.
Contact: Rupert P.J. Scott
Phone: 011-44-1295-810094
Fax: 011-44-1295-811284

MIDDLE EAST

Israel

'OExporto' Investment Co.
Phone: 011-03-517-3310
Fax: 011-03-510-2780

Prodtec International Ltd.
Contact: Uri Pardo
Phone: 011-972-3-922-0472
Fax: 011-972-3-922-3750

Vi Ar Home Shopping Ltd.
Contact: Ruth Benozaiq
Phone: 011-9723-546-9340
Fax: 011-9723-546-9077

Saudi Arabia

Tihama Group
Contact: Sharaf Aldabbagh
Phone: 011-966-2-653-4321
Fax: 011-966-2-651-1089

United Arab Emirates

Broadman Trading Est.
Contact: Arshad Waheed
Phone: 011-9716-539195
Fax: 011-9716-539196

NORTH AMERICA

Canada

Apple Box Productions
Contact: Hans J. Dys
Phone: 403-944-0011
Fax: 403-438-5800

Atlantel Inc.
Contact: France Veilet
Phone: 514-871-1095
Fax: 514-651-2344

Channel 500
Contact: Rod Bell
Phone: 416-588-3677
Fax: 416-532-7736

City Entertainment
Contact: Richard Hazell
Phone: 604-251-4655
Fax: 604-251-5940

Fantom Technologies
Contact: Allan Millman
Phone: 416-622-9740
Fax: 416-626-0674

Integrated Messaging Inc.
Contact: Sheldon Stoller
Phone: 800-561-3734
Fax: 204-788-7718

Interwood Marketing Group
Contact: Robert Woodrooffe
Phone: 905-669-5151
Fax: 905-669-5511

Jaylar Productions Ltd.
Contact: Michael Spivak
Phone: 416-360-4321
Fax: 416-362-7642

Link to Life Seminars, Inc.
Contact: Brian Brass
Phone: 416-398-5033
Fax: 416-398-5034

Northern Response (Canada) Ltd.
Contact: Richard Stacey
Phone: 416-261-6699
Fax: 416-281-4159

Obus Forme
Contact: Brian Roberts
Phone: 416-785-1388
Fax: 416-785-5862

Opportunity TV
Contact: Grant Buchanan
Phone: 403-430-2800
Fax: 403-437-7969

Quality Special Products
Contact: Ed LaBuick
Phone: 416-291-5590
Fax: 416-291-7537

Siftex
Contact: Peter Gumpesberger
Phone: 905-472-0959

Tasha International Inc.
Contact: Amin Jivraj
Phone: 403-430-9098
Fax: 403-430-9644

Television Bureau of Canada
Contact: Wendy Miles
Phone: 416-923-8813
Fax: 416-923-8739

The Production Partners
Contact: Ed Crain
Phone: 416-363-0874
Fax: 416-504-7390

Touch TV
Contact: Agnes Jamuszidewicz
Phone: 514-285-1424
Fax: 514-285-2400

Videoway Communications
Contact: Pierre Dion
Phone: 514-985-8458
Fax: 514-985-8452

UNITED STATES

Arizona

Apex Media Sales, Inc.
Contact: Dennis Hart
Phone: 602-596-6320
Fax: 602-596-6322

Landin Media
Contact: Bob Dickenson
Phone: 602-553-4080
Fax: 602-553-4090

Nancy Langston & Associates
Contact: Nancy Langston
Phone: 602-953-8558
Fax: 602-953-8559

Professional Marketing Associates
Contact: Lou Hagen
Phone: 602-829-0131
Fax: 602-829-9202

Universal Teleservices Corporation
Contact: Randy Warren
Phone: 800-387-2850
Fax: 602-948-8829

California

3-G Video Cassette Corp.
Contact: Eyal Erster
Phone: 818-888-6583
Fax: 818-888-6573

Abflex U.S.A., Inc.
Contact: Jaeson Cayne
Phone: 619-438-5800
Fax: 619-438-5802

Access TV
Contact: Bill Bernard
Phone: 714-442-6170
Fax: 714-757-1528

American Video Group
Contact: John Berzner
Phone: 800-571-8433
Fax: 310-473-5299

ASI Market Research Inc.
Contact: Shelly Zalls
Phone: 818-982-6800
Fax: 818-962-0440

Audio Video Color Corp.
Contact: Moshe Begim
Phone: 818-982-6800
Fax: 818-982-0440

Bieler Marketing Associates
Contact: Peter Bieler
Phone: 213-550-4646
Fax: 213-962-1811

Body By Jake Enterprises
Contact: Phil Scotti
Phone: 619-464-7100
Fax: 619-464-7181

BodyLines Inc.
Contact: William T. Sautter
Phone: 415-508-0920
Fax: 415-508-1910

Brentwood Marketing
Contact: Gerald Bagg
Phone: 310-447-9676
Fax: 310-447-9680

Brian Bennett Music
Contact: Brian Bennett
Phone: 310-859-8100
Fax: 310-859-2991

Browning, Jacobson & Klein
Contact: Kenneth Browning
Phone: 310-247-8777
Fax: 310-247-1827

Catalyst Computer Services
Contact: Richard Shaw
Phone: 310-836-5755
Fax: 310-838-3684

Comar Acquisitions, Inc.
Contact: Bruce Gersh
Phone: 805-294-2700
Fax: 805-294-2717

Convention Cassettes Unlimited
Contact: Rex Slezak
Phone: 619-773-4498
Fax: 619-773-9671

Creative Age Publications, Inc.
Contact: Deborah Carver
Phone: 818-782-7328
Fax: 818-782-7450

Minnesota

K-Tel International
Phone: 612-559-6800
Fax: 612-559-6815

New York

Welcome USA/Arich Inc.
Phone: 212-249-1800
Fax: 212-247-2231

SOUTH AMERICA

Argentina

Imagem Satelital S.A.
Phone: 011-541-495-500
Fax: 011-541-495-101

Sprayette S.A.
Phone: 011-541-585-8500
Fax: 011-541-585-8599

VIGRA s.r.l.
Phone: 011-54-1-325-3000
Fax: 011-54-1-394-7000

The Sales Channel S.A.
Phone: 011-541-326-5523
Fax: 011-541-326-5523

Showtime S.A.
Phone: 011-541-546-8000
Fax: 011-541-548-8001

Sprayette
Phone: 011-541-584-0306
Fax: 011-541-582-0976

Brazil

B.L.I. International de Comercio Ltda.
Phone: 011-5511-821-9776
Fax: 011-5511-829-4559

Fulfillment Servicos Ltda.
Phone: 011-5511-421-2460
Fax: 011-5511-870-1649

Grupo Imagem
Phone: 011-5511-813-7055
Fax: 011-5511-814-8507

Chile

Arcadia Chile S.A.
Phone: 011-50-2-737-6912
Fax: 011-562-334-1713

The Open Market S.A.
Phone: 011-50-2-737-6912
Fax: 011-56-2-737-6912

Colombia

Global Marketing
Phone: 011-571-629-0066
Fax: 011-571-629-0892

Interproject
Phone: 011-571-619-7585
Fax: 011-571-215-1871

Ecuador

TVentas
Phone: 011-5932-448-50
Fax: 011-5932-448-57

El Salvador

T.V. Offer
Phone: 011-503-298-6088
Fax: 011-503-223-1515

Peru

Teleshop S.A.
Phone: 011-511-472-8744
Fax: 011-511-472-8744

Venezuela

Jeica
Phone: 011-582-561-3293
Fax: 011-582-563-8119

APPENDIX E

Sample Storyboard

"The Art of Buying a Car" (Nissan Altima)

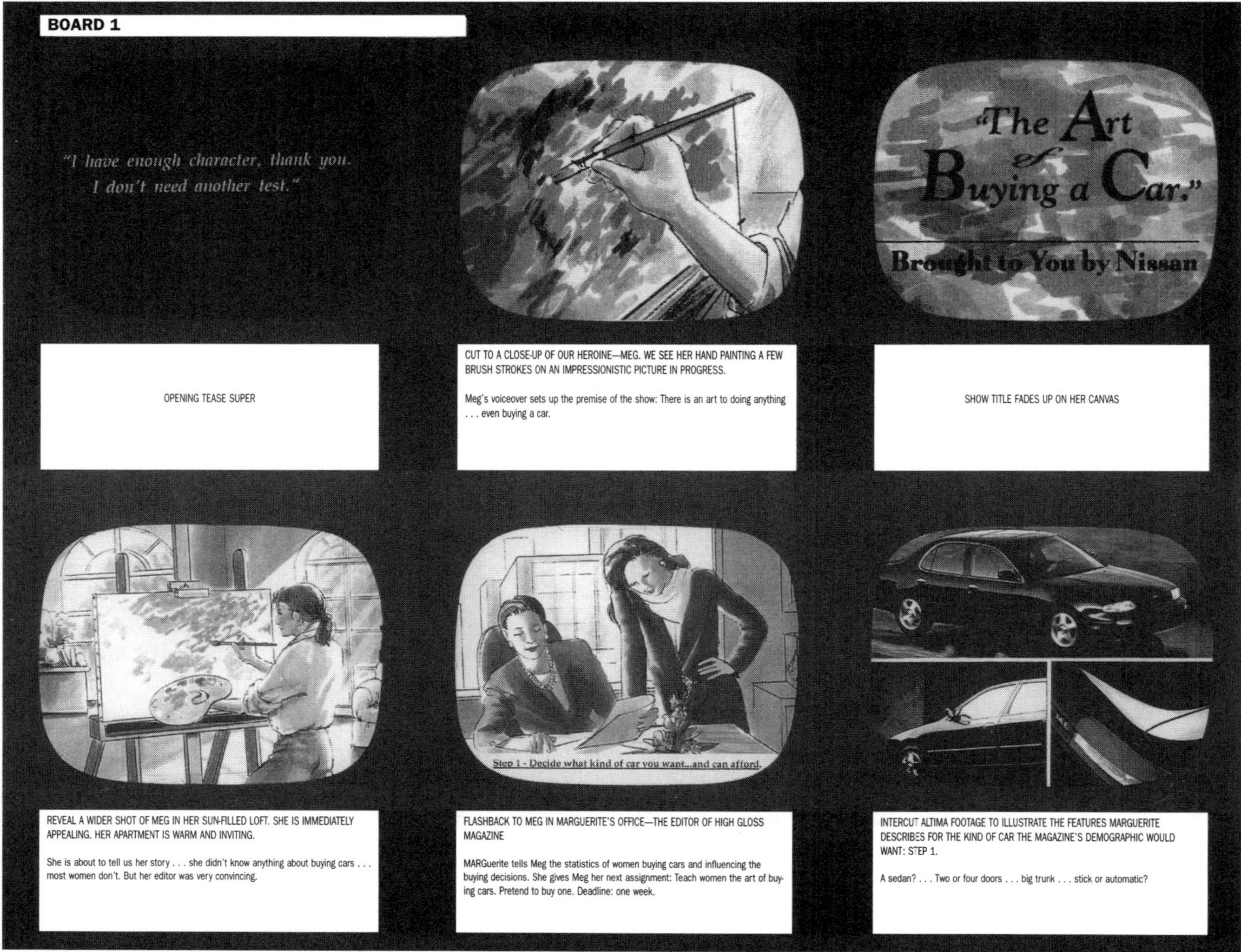
BOARD 1
"I have enough character, thank you. I don't need another test."
OPENING TEASE SUPER
CUT TO A CLOSE-UP OF OUR HEROINE—MEG. WE SEE HER HAND PAINTING A FEW BRUSH STROKES ON AN IMPRESSIONISTIC PICTURE IN PROGRESS.
Meg's voiceover sets up the premise of the show: There is an art to doing anything . . . even buying a car.
"The Art of Buying a Car."
Brought to You by Nissan
SHOW TITLE FADES UP ON HER CANVAS
REVEAL A WIDER SHOT OF MEG IN HER SUN-FILLED LOFT. SHE IS IMMEDIATELY APPEALING. HER APARTMENT IS WARM AND INVITING.
She is about to tell us her story . . . she didn't know anything about buying cars . . . most women don't. But her editor was very convincing.
Step 1 - Decide what kind of car you want...and can afford.
FLASHBACK TO MEG IN MARGUERITE'S OFFICE—THE EDITOR OF HIGH GLOSS MAGAZINE
MARGuerite tells Meg the statistics of women buying cars and influencing the buying decisions. She gives Meg her next assignment: Teach women the art of buying cars. Pretend to buy one. Deadline: one week.
INTERCUT ALTIMA FOOTAGE TO ILLUSTRATE THE FEATURES MARGUERITE DESCRIBES FOR THE KIND OF CAR THE MAGAZINE'S DEMOGRAPHIC WOULD WANT: STEP 1.
A sedan? . . . Two or four doors . . . big trunk . . . stick or automatic?

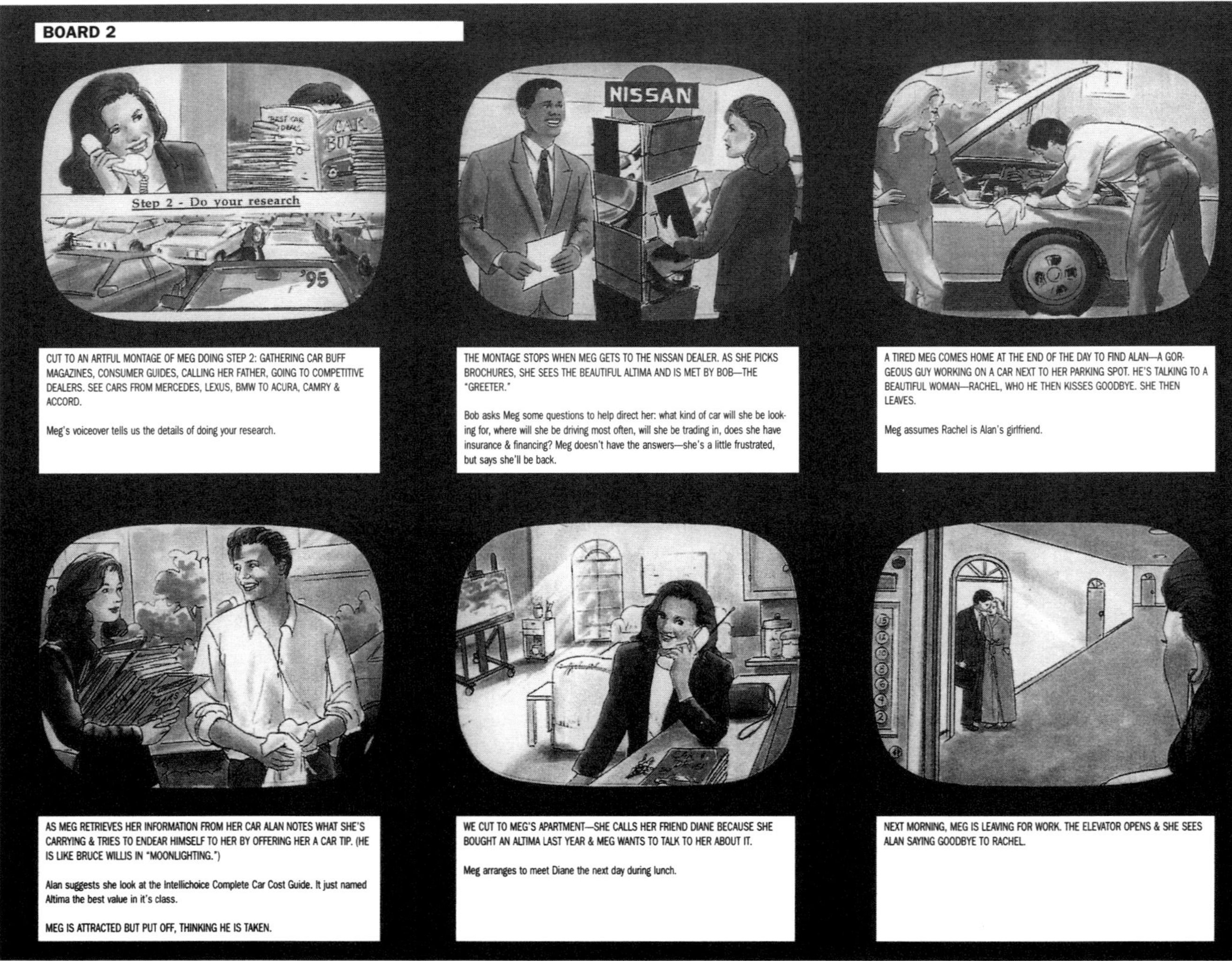
BOARD 2
Step 2 - Do your research
'95
CUT TO AN ARTFUL MONTAGE OF MEG DOING STEP 2: GATHERING CAR BUFF MAGAZINES, CONSUMER GUIDES, CALLING HER FATHER, GOING TO COMPETITIVE DEALERS. SEE CARS FROM MERCEDES, LEXUS, BMW TO ACURA, CAMRY & ACCORD.
Meg's voiceover tells us the details of doing your research.
NISSAN
THE MONTAGE STOPS WHEN MEG GETS TO THE NISSAN DEALER. AS SHE PICKS BROCHURES, SHE SEES THE BEAUTIFUL ALTIMA AND IS MET BY BOB—THE "GREETER."
Bob asks Meg some questions to help direct her: what kind of car will she be looking for, where will she be driving most often, will she be trading in, does she have insurance & financing? Meg doesn't have the answers—she's a little frustrated, but says she'll be back.
A TIRED MEG COMES HOME AT THE END OF THE DAY TO FIND ALAN—A GORGEOUS GUY WORKING ON A CAR NEXT TO HER PARKING SPOT. HE'S TALKING TO A BEAUTIFUL WOMAN—RACHEL, WHO HE THEN KISSES GOODBYE. SHE THEN LEAVES.
Meg assumes Rachel is Alan's girlfriend.
AS MEG RETRIEVES HER INFORMATION FROM HER CAR ALAN NOTES WHAT SHE'S CARRYING & TRIES TO ENDEAR HIMSELF TO HER BY OFFERING HER A CAR TIP. (HE IS LIKE BRUCE WILLIS IN "MOONLIGHTING.")
Alan suggests she look at the Intellichoice Complete Car Cost Guide. It just named Altima the best value in it's class.
MEG IS ATTRACTED BUT PUT OFF, THINKING HE IS TAKEN.
WE CUT TO MEG'S APARTMENT—SHE CALLS HER FRIEND DIANE BECAUSE SHE BOUGHT AN ALTIMA LAST YEAR & MEG WANTS TO TALK TO HER ABOUT IT.
Meg arranges to meet Diane the next day during lunch.
NEXT MORNING, MEG IS LEAVING FOR WORK. THE ELEVATOR OPENS & SHE SEES ALAN SAYING GOODBYE TO RACHEL.

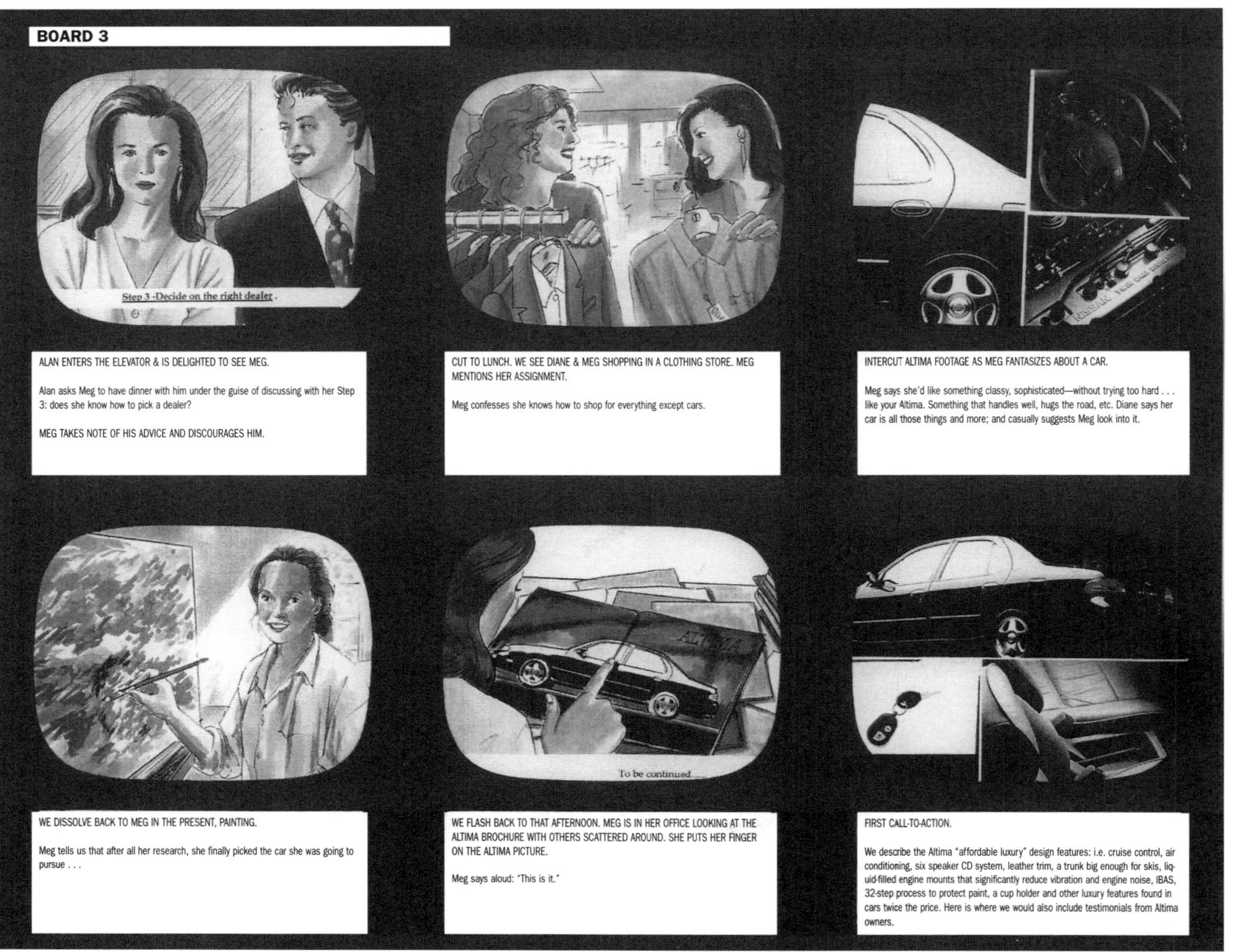
BOARD 3
Step 3 -Decide on the right dealer.
ALAN ENTERS THE ELEVATOR & IS DELIGHTED TO SEE MEG.
Alan asks Meg to have dinner with him under the guise of discussing with her Step 3: does she know how to pick a dealer?
MEG TAKES NOTE OF HIS ADVICE AND DISCOURAGES HIM.
CUT TO LUNCH. WE SEE DIANE & MEG SHOPPING IN A CLOTHING STORE. MEG MENTIONS HER ASSIGNMENT.
Meg confesses she knows how to shop for everything except cars.
INTERCUT ALTIMA FOOTAGE AS MEG FANTASIZES ABOUT A CAR.
Meg says she'd like something classy, sophisticated—without trying too hard . . . like your Altima. Something that handles well, hugs the road, etc. Diane says her car is all those things and more; and casually suggests Meg look into it.
WE DISSOLVE BACK TO MEG IN THE PRESENT, PAINTING.
Meg tells us that after all her research, she finally picked the car she was going to pursue . . .
To be continued.....
WE FLASH BACK TO THAT AFTERNOON. MEG IS IN HER OFFICE LOOKING AT THE ALTIMA BROCHURE WITH OTHERS SCATTERED AROUND. SHE PUTS HER FINGER ON THE ALTIMA PICTURE.
Meg says aloud: "This is it."
FIRST CALL-TO-ACTION.
We describe the Altima "affordable luxury" design features: i.e. cruise control, air conditioning, six speaker CD system, leather trim, a trunk big enough for skis, liquid-filled engine mounts that significantly reduce vibration and engine noise, IBAS, 32-step process to protect paint, a cup holder and other luxury features found in cars twice the price. Here is where we would also include testimonials from Altima owners.

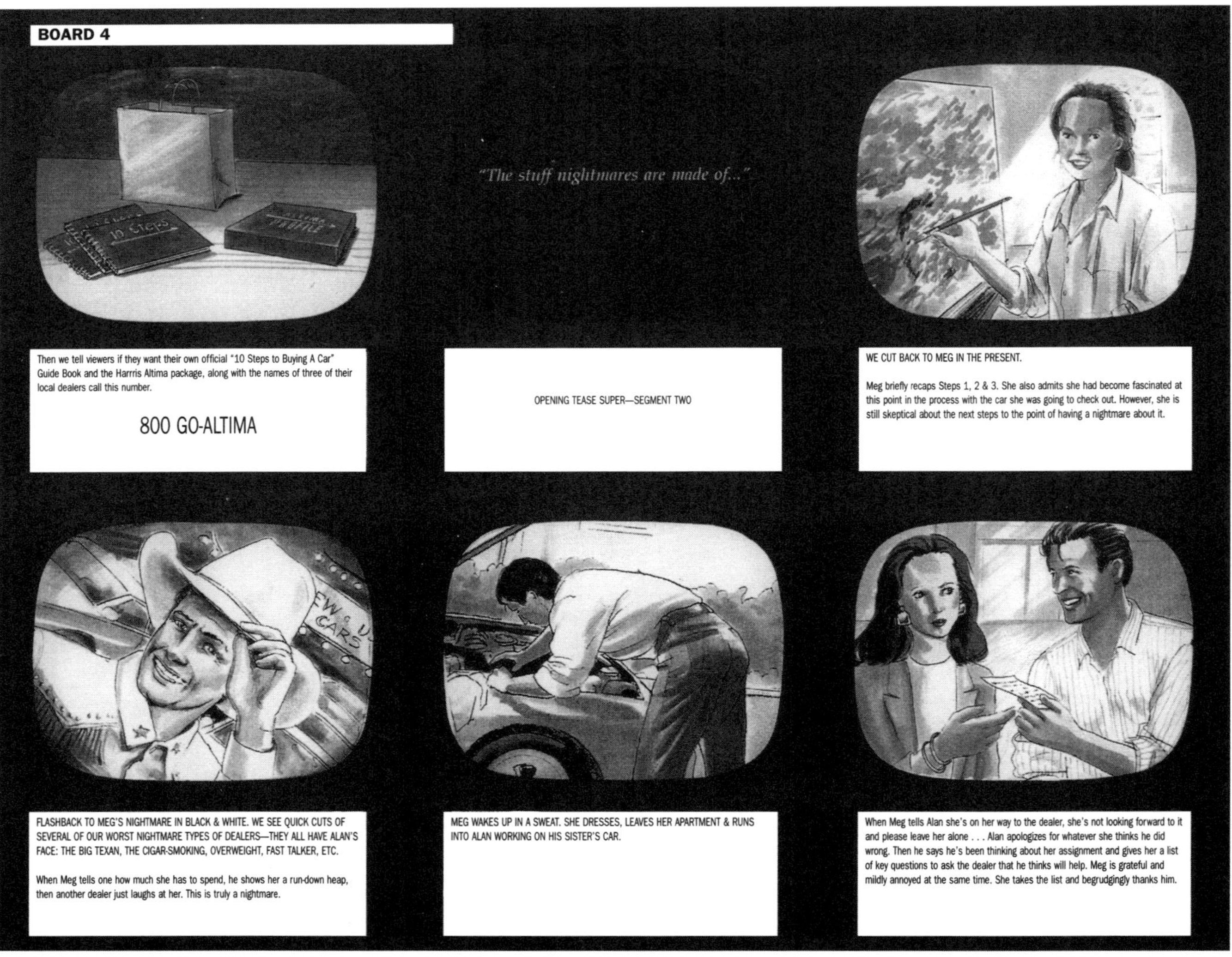
BOARD 4
"The stuff nightmares are made of..."
Then we tell viewers if they want their own official "10 Steps to Buying A Car" Guide Book and the Harrris Altima package, along with the names of three of their local dealers call this number.
800 GO-ALTIMA
OPENING TEASE SUPER—SEGMENT TWO
WE CUT BACK TO MEG IN THE PRESENT.
Meg briefly recaps Steps 1, 2 & 3. She also admits she had become fascinated at this point in the process with the car she was going to check out. However, she is still skeptical about the next steps to the point of having a nightmare about it.
FLASHBACK TO MEG'S NIGHTMARE IN BLACK & WHITE. WE SEE QUICK CUTS OF SEVERAL OF OUR WORST NIGHTMARE TYPES OF DEALERS—THEY ALL HAVE ALAN'S FACE: THE BIG TEXAN, THE CIGAR-SMOKING, OVERWEIGHT, FAST TALKER, ETC.
When Meg tells one how much she has to spend, he shows her a run-down heap, then another dealer just laughs at her. This is truly a nightmare.
MEG WAKES UP IN A SWEAT. SHE DRESSES, LEAVES HER APARTMENT & RUNS INTO ALAN WORKING ON HIS SISTER'S CAR.
When Meg tells Alan she's on her way to the dealer, she's not looking forward to it and please leave her alone . . . Alan apologizes for whatever she thinks he did wrong. Then he says he's been thinking about her assignment and gives her a list of key questions to ask the dealer that he thinks will help. Meg is grateful and mildly annoyed at the same time. She takes the list and begrudgingly thanks him.

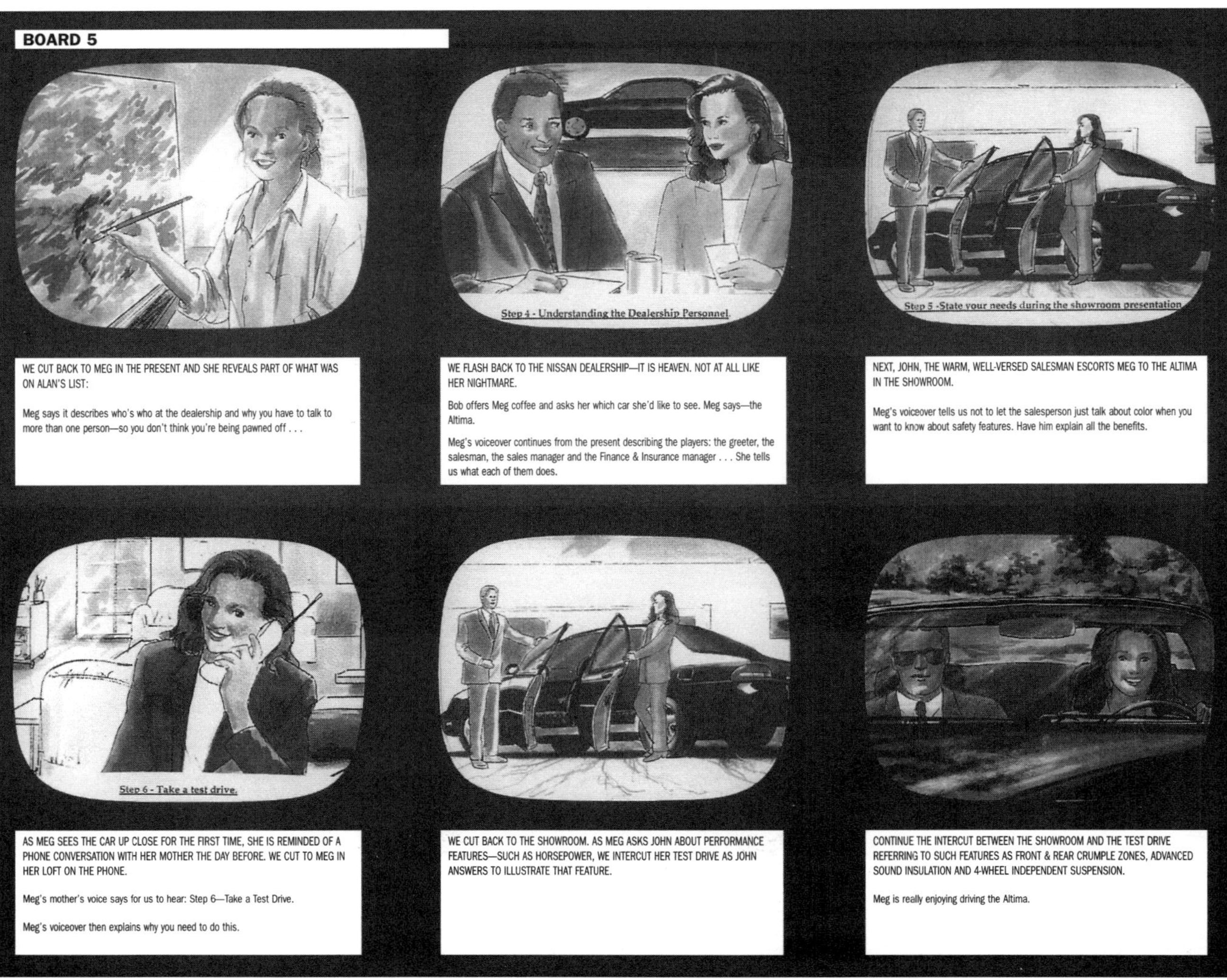
BOARD 5
WE CUT BACK TO MEG IN THE PRESENT AND SHE REVEALS PART OF WHAT WAS ON ALAN'S LIST:
Meg says it describes who's who at the dealership and why you have to talk to more than one person—so you don't think you're being pawned off . . .
Step 4 - Understanding the Dealership Personnel.
WE FLASH BACK TO THE NISSAN DEALERSHIP—IT IS HEAVEN. NOT AT ALL LIKE HER NIGHTMARE.
Bob offers Meg coffee and asks her which car she'd like to see. Meg says—the Altima.
Meg's voiceover continues from the present describing the players: the greeter, the salesman, the sales manager and the Finance & Insurance manager . . . She tells us what each of them does.
Step 5 -State your needs during the showroom presentation
NEXT, JOHN, THE WARM, WELL-VERSED SALESMAN ESCORTS MEG TO THE ALTIMA IN THE SHOWROOM.
Meg's voiceover tells us not to let the salesperson just talk about color when you want to know about safety features. Have him explain all the benefits.
Step 6 - Take a test drive.
AS MEG SEES THE CAR UP CLOSE FOR THE FIRST TIME, SHE IS REMINDED OF A PHONE CONVERSATION WITH HER MOTHER THE DAY BEFORE. WE CUT TO MEG IN HER LOFT ON THE PHONE.
Meg's mother's voice says for us to hear: Step 6—Take a Test Drive.
Meg's voiceover then explains why you need to do this.
WE CUT BACK TO THE SHOWROOM. AS MEG ASKS JOHN ABOUT PERFORMANCE FEATURES—SUCH AS HORSEPOWER, WE INTERCUT HER TEST DRIVE AS JOHN ANSWERS TO ILLUSTRATE THAT FEATURE.
CONTINUE THE INTERCUT BETWEEN THE SHOWROOM AND THE TEST DRIVE REFERRING TO SUCH FEATURES AS FRONT & REAR CRUMPLE ZONES, ADVANCED SOUND INSULATION AND 4-WHEEL INDEPENDENT SUSPENSION.
Meg is really enjoying driving the Altima.

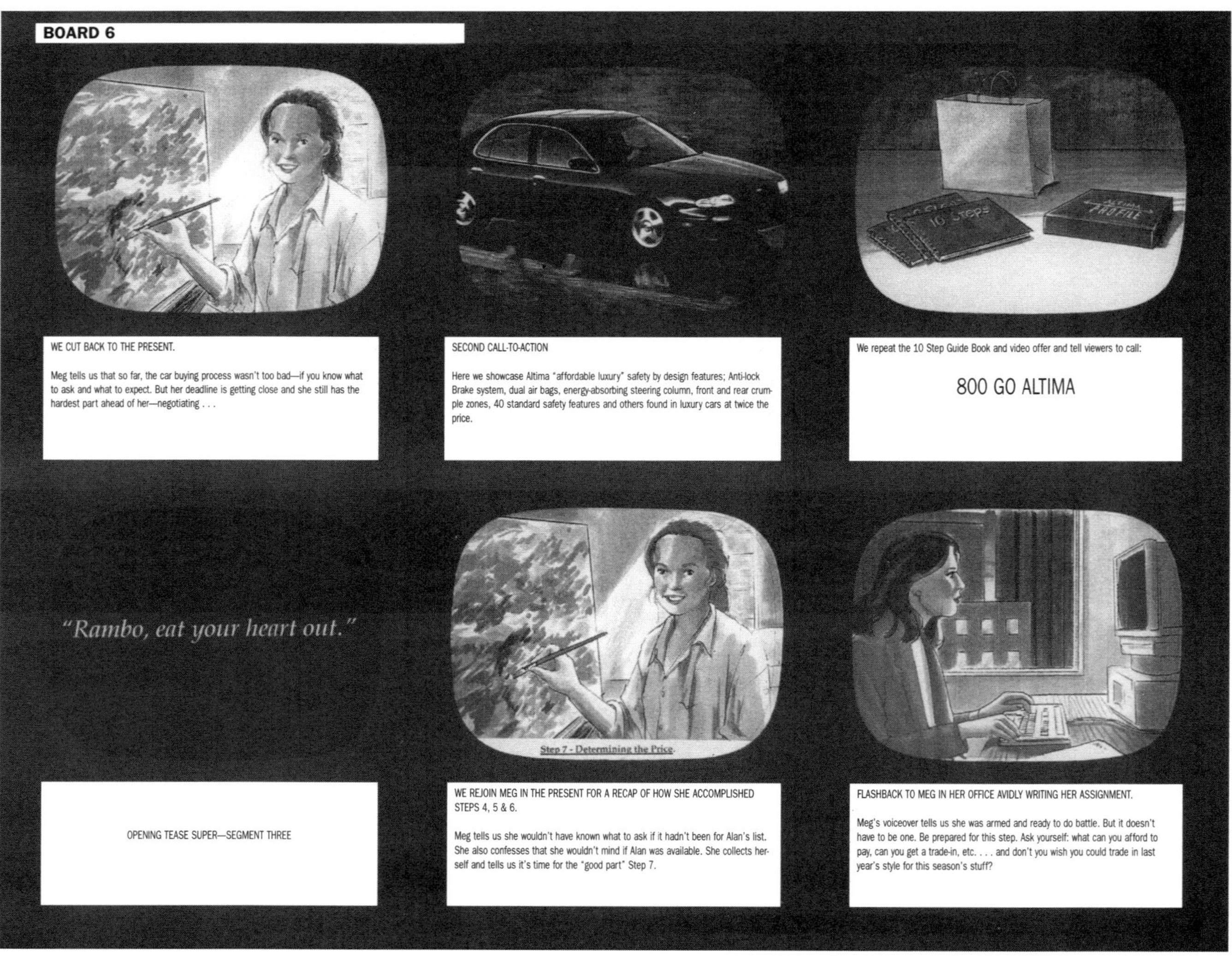
BOARD 6
WE CUT BACK TO THE PRESENT.
Meg tells us that so far, the car buying process wasn't too bad—if you know what to ask and what to expect. But her deadline is getting close and she still has the hardest part ahead of her—negotiating . . .
SECOND CALL-TO-ACTION
Here we showcase Altima "affordable luxury" safety by design features; Anti-lock Brake system, dual air bags, energy-absorbing steering column, front and rear crumple zones, 40 standard safety features and others found in luxury cars at twice the price.
We repeat the 10 Step Guide Book and video offer and tell viewers to call:
800 GO ALTIMA
"Rambo, eat your heart out."
OPENING TEASE SUPER—SEGMENT THREE
Step 7 - Determining the Price.
WE REJOIN MEG IN THE PRESENT FOR A RECAP OF HOW SHE ACCOMPLISHED STEPS 4, 5 & 6.
Meg tells us she wouldn't have known what to ask if it hadn't been for Alan's list. She also confesses that she wouldn't mind if Alan was available. She collects herself and tells us it's time for the "good part" Step 7.
FLASHBACK TO MEG IN HER OFFICE AVIDLY WRITING HER ASSIGNMENT.
Meg's voiceover tells us she was armed and ready to do battle. But it doesn't have to be one. Be prepared for this step. Ask yourself: what can you afford to pay, can you get a trade-in, etc. . . . and don't you wish you could trade in last year's style for this season's stuff?

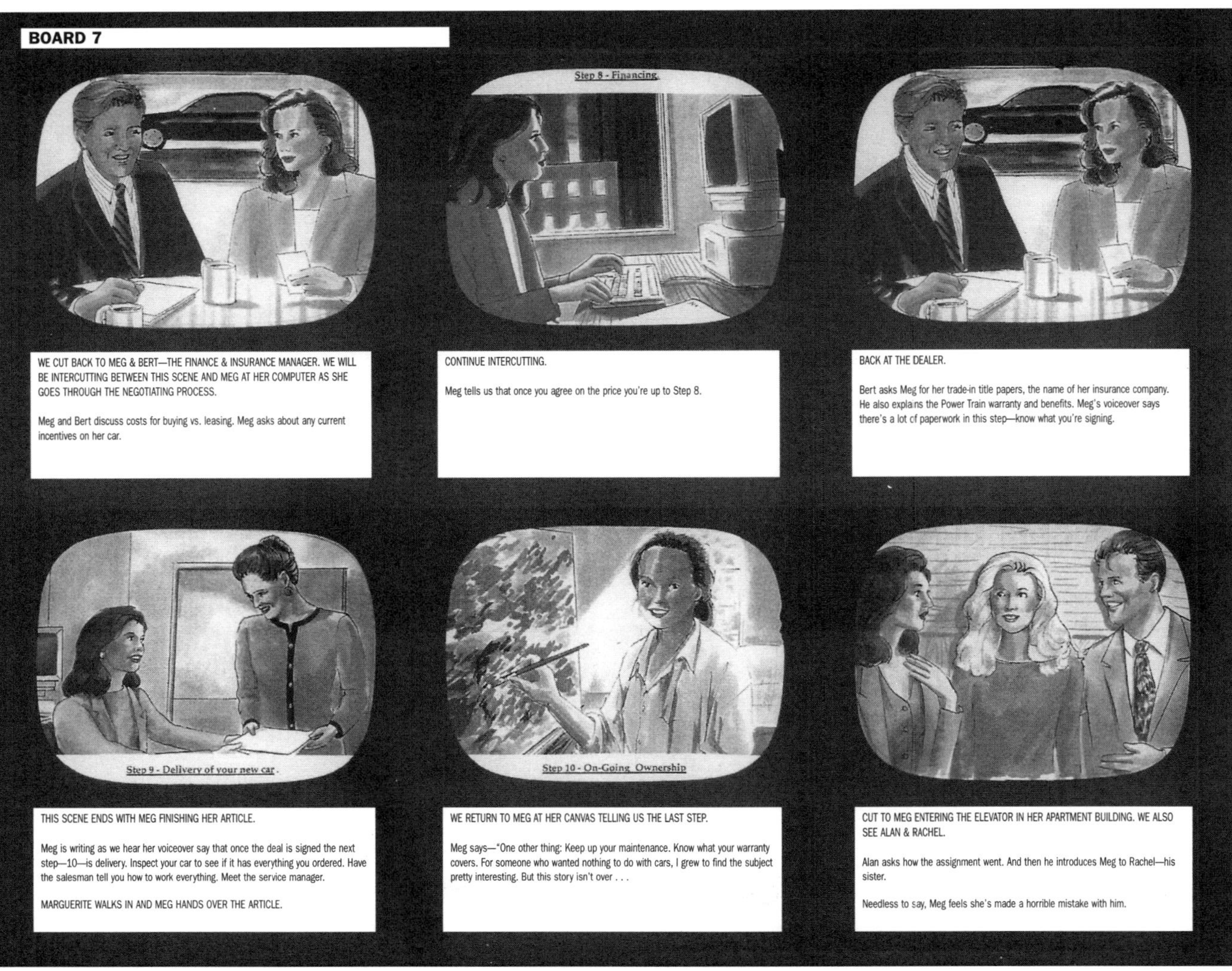
BOARD 7
WE CUT BACK TO MEG & BERT—THE FINANCE & INSURANCE MANAGER. WE WILL BE INTERCUTTING BETWEEN THIS SCENE AND MEG AT HER COMPUTER AS SHE GOES THROUGH THE NEGOTIATING PROCESS.
Meg and Bert discuss costs for buying vs. leasing. Meg asks about any current incentives on her car.
Step 8 - Financing
CONTINUE INTERCUTTING.
Meg tells us that once you agree on the price you're up to Step 8.
BACK AT THE DEALER.
Bert asks Meg for her trade-in title papers, the name of her insurance company. He also explains the Power Train warranty and benefits. Meg's voiceover says there's a lot of paperwork in this step—know what you're signing.
Step 9 - Delivery of your new car.
THIS SCENE ENDS WITH MEG FINISHING HER ARTICLE.
Meg is writing as we hear her voiceover say that once the deal is signed the next step—10—is delivery. Inspect your car to see if it has everything you ordered. Have the salesman tell you how to work everything. Meet the service manager.
MARGUERITE WALKS IN AND MEG HANDS OVER THE ARTICLE.
Step 10 - On-Going Ownership
WE RETURN TO MEG AT HER CANVAS TELLING US THE LAST STEP.
Meg says—"One other thing: Keep up your maintenance. Know what your warranty covers. For someone who wanted nothing to do with cars, I grew to find the subject pretty interesting. But this story isn't over . . .
CUT TO MEG ENTERING THE ELEVATOR IN HER APARTMENT BUILDING. WE ALSO SEE ALAN & RACHEL.
Alan asks how the assignment went. And then he introduces Meg to Rachel—his sister.
Needless to say, Meg feels she's made a horrible mistake with him.

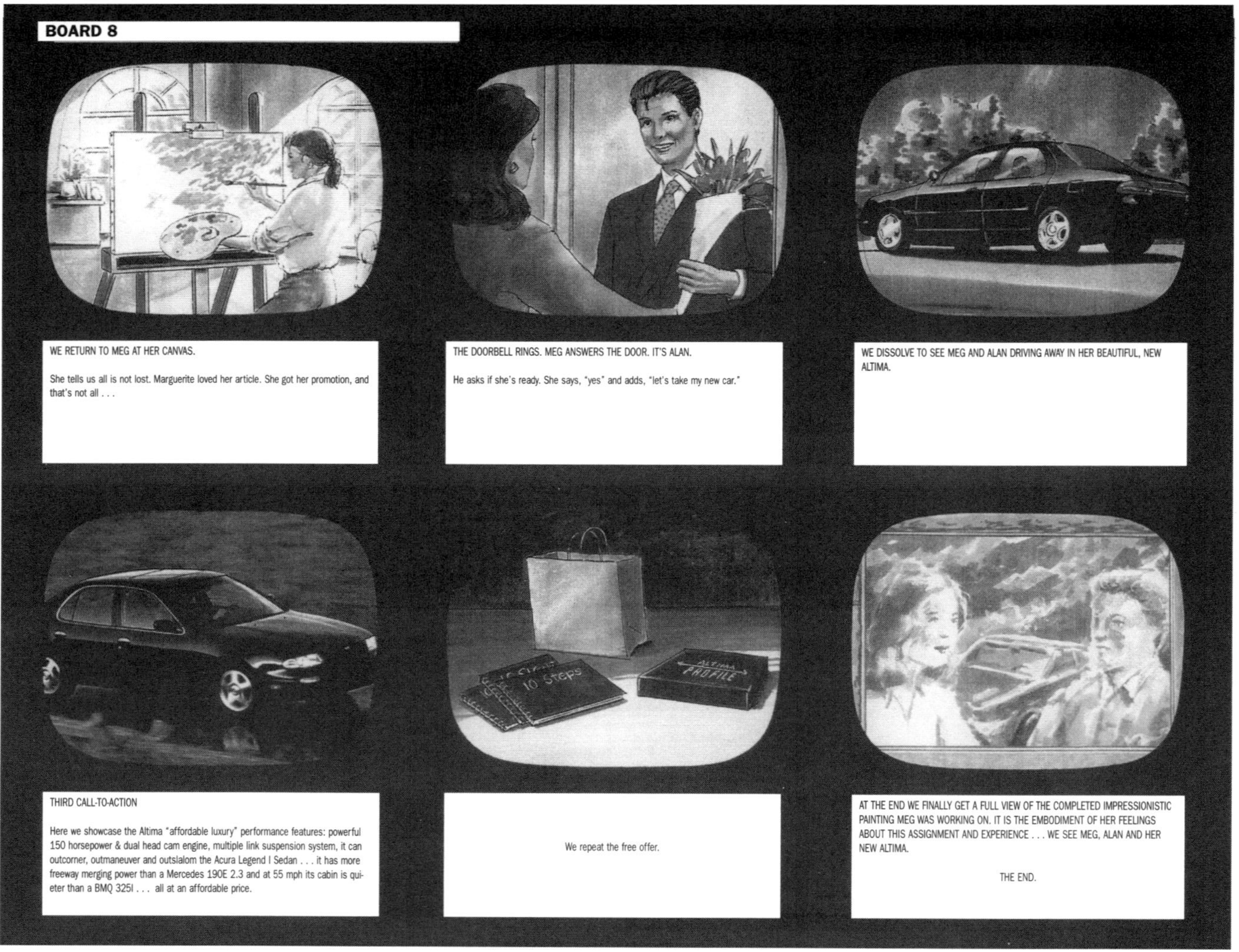
BOARD 8
WE RETURN TO MEG AT HER CANVAS.
She tells us all is not lost. Marguerite loved her article. She got her promotion, and that's not all . . .
THE DOORBELL RINGS. MEG ANSWERS THE DOOR. IT'S ALAN.
He asks if she's ready. She says, "yes" and adds, "let's take my new car."
WE DISSOLVE TO SEE MEG AND ALAN DRIVING AWAY IN HER BEAUTIFUL, NEW ALTIMA.
THIRD CALL-TO-ACTION
Here we showcase the Altima "affordable luxury" performance features: powerful 150 horsepower & dual head cam engine, multiple link suspension system, it can outcorner, outmaneuver and outslalom the Acura Legend I Sedan . . . it has more freeway merging power than a Mercedes 190E 2.3 and at 55 mph its cabin is quieter than a BMQ 325I . . . all at an affordable price.
10 Steps
ALTIMA PROFILE
We repeat the free offer.
AT THE END WE FINALLY GET A FULL VIEW OF THE COMPLETED IMPRESSIONISTIC PAINTING MEG WAS WORKING ON. IT IS THE EMBODIMENT OF HER FEELINGS ABOUT THIS ASSIGNMENT AND EXPERIENCE . . . WE SEE MEG, ALAN AND HER NEW ALTIMA.
THE END.

APPENDIX F

Sample Script: "The Art of Buying a Car" (Nissan Altima)

Segment One

FADE IN:
INT. REGISTER NEWSPAPER OFFICE—MEG'S WORK AREA—DAY

MEG

Leslie, I need that photo of the Mayor by 3:00 this afternoon. Thanks.

Hey, there's our new Dad.

EXT. MEG'S APARTMENT BUILDING—DAY

A Spanish duplex on a tree-lined L.A. street. A shiny new Nissan Altima is parked in the driveway. MEG MOORE, an attractive woman in her thirties, comes out of the font door of the building carrying a suitcase. She brings it over to the Altima.

Source: Nissan Motor Corporation U.S.A.

During the following MEG crosses to the trunk, opens it and puts in the suitcase.

MEG
(to camera)

If you had told me a month ago that I would take a whole week off work to go on a road trip, I would've said, "MEG Moore—relax? No chance!" But that was before the biggest challenge of my career, one that changed my life. An assignment on how to buy a car at the newspaper where I work. Having never bought a new car before, it wasn't exactly what I was looking forward to. But somehow I learned that buying a car can be a great experience. If you know what you're doing. It all started on a typical morning at the Register . . .

* * *

SC. 3 INT. MARGUERITE'S OFFICE

The office is spacious and well appointed. MARGUERITE, a tailored woman in her late forties, is the Managing Editor of the Sunday magazine section. She comes out from behind her desk as MEG enters.

MEG

Yes?

MARGUERITE

Hey Meg. I know how you hate it when I beckon you to my office, but I really need to talk to you about the feature editor job.

MEG

We've been waiting a long time for this.

MARGUERITE

It doesn't look like it's going to be that easy.

MEG

What?

MARGUERITE

Well, you know I'd really like for you to get the job . . . but

MEG

That makes three of us. You, me and my credit cards.

MARGUERITE

There's some reporter in the Chicago office that the paper's been trying to bring in here for months. And the guy's starting here today . . . looks like the boss really wants to hire him for the feature editor job.

MEG

So he just walks in here and takes it?

MARGUERITE

No, not necessarily. I've talked Pendleton into letting you both get a shot at it.

The intercom buzzes.

SECRETARY (o.s.)

MARGUERITE, Mr. Clark is here to see you.

MEG responds with suspicion to the name.

MARGUERITE
(to MEG)

Your competition's here. You want to meet him?

MEG

Why not?

MARGUERITE
(into intercom)

Send him in.

ALAN CLARK enters. He's a handsome, energetic guy with a little too much confidence. He and Meg react on seeing each other.

MEG

Oh great.

ALAN

Oh and a big hello to you too, Meg.

MARGUERITE

You two know each other?

MEG

We've met.

MARGUERITE

Well I, I guess . . . that's a, that's good, Okay, here's the situation. You'll both be writing a story for the Sunday magazine section. The best one gets the feature editor job. It's as simple as that. And the story will be on buying a car.

MEG

Well, that's a good one for him. What's mine?

MARGUERITE

Buying a car. Next week is the yearly auto buyer's issue.

ALAN

Ahh, I know it well.

MEG

I can write about cars.

MARGUERITE

Well, this article should be helpful to anyone even thinking about buying a car. So, please try to find an interesting angle.

* * *

CUT TO:

SC.4 INT. MEG'S WORK AREA

MEG is typing a little too intensely into her computer.

* * *

SC. 4

EVELYN

Just think about what you'd want in a car if you were going to get one for yourself.

MEG

Let me see, what would I want? A sportscar . . .

no . . . maybe something with four doors . . . definitely air conditioning . . . and price would be a factor. But, you know, you're right, I need to narrow my choices down—that's my first step . . .

Meg starts typing into her computer.

CLOSE ON COMPUTER SCREEN.

MEG has typed:
"HOW TO BUY A CAR" BY MEG MOORE
STEP #1. DECIDE ON THE TYPE OF CAR
*STYLE & DESIGN
*FEATURES & OPTIONS
*YOUR BUDGET

CUT TO:

SC. 5 INT. PARKING GARAGE

MEG enters and heads for her car.

MEG (v.o.)
The last time I went to a car dealership was . . . never. I bought my old car from my mechanic . . .

MEG reaches her car. It's an old Honda Accord (WITHOUT ITS LOGO).

SC. 6 INT. MEG'S CAR

She tries to start the car but it won't turn over. She tries again, to no avail.

MEG (v.o.)

So, I called my girlfriend Diane to come get me, or should I say my best friend. It was the third time she had to pick me up this month.

CUT TO:

SC. 7 EXT. OFFICE BUILDING—DAY

MEG is waiting with a styrofoam cup of coffee, checking her watch. Her girlfriend DIANE pulls up in a new Pebble Beige Altima GLE.

SC. 8 INT. ALTIMA

As MEG climbs into the passenger side. DIANE is a stylish woman about MEG's age. They drive off. During the following the camera shows us the various features of the Altima interior.

* * *

DIANE

Oh yeh, when does Frank remember our anniversary. I picked out this GLE myself. I didn't know where to start. I looked through a bunch of consumer magazines, went to a lot of dealers—and I discovered the Altima. This car gives me more luxury features than I ever thought I could afford.

SC. 8

MEG

It's really comfortable.

DIANE

Oh yeh, I love driving my clients to lunch in it.

MEG

You know, the story I have to write is on how to buy a car.

DIANE

Really? I could've used a story like that. You know, the process can be intimidating. I thought I'd get lost with all the, uh, car lingo.

MEG

My article should help people through all that. I just have to figure out a good angle first.

DIANE

Oh, I know someone that could definitely help you out with that.

MEG

Don't say Alan.

DIANE

No, his name is Bob. He's the guy that sold me this car.

MEG

Well, I'll hear him out. But you can't tell him I'm writing a story, it's got to be as if I'm really buying one.

* * *

CUT TO:

SC. 9 INT. NISSAN DEALERSHIP

A bright, welcoming showroom displaying various models of Nissan automobiles, including two or three Altimas.

SC. 9

During the following BOB walks the women over to a black Altima.

MEG

I don't know about this one. It looks a little pricey.

BOB

Well, that's what's so nice about the Altima. It has all the features of a luxury car but it costs much less.

* * *

MEG (v.o.)

I knew I had to see a lot of cars as research for my story . . .

DISSOLVE TO: SC 10 USED CAR LOT

The consummate car salesman (MARTY) approaches MEG.

MARTY

So you wanna buy yourself a car today?

MEG

I'm really just looking.

MARTY

Nah, I got all day. That's my job. Marty Martin. Nice to meet you. Got a trade in?

MEG points to her beat-up car.

MARTY (cont'd)

I guess not.

* * *

CUT TO:

SC. 13 INT. MEG'S BEDROOM.

ON SCREEN A GRAPHIC READS:

STEP #2. CONDUCT RESEARCH

*FRIENDS AND FAMILY RECOMMENDATIONS

*CAR AND CONSUMER MAGAZINES

MEG (v.o.)

I talked to friends, collected brochures, read consumer and car magazines. I also found the Intellichoice Car Cost Guide. It rated the Altima as a best value in its class, measuring vehicle expenses over a five year period. I knew then it was the best car for my story too.

* * *

MEG EXITS.

ON SCREEN A GRAPHIC READS:

STEP #3. SELECT A DEALERSHIP

*CONVENIENT LOCATION

*SERVICE HOURS

SC. 15

ALAN notices she left the Altima brochure behind. He picks it up and it piques his interest. He puts his feet on his desk and begins to read.

FADE OUT

END OF SEGMENT ONE

First Call-to-Action

Open on stage with product display to one side. An attractive, smart woman, 28–33 years of age walks brightly into frame.

	Video	Audio
1.	Woman walks in front of the Altima and addresses camera: **SUPER: Nissan Logo in lower right hand corner.**	Do ***you*** know the art of buying a car? There's **so much** to know . . . like: where to go . . . what to look for . . . how to get the best deal . . . So where can you go for help?
2.	*Shot of 10 Steps Guide* **SUPER: FREE** **800 #** **Limited Time Only**	*Well, the answers are right here in this valuable information packed guide from Nissan* . . . everything you need to turn buying a car into an art. No matter which car you choose. And it's yours—FREE, just by calling this 800#.
3.	Move in on 10 Steps Guidebook	The enlightening "10 Steps to Buying a New Car" guide . . . is a simple, trusty road map to successfully finding and buying the car of your dreams.
4.	Guidebook	Even people who've bought cars before will discover great tips . . . like how to decide on which car you want, how to conduct research and the smart way to select a dealership.

5. *Altima Footage*	*And if you're looking for an elegant,* affordable *luxury car. Nissan has the answer for that too. The Nissan Altima!*
6. Footage clips and graphic supers listing GLE features: **power mirrors, windows and doorlocks, power sunroof, automatic temperature control, six-speaker AM/FM cassette stereo and CD player, available leather**	The Altima GLE comes standard with premium design features like power mirrors, windows and doorlocks, power sunroof, automatic temperature control and a 6-speaker CD audio system found in luxury cars costing **twice** the price . . .
7. Footage and graphically list feature supers: **side-door guard beams, front and rear crumple zones, dual air bags**	The Altima also has 50 standard safety features including side-door guard beams, crumple zones and dual air bags—like the Mercedes C220 . . .
8. Footage and Super-Toe Control Animation	and Super Toe Control rear wheel suspension to help you feel secure during abrupt lane changes and evasive maneuvers. It's quality that goes beyond your expectations.
9. *J.D. Power Award* ***SUPER: "Best Mid-Size Car Under $20,000 in initial quality" J.D. Power and Associates 1996 Quality Study***	*That's why, in initial quality, J.D. Power and Associates rated the Altima the "best mid-size car under $20,000."*
10. Return to woman at display **800# Limited Time Only**	And if you call this toll-free number now, you'll receive an exclusive gift—the Altima:Extra Sales and Service Card . . . which gives you all these VIP benefits: And when you buy or lease a new Altima, you'll get **40% off** its theft deterrent system with remote keyless entry . . . **or,** a Gold Preferred Security Plus with 24 hour roadside assistance . . .
11. She shows us Altima:Extra card graphically list features: ***Specially trained dealer contacts** ***Appointment scheduling** ******Quick*** **Financing Option** ***Theft deterrent system—40% off** ***Gold Preferred Security Plus**	

extended service contract— just $1.00 **SUPER: Limited time only theft deterrent system. Dealer sets actual price. Gold Preferred Security Plus Plan 36 month/45,000 mile limited coverage. Restrictions/deductible apply. See dealer for details.**	for just $1.
12. *Gift Certificate* ***SUPER: Free 800 #***	*Plus, you'll get a valuable gift certificate for your personal copy of the "10 Steps to Buying a New Car" guide.*
13. Map of Denver Area (Houston Area) **SUPER: Names and addresses of dealers**	You'll also receive a list of all participating Nissan dealers in your area.
14. See woman in front of display.	So call now. Turn your next car buying experience into an art.
15. **CUT TO NISSAN LOGO AND SUPER: Enjoy the Ride.**	

Segment Two

FADE IN:

SC. 16 ext. MEG'S APARTMENT—DAY (THE PRESENT)

MEG puts the last suitcase into the trunk and turns to camera.

MEG

I realized how important it is for people to know the basic steps of buying a car and I found the first three—I'd decided a good car for my story would be a Nissan Altima, I'd done my research, and I'd picked a dealership. Now two days had gone by and there were only three more until my story was due. I needed all the help I could get . . . I guess Alan did, too. . . .

DISSOLVE TO:

SC. 17/18/19 INT. NISSAN DEALERSHIP—DAY

ALAN is at the dealership. He is in a conversation with BOB. BOB's daughter SUSANNAH is at his desk, doing her homework.

BOB

The Z is an outstanding sportscar.

ALAN

Oh yeh, I know, a friend of mine has one. He loves it. What if I wanted a car that was roomier, do you have something that's still as much fun to drive?

BOB

That would be the Altima.

BOB starts to walk ALAN over to an Altima. MEG enters the showroom and is surprised to find ALAN there.

* * *

SC 20 INT. NISSAN SHOWROOM—CONTINUOUS

ON SCREEN A GRAPHIC READS:

STEP #4. HOW THE DEALERSHIP WORKS

*IT'S A TEAM APPROACH

As MEG enters and BOB greets her.

BOB

Where'd your husband go?

SC. 20

MEG

Oh, we're getting a divorce. Anyway, Bob, I really like the Altima. What's my next step?

BOB

Well, maybe I should tell you a little bit about how a dealership works.

MEG

Don't I just say I want to buy a car and then you sell me one?

BOB

Oh, you'll be getting a lot more attention than that here. We have different people especially trained to help you through the entire procedure . . . Once I've answered all your questions, I'll show you everything I can about the car. Now, my boss is the sales manager who oversees the trade-ins and approves all the transactions. If you decide to buy the car then you'll meet Jim, who's our finance and insurance manager. And once it's yours, our service experts will be at your service.

MEG

That's a lot of helpful people.

* * *

Meg types into the computer.

CUT TO:

SC. 27 INT. NISSAN DEALERSHIP - DAY

MEG and BOB are standing beside the Altima GLE. She takes notes as BOB shows her some features.

ON SCREEN A GRAPHIC READS:

STEP #5. REQUEST A SHOWROOM PRESENTATION

*STATE YOUR NEEDS

*CHECK OUT THE CAR

MEG

I have pretty long legs. Can I sit inside to see if I fit?

BOB

Absolutely.

Bob opens the drivers door and *Meg* sits inside.

BOB

Comfortable?

MEG

Umhmm.

BOB

You know the Altima has power windows and doorlocks and more head and leg room than the Mercedes C280. Have enough room?

* * *

ON SCREEN WE SEE THE GRAPHIC:

STEP #6. TAKE A TEST DRIVE

*DUPLICATE YOUR NORMAL DRIVING CONDITIONS SC. 28

As the Altima cruises along.

SC. 29 INT. ALTIMA

MEG is driving. BOB is on the passenger side.

MEG (v.o.)

I drove on the types of roads I usually take. I never knew you could travel these streets without bouncing. It was smooth and quiet—and the car really did handle corners well. I wasn't ready to handle what was around the next corner though . . .

* * *

End of Segment Two

Second Call-to-Action

Open on stage with Altima at center. Talent is lively . . .

1.	Woman walks to center stage and addresses camera **SUPER: Nissan logo in lower right hand corner**	ABS, DOHC, Non-CFC, MSRP . . . sequential multipoint fuel injection. Yes, car lingo can be intimidating . . .
2.	She walks toward product display and shows us the Car Shopping Kit.	Well, now you can solve the mysteries of buying a car **and** turn it into an art . . .
3.	*Shot of 10 Step Guide* **SUPER: Free 800# Limited Time Only**	*with this information and revealing guide from Nissan.* It's yours—**FREE,** just by calling this 800 #.

REMAINDER REPEATS CALL-TO-ACTION 1.

Segment Three

FADE IN:

SC. 33 EXT. MEG'S APARTMENT BUILDING—DAY (PRESENT)

MEG
(to camera)

Test driving the Altima was fun, but afterwards I had to face the reality that my story was due in less than twenty-four hours. I felt as informed as I could be about the car, but before I could write, I knew I had to learn the process of determining the price . . .

DISSOLVE TO:

SC. 34 INT. NISSAN DEALERSHIP - DAY

MEG is seated across from BOB at the sales desk.

ON SCREEN WE SEE THE GRAPHIC:

STEP #7. DETERMINE THE PRICE.

*KNOW YOUR PRIORITIES & SPENDING LIMITS

*BUYING VS. LEASING

*TRADE-IN

MEG (v.o.)

I had to really be prepared for this step. You have to know your priorities and spending limits because there's a lot involved here. I admit I was feeling some trepidation . . .

During the following, BOB writes on a pad.

* * *

BOB and MEG continue talking as he writes some figures on a pad.

MEG (v.o.)

I should've expected this to take a little time. I asked about buying versus leasing—it just depends on what your needs are. We eventually arrived at a fair price for both of us. And when we talked about a trade-in, you wouldn't believe what Bob offered me for my old car . . .

BOB

We think it's a classic.

BOB laughs and shows her the numbers he'd written.

MEG (v.o.)

I was getting close to the point where I could finish my story. But I was worried that all this research was taking up valuable time while Alan was finishing his.

* * *

BOB walks MEG over to JIM, a friendly looking, grey-haired man.

SC. 37 INT. SALES OFFICE

As JIM brings MEG in and seats her at his desk. During the following he will lead her through various documents.

ON SCREEN WE SEE THE GRAPHIC:

STEP #8. FINANCING

*FUNDING ALTERNATIVES & CREDIT APPROVAL

*TOTAL PRICE INCLUDES ADD-ONS

*PROVIDE DOCUMENTATION

BOB

Hi Jim, meet Meg.

JIM

Hi Meg, Jim Haskins, how are you?

MEG

Hi. I'm good.

BOB

He's our Finance and Insurance Manager. So you're in good hands.

* * *

CUT TO:

SC. 39 INT. MEG'S BEDROOM—NIGHT

A totally relaxed MEG is sound asleep. With a big smile on her face.

MEG (v.o.)

That night all my dreams were sweet ones. Especially the one where they were painting my name on the feature editor's parking spot.

CUT TO:

SC. 40 INT. REGISTER HALLWAY—DAY

A fresh looking MEG heads for MARGUERITE's office carrying her story in a folder.

A dishevelled, unshaven, and bleary-eyed ALAN rounds the corner with his story in hand.

* * *

MEG smiles, and they head for MARGUERITE's office . . .

CUT TO:

SC. 41 INT. MARGUERITE'S OFFICE

MARGUERITE is at her desk. MEG and ALAN enter and place their stories in front of her.

MARGUERITE

Well, I'm impressed. A day early.

MEG/ALAN

What??!

MARGUERITE

Kidding. Okay, thank you both for your very hard work and you'll know whose story won and who earned the promotion tomorrow when you see it in print.

DISSOLVE TO:

SC. 42 INT. MEG'S OFFICE AREA—DAY

MEG (V.O.)

Well, the day of reckoning had come. I knew if the job wasn't mine, it would be going to someone very qualified. But not more qualified than me.

ALAN comes into MEG's office area. In his hand he has the Sunday Magazine section.

ALAN

Ah, congratulations are in order!

* * *

ALAN

Well, see they put your name first!

He shows her the article.

ALAN

"The Art of Buying a Car" and "Finding Affordable Luxury."

MEG

I can't believe it. Marguerite combined our stories.

* * *

DISSOLVE TO:

SC. 43 EXT. NISSAN DEALERSHIP - DAY

BOB is showing MEG around her new Altima.

ON SCREEN WE SEE THE GRAPHIC:

STEP #9. TAKE DELIVERY

*INSPECT THE VEHICLE AND OWNER'S MANUAL

*MEET SERVICE MANAGER

MEG (v.o.)

Needless to say, after learning everything I could about the Altima, I came to realize I deserved to have one for myself. When I took delivery of my car, I went through the owner's manual, got an explanation of everything, and even met the service manager.

MEG is thanking the SERVICE MANAGER. BOB gives her the keys and shakes her hand. MEG gets in the car and drives off the lot.

DISSOLVE TO:

SC. 44 EXT. MEG'S APARTMENT BUILDING—DAY (PRESENT)
ON SCREEN WE SEE THE GRAPHIC:

STEP #10. CARING FOR YOUR NEW CAR

*KEEP UP YOUR MAINTENANCE SCHEDULE

MEG is parking the car. MEG (to camera)

Now that I made the investment, I'm really going to take good care of this car. So, I'll be going back to see Bob and the Nissan guys to make sure this car runs well for the rest of its life—they told me they had customers whose Altimas lived to well over a hundred-thousand. (then)

MEG finished parking. MEG (v.o.)

So I came to realize there's more to life than work. And Alan and I, we found a great way to make our partnership work that's not just about work . . .

ALAN comes out of the building with a suitcase. He gives MEG a kiss and throws his suitcase in the trunk of the Altima. MEG is climbing into the driver's side . . .

From car interior as they pull out of the driveway. ALAN (v.o.)

Hey, I thought you said you were going to let me drive.

MEG (v.o.)

Not this trip, partner.

SC. 45 EXT. ROAD

As they ride into the distance.

FADE OUT

END OF SEGMENT THREE

Third Call-to-Action

Open on stage with Altima at center. Talent is lively . . .

	Video	Audio
1.	Woman walks to center stage addresses camera **SUPER: Nissan logo in lower right hand corner**	Do you know the art of financing a new car? How about figuring out best price? Then there's your old car to deal with—should you sell it yourself or trade it in? You know, there is an art to buying a car. And it's not that hard to figure out . . .
2.	*Shot of 10 Step Guide* SUPER: FREE 800 # **Limited Time Only**	*If you have this information packed guide from Nissan.* It's yours—**FREE,** just by calling this 800 #.

NOTE: REMAINDER OF CALL-TO-ACTION IS THE SAME AS CALL-TO-ACTION 1.

CREDIT

PROGRAM DISCLAIMER

THE END

APPENDIX G

Sample Production Budget

PROGRAM FORM

Bid Date: **4/6/95**
Disc Number:
Job Number:

PROJECT NAME:	I				**CLIENT:**	**Hawthorne Communications**
Script Writing Fee:					Contact:	
Pre Production:	14	Days			Phone:	
Set Build:		Days			Fax:	
Pre Light:	1	Days				
Studio Shoot:	1	Days			**HMCI**	
Location:	6	Days			Acct Rep:	
Betacam SP:		Tapes			Exec Prod:	
Film Format:	16	mm	Footage:	16000	Writer:	**TBD**
Film Transfer:	16	Hours			Producer:	
Avid Offline:	50	Hours			Director:	**TBD**
Online Edit:	16	Hours			Editor:	**TBD**
Audio Mix:	12	Hours	10	Hour day		
Music Composing Fee:	10000		10	1.5 O.T.	Length:	**28:30**

SUMMARY OF ESTIMATED PRODUCTION COSTS			**ESTIMATED**	**ACTUAL**	**VARIANCE**
1000 SCRIPT FEES		Page 1			
2000 PRODUCTION CREW (A&B)		Page 1	**123695**		
3000 PRODUCING EXPENSES (A&B)		Page 1	**6125**		
3100 CASTING		Page 2	**6305**		
3200 WARDROBE & MAKE-UP		Page 2	**21880**		
3300 ART DIRECTION		Page 2	**31570**		
3400 STUDIO RENTAL & EXPENSES		Page 3	**3300**		
3500 LOCATION EXPENSES		Page 3	**25585**		
3600 CAMERA/SOUND EQUIPMENT		Page 4	**34875**		
3700 FILM/VIDEO/AUDIO STOCK & PROCESSING		Page 4	**9936**		
4000 CAST		Page 4			
5000 EDITING		Page 5	**41350**		
6000 MUSIC & AUDIO RECORDING		Page 5	**15395**		
7000 VIDEO DUBS		Page 5			
		Sub Total Direct Costs	**320016**		
	Overhead/Fee	25%	**79985**		
		TOTAL	**400000**		
	Contingency		$40,000		

Comments:

Talent payments not included
Talent expenses (including meals and craft service) not included.

Summary Page 778503

####	SCRIPT WRITING				ESTIMATE		ACTUAL
####	Script Writer						
####	Research						
####	Travel						
####	Per Diem						
				TOTAL 1000		**TOTAL 1000**	

PRODUCTION		**PRE-PRODUCTION**							EST..		**SHOOT**							EST..	ACTUAL
####	**CREW**	DAYS	RATE	Hrs	2	1.5x $	2x	2x $	TOTAL	####	DAYS	RATE	Hrs	2	1.5x $	2x	2x $	TOTAL	TOTAL
####	Exec Prod	2	####	#					4000	####		####							
####	Producer	15	500	#					7500	####	7	500	#					3500	
####	Prod Mangr		350							####		350							
####	Prod Coord	14	275	#					3850	####	7	275	#					1925	
####	Loc Scout	5	400	#					2000	####		300							
####	Director	7	####	#					8750	####	7	####	#					14000	
####	1st A.D.	3	475	#					1425	####	7	475	#					3325	
####	2nd A.D.	1	225	#					225	####	6	250	#					1500	
####	Cinmatgrphr	1	####	#					1000	####	7	####	#	8	###			10660	
####	Asst Camera	1	375	#					375	####	7	375	#	10	563			3188	
####	Gaffer	1	375	#					375	####	7	375	#	10	563			3188	
####	Best Boy	1	300	#					300	####	7	350	#	10	525			2975	
####	Key Grip	1	350	#					350	####	7	375	#	10	563			3188	
####	Grip	1	250	#					250	####	6	350	#	10	525			2625	
####	Dolly Grip		275							####	6	300	#	10	450			2250	
####	Rigging Grip		325							####	1	325	#	4	195			520	
####	Mixer		350							####	7	375	#	10	563			3188	
####	Boom Man		250							####	6	325	#	8	390			2340	
####	VTR Recdst		300							####	6	350	#	10	525			2625	
####	Script Sup'r		300							####	6	375	#					2250	
####	Tele Promtr		200							####		200							
####	Still Photo		300							####		300							
####	Home Econ		400							####		400							
####	Asst Hm Ec		275							####		275							
####	Prd Asst	15	175	#					2625	####	12	175	#					2100	
####	Craft Service	2	200	#					400	####	7	200	#					1400	
####	Runners	5	125	#					625	####	7	125	#					875	
####										####									
####										####									
								Sub total	34050								Sub total	67620	
								P&W	6810								P&W	15215	
								TOTAL 2000	**40860**								**TOTAL 2050**	**82835**	

PRODUCING EXPENSES											
####		NBR	RATE	**Pre-Production**	ESTIMATE	####	NBR	RATE	**Shoot**	EST..	ACTUAL
####	Phone/Fax	20	10		200	####	10	25		250	
####	Ex Mail	20	25		500	####	12	25		300	
####	Messengers	15	10		150	####	15	10		150	
####	Transptn	4	75		300	####	3	75		225	
####	Airfares		850			####		850			
####	Per Diems		150			####		150			
####	Insurance	1	400		400	####	7	400		2800	
####	Misc.	1	350		350	####	1	500		500	
				TOTAL 3000	**1900**				**TOTAL 3050**	**4225**	

Page 1

3100	CASTING	DAYS	RATE	Hrs	2	1.5x $	2x	2x $	ESTIMATE	ACTUAL
3101	Casting Director	6	400	10					2400	
3102	Casting Asst	5	200	10					1000	
3103	Casting Facilities -Test.		500							
3104	Casting Facilities - LA	5	400						2000	
3105	Materials		50							
3106	Telephone/Fax	5	15						75	
3107	Messengers/Express	5	30						150	
3108	Meals		25							
3109	Misc.									
								Sub Total	5625	
								P&W	680	
								Total 3100	**6305**	

3200	WARDROBE/MAKE-UP	DAYS	RATE	Hrs	2	1.5x $	2x	2x $	ESTIMATE	ACTUAL
3201	Make-up Artist	7	500	10	10	750			4250	
3202	Hairdresser	6	500	10					3000	
3203	Wqrdrobe Stylist	11	500	10					5500	
3204	Assistants	10	150	10					1500	
3205	Wardrobe Purchased	1	3500						3500	
3206	Wardrobe Rented	1	1000						1000	
3207	Special Make-up									
3208	Kit Rentals	7	40						280	
3209										
3210	Misc.									
								Sub Total	19030	
								P&W	2850	
								Total 3200	**21880**	

3300	ART DIRECTION	DAYS	RATE	Hrs	2	1.5x $	2x	2x $	ESTIMATE	ACTUAL
3301	Art Director		500							
3302	Asst Art Director		300							
3303	Set Decorator	9	500	10					4500	
3304	Asst Set Decorator	12	375	10					4500	
3305	Prop Master	7	375	10	12	675			3300	
3306	Set Prep/Wrap	2	150	10					300	
3307	Construction Crew	4	200	10					800	
3308	Construction Materials	1	3500						3500	
3309	Set Furnishings	1	5000						5000	
3310	Props	1	4500						4500	
3311	Foliage/Landscape									
3312	Cars/Boats/Etc	1	1000						1000	
3313	Animals	1	350						350	
3314	Animal Trainer	1	500						500	
3315	Specials EFX									
3316	Transportation	1	800						800	
3317										
3318	Misc.									
								Sub Total	29050	
								P&W	2520	
								Total 3300	**31570**	

Page 2

3400	STUDIO RENTAL	DAYS	RATE	Hrs	2	1.5x $	2x	2x $	ESTIMATE	ACTUAL
3401	Studio Supervisor	2	250	10					500	
3402	Build Days	1	700						700	
3403	Pre Light Days		450							
3404	Shoot Days	1	900						900	
3405	Strike Days		450							
3406	Electricity	2	150						300	
3407	Paint/Prep Stage		200	Nbr						
3408	Craft Services	2	6	25					300	
3409	Lunches	2	12	25					600	
3410	Dinners		16	20						
3411	Meal Penalties		15	20						
3412	Per Diems		50	20						
3413	Lodging		100	20						
3414	Airfares		750							
3415	Transportation									
3416	Photo Film/Processing									
3417	Security Services									
3418										
3419										
3420										
								Sub Total	3300	
								P&W		
								Total 3400	**3300**	

3500	LOCATION EXPENSES	DAYS	RATE	NBR	2	1.5x $	2x	2x $	ESTIMATE	ACTUAL
3501	Location Manager	4	300	10					1200	
3502	Permits/Location Fees	1	15000	1					15000	
3503	Road Barriers	6	12	1					72	
3504	Dressing Room Vehicle	5	300	1					1500	
3505	Passenger Vehicles	8	75	1					600	
3506	Limo/Taxi/Passengers									
3507	Parking/Gas	8	75	1					600	
3508	Mileage		0							
3509	Airfares		850							
3510	Lodging		100							
3511	Craft Services	6	12	25					1800	
3512	Lunches	6	13	25					1950	
3513	Dinners		16	20						
3514	Meal Penalties									
3515	Photo Film/Processing	5	75	1					375	
3516	Security Services	1	300	4					1200	
3517	Breakfast	8	7	8					448	
3518	cell phones	6	100	1					600	
3519										
3520										
								Sub Total	25345	
								P&W	240	
								Total 3500	**25585**	

3600	CAMERA EQUIPMENT	DAYS	RATE	ESTIMATE	ACTUAL
3601	Video Camera Package		750		
3602	Film Camera Package	6	1500	9000	
3603	Sound Package	6	375	2250	
3604	Grip Truck	7	400	2800	
3605	Standard Lighting Package	7	850	5950	
3606	Additional Lighting Rental	5	1000	5000	
3607	Generator	6	400	2400	
3608	Dolly Rental	7	200	1400	
3609	Crane Rental		500		
3610	Video Tap & VTR	7	300	2100	
3611	Helicopter (Hourly)		600		
3612	Tyler Mount (Two day minimum)		650		
3613	Camera Car	1	850	850	
3614	Walkie Talkies	7	75	525	
3615	Production Supplies	7	300	2100	
3616	Teleprompter	1	500	500	
3617					
3618					
3619	Misc.				
			Total 3600	**34875**	

3700	FILM-VIDEO STOCK & PROCESSING	NUMBER	RATE	ESTIMATE	ACTUAL
3701	Video Tape - Betacam		33.00		
3702	Video Tape - Other				
3703	16mm Film Stock (ft)	16000	0.35	5600	
3704	35mm Film Stock (ft)		0.52		
3705	Processing (ft)	16000	0.24	3840	
3706	Workprint (ft)		0.15		
3707	Audio Tape	9	10.00	90	
3708	Shipping	7	50.00	350	
3709	Video Tap Tape	7	8.00	56	
3710	Stock Footage				
3711	Stock Footage - Demo Fee				
3712					
3713	Misc.				
			Total 3700	**9936**	

4000	CAST	DAYS	NUMBER	RATE	ESTIMATE	ACTUAL
4001	Principals			400		
4002						
4003						
4004	Group Player			200		
4005	Extras			150		
4006	Narrator			400		
4007	Travel					
4008	Lodging					
4009	Per Diems					
4010	Payment Service					
4011			P/W	0		
4012			Agency Fee	0		
				Total 4000		

Page 4

5000	EDITING	HOURS	RATE	ESTIMATED	ACTUAL
5001	Post Production Supervisor		40		
5002	Editor, Producer or Director	18	500	9000	
5003	Supervisor - Film Transfer	16	50	800	
5004	Film to Tape - Best Light	10	350	3500	
5005	Film to Tape - Timed	15	400	6000	
5006	Audio Synching	8	175	1400	
5007	Avid-Logging Selects	8	75	625	
5008	Avid-Digitizing	10	100	1000	
5009	Avid - Off-Line Edit	50	150	7500	
5010	On-Line Edit	16	375	6000	
5011	Abekas Recorder		120		
5012	Graphic Designer		100		
5013	Paint Box System	4	225	900	
5014	Computer Graphics	10	400	4000	
5015	D-2 Video Tapes	3	175	525	
5016	Betacam Tapes		33		
5017	Travel - Film Transfer		300		
5018	Per Diems - Film Transfer		100		
5019	Meals		10		
5020	Shipping	1	100	100	
5021	Tape to Tape Dubs for Edit		100		
5022	Dubs - Small Format		35		
			Sub Total 5000	**41350**	

6000	MUSIC & AUDIO RECORDING	HOURS	RATE	ESTIMATE	ACTUAL
6001	Composer			8000	
6002	Needle Drop Fees - Music & EFXs		75		
6003	Music/EFX Search		75		
6004	Narration Recording	7	200	1400	
6005	Audio Editing		100		
6006	Sweetening	16	200	3200	
6007	Mix	12	200	2400	
6008	Lay-up and Layback	2	135	270	
6009	Audio Tape	1	100	100	
6010	Misc. Materials	1	25	25	
6011	Travel				
6012	Per Diems/Meals				
6013	Shipping				
6014					
6015	Misc.				
			Sub Total 6000	**15395**	

7000	VIDEO DUBS	NBR	RATE	ESTIMATE	ACTUAL
7001	D-2 Duplicate Masters				
7002	1 inch Broadcast				
7003	3/4 inch U-matic				
7004	1/2 inch VHS				
7005	Special Packaging				
7006					
7007	Misc.				
			Sub Total 7000		

Page 5

Glossary

A

ad agency (general): hired by businesses to market products using traditional advertising avenues (print, spot TV, etc.). May consult with specialized infomercial agencies to maximize resources and create complementary campaigns.

ad agency (infomercial): hired by corporations and product owners to execute their infomercial program (on a fee or commission basis). Provides one or more of the following infomercial services: product assessment, marketing strategy, creative, production, media planning/buying/analysis, and back-end management. Infomercial ad agencies differ from infomercial direct marketers, who retain product ownership.

ad allowable: a dollar amount determined to be the maximum media expense per unit sold in order to make a minimum profit. Approximately the gross profit per unit, less all direct selling costs, except media time.

adjacency: commercial spot time purchased adjacent to or within a specific program that targets the advertiser's ideal demographic. For example, if Richard Simmons appeared as a guest on *Late Night with David Letterman,* his media buying agency might purchase an "adjacency" for "Deal A Meal" immediately before, after, or during the show.

ADO: acronym for Ampex's digital video effects (DVE) system.

affidavit: the document that TV station and cable network sales departments create and send their agency clients confirming their allotted commercial run times and specific prices paid.

affiliate: any broadcast TV station that is financially compensated for local telecasting of national programs for a network (ABC, CBS, NBC, Fox, Paramount, Warner).

aftermarketing: see **back-end sales**.

airing: the broadcast of an infomercial in a specific time slot.

airtime: media time periods a network or broadcast station has available for infomercial placements.

analog: audio and video presented or collected in a continuous form as voltage measurement.

analog editing: editing systems manipulating audio and video recorded in analog form.

Area of Dominant Influence (ADI): a television marketing area defined by Arbitron. Each county in the U.S. is assigned to only one market, according to where the majority of household viewing hours are directed.

auction format: an infomercial program structure that mirrors an auction. For example, "Telephone Auction" successfully aired in 1985–86, presenting products for live audience bidding. As bids peak on each product, the auctioneer dramatically reveals the actual bargain price for the TV audience, which is usually significantly lower.

avail: a spot or infomercial time period available for purchase.

average take: term used by continuity marketers to describe the average number of orders a consumer will make once entering a continuity program. For example, a music club member may take an average of six CDs before canceling their membership.

B

back-end sales: product transactions that occur after the initial direct television sale generated by an infomercial or short-form DRTV spot. These additional sales of the advertised item and related products can be generated via inbound telemarketing (upsells), outbound telemarketing, direct mail, continuity and club programs and catalogs. Back-end sales can account for 20 percent to 90 percent of all product sales; this does not include retail sales.

bad debt: at any point in an infomercial/DRTV campaign, the sum of all outstanding debt incurred due to consumers' unpaid invoices, bounced checks or unauthorized credit card charges.

beauty shots: term for flattering film or video shots of a DRTV product; usually shot in studios on a light table or cyc.

Beta SP: Sony's professional, half-inch video tape format and the equipment that shoots, records and edits the format.

bicycle tape: the practice of reusing an infomercial recorded on videotape. The same tape can potentially be sent to many broadcast stations for viewing or broadcasting, thus reducing tape duplication costs. Primarily used for infomercial demo tapes.

billboard: the graphic page or pages at the end of a CTA that lists product price, shipping and handling charges, guarantees, "send check" address, 800/888 telephone number, etc. Also called "tag page."

bonus: an attractive extra product or service added to the key infomercial product.

book/booked: to buy or to have bought; as in "book media" or "booked media."

border market: a "Nielsen-Designated-Market" Area whose broadcast TV stations' signals and viewership spills over into Canada. These are markets such as Seattle, Fargo, Detroit, Buffalo, Burlington, Vermont, etc.

brandmercial: a new breed of infomercial where an arresting creative treatment of authentic brand image generates a lead or sale. Brand identity is magnified.

B-roll: footage shot expressly to "cover" narration or interview copy. The audio from these shots is generally used as background audio or "sound under." Same as cover footage.

C

"Call Now!" motivators: use of premiums, bonuses, discounts, sweepstakes, etc. in addition to the principal infomercial product; designed to motivate viewers to call immediately. A good "motivator" can double response. Marketers are cautioned to fully substantiate and fulfill all claims. If your infomercial states: "$10 off for all callers in the next hour," you must strictly adhere to the offer.

call to action (CTA): the segments of an infomercial that "ask for the order." An infomercial can have one, two, three, or more CTAs. Each infomercial CTA is typically a minimum of two minutes long, reviews the product's main features and benefits, and states product guarantee, price point, warranties, "send check" address, 800/888 number, credit cards accepted, etc.

campaign: term used to describe a product's advertising plan and execution, from development, through production and media placement.

CD-ROM: computer term for compact disc-read only memory, which—in a marketing context—is used more and more to sell and promote products, particularly in catalog form.

channel surfing: the use of a remote control to window shop multiple cable channels, stopping only briefly on each channel.

chip camera: a technologically advanced video camera that records images using silicon microchips. This video is more stable and not subject to the drifting and burning typical of older tube cameras.

clearance: a term used by short-form media buyers to indicate what portion of their media order in any day, week or campaign was actually broadcast. If a media buyer requests that $10,000 of short-form media be telecast in a week, but only $5,000 airs, the clearance is

50%. Decreasing clearance percentages over the past decade have been a problem for short-form direct marketers and media buyers.

clutter: a term used primarily by the spot image/awareness TV advertising industry to denote multiple commercial messages in a short period of time, thus making it difficult for an individual spot commercial to stand out from the crowd. Commercial breaks can last two to four minutes, and possibly have as many as eight to 16 different commercial messages.

COD: acronym for "cash on delivery." The most common method of payment in Europe; rarely used today for North American infomercial/DRTV sales. Refusal rate is often 50 percent or higher, making it too costly except when a product's gross margin is very high (10-to-1) and therefore able to absorb refusal costs. "Sorry, no CODs" is a common graphic on infomercial billboards.

color correction: a technical process involving the electronic manipulation of colors on transferred film or video. Color correction is done to enhance color or correct lighting or equipment problems resulting in off-colored images during shooting.

comparables: a media time slot or slots that previously aired an infomercial with a product of similar demographic appeal to the product being analyzed.

component: recording and transmission of the individual color, luminance and chroma characteristics of a video signal without combining them first as in a composite signal.

composite: combining, recording and transmission of a video signal's color, luminance and chroma values and characteristics as one signal.

composition: the demographic make-up of a specific viewing audience.

contingency: a percentage (usually 10%) of a production budget that is set aside for potential cost overruns.

continuing media: specific infomercial media time slots that produce profitable results week after week and are continually rebooked.

continuity program: an infomercial/DRTV product purchasing program that encourages consumers to purchase the first in a series of products, often for a lower-than-normal price, then continue purchasing the entire series for a higher price. Extensively used for music and book series. Concept also employed successfully for beauty, diet products and self-development products.

copy: term used by advertisers and agencies to specify the written or spoken words in a commercial. The term "copywriter" is most often used in traditional advertising to denote the writer of copy. In the infomercial industry, the copywriter is more often referred to as a "scriptwriter," due to the length of copy written, which can range from 30 to 40 pages.

cost of goods (COG): the direct costs associated with the manufacturing and packaging of a specific product.

cost per lead (CPL): the average cost of television media to generate one lead or telephone request for more product information.

cost per order (CPO): the average cost of television media to generate one product order. The figure is determined by taking the cost of a specific infomercial telecast and dividing it by the number of orders received. A $1,000 time period that generates 100 product orders would have a CPO of $10.

cost per rating point (C/RP): the cost of buying one rating point in a specific time period or general program category (news, talk show, soap operas).

coverage: total number of different people or homes reached by a specific ad campaign.

cover footage: same as **B-roll**.

creative: term used to describe the concept and scripting phases of the production process; and/or a person who is involved in these processes, as in "the creative department."

credit card %: the percentage of total DRTV orders purchased with a credit card versus check or COD.

CTA: see **call to action**

cumulative/CUME: synonyms for **reach**.

customer service: in infomercials, this typically refers to a bank of telephone operators or telephone service representatives (TSRs) who manage the shipping, payment, returns and product questions from customers. Customer service can make or break product manufacturers' infomercial campaigns.

cyc: a seamless curved studio wall, floor to ceiling, which is used as a background for shooting film or video.

D

daypart: refers to the various multiple hour segments of television's 24-hour broadcast day. Dayparts are typically segmented as follows:

6a–9a	-	Early Morning
9a–12n	-	Morning
12n–4p	-	Daytime
4p–6p	-	Early Fringe
6p–7p	-	Early News
7p–8p	-	Prime Access
8p–11p	-	Prime
11p–11:30p	-	Late News
11:30p–1a	-	Late Fringe
1a–6a	-	Late Night

demo format: an infomercial program structure that places the product center stage; generally shot in a studio, with or without a studio audience; always has a product demonstrator talking directly to the camera, or to a companion interviewer, while demonstrating the product. "Amazing Discoveries" is a classic demo formatted infomercial.

Designated Market Area (DMA): Nielsen's term to describe a specific TV market area. Nielsen counts 212 distinct TV markets in the U.S. (Similar to ADI.)

digital: audio and video recorded in quantities represented by digits, usually in the binary system.

digital editing: also called non-linear editing. The use of editing equipment that translates analog video into digitized video to manipulate it more quickly. Digital editing can decrease analog editing time by as much as two-thirds.

digital video effects (DVE): also known as ADO, refers to equipment that digitizes video to manipulate it within the frame. Typical digital video effects include page turns, image flipping, zooming, squeezing, sparkle trails, exploding images, etc.

direct marketer: a company that manufactures or sources products, then executes an infomercial campaign while retaining ownership in the product sales. Often pays a royalty of 3 to 10 percent of sales to original owners.

direct marketing: the marketing of goods and services directly from manufacturer or wholesaler, bypassing retail to the consumer. Typical direct marketing channels are through mail, newspapers, magazines, and TV.

direct response (DR): the marketing and sales methodology of bypassing standard retail stores to make a product sale directly with the consumer. Basic direct response channels are: television, radio, mail, print (newspapers and magazines), catalogs, phone, electronic kiosks, online services, CD-ROM and—the grand daddy of them all—carnival pitch men.

direct response television (DRTV): the all-inclusive term that describes anything sold directly over television, generally bypassing traditional retail stores. DRTV is comprised of three primary marketing subgroups of short form, long form (infomercials) and live home shopping.

distributor: in the infomercial industry, similar to infomercial direct marketer. A company that owns the rights to a product or infomercial and finances their own infomercial campaigns.

documercial: the infomercial program format that uses production/creative techniques derived from the traditional documentary form. These may include on-camera spokespersons, live or taped interviews, multiple location shooting; voice-over narrator, real people features—all interwoven into a seamless half hour. Similar to *60 Minutes* or *20/20*, the format is based on actuality, i.e. no fictional elements are presented unless denoted as "dramatizations."

drag: a term referring to DRTV orders that come in long after the commercial telecast time. In the infomercial industry, 75% to 95% of all orders will be made within 60 minutes of a specific telecast. Additional orders made over the next one to seven days are known as drag orders.

driving retail: using an infomercial campaign to directly impact and lift retail sales. Braun was the first major manufacturer to use this strategy in 1992 for their single-stem food mixer. Infomercial product sales at retail can be as much as two to five times the direct TV sales volume and significantly increase existing retail volume.

DRTV: See **direct response television**.

dub master: the dub of the master with a specific 800/888 number edited in from which other dubs with the same 800/888 number will be sent to different market TV stations.

dubs/dubbing: the video duplication of an infomercial for distribution to TV stations and cable networks for airing.

E

effective frequency: the estimated number of times an individual must see a specific brand-awareness spot commercial in order to produce a positive change in awareness and attitude about the product.

effective reach: the percentage of the target demographic that sees a specific brand-awareness commercial the estimated number of times necessary to produce a positive change in awareness and attitude about the product.

electronic marketing: the direct response, marketing and sales methodology that uses electronic media, such as, TV, radio, online services, CD-ROM and electronic kiosks.

electronic media: the media of television, radio, fax, phone, kiosks, CD-ROM and Internet. As distinguished from print (newspaper, magazines, catalogs, letters) and outdoor media.

electronic retailing: see **electronic marketing**.

erosion: refers to the "diminishing effect" on viewership, media buy and response volume. After a specific infomercial has aired for a number of weeks or months, order response levels begin to drop or "erode."

F

feature: among infomercial producers and directors, a term used to describe a lengthy (one- to ten-minute) profile of an individual, usually a product inventor or consumer testimonial. Often shot "news style," the feature is usually structured to tell a story about how the product has impacted a person's life.

Federal Communications Commission (FCC): Government regulatory body that oversees electronic communications, including television.

Federal Trade Commission (FTC): Government regulatory body that oversees commercial advertising and trade practices.

film look: an electronic process that gives video a softer, more film-style look.

film to tape transfer: the process of transferring the film image to video tape by projecting the film into a video camera. The videotape of the film is then edited electronically versus physically cutting and rejoining the film as traditional film editing is performed.

firesale: term used to describe the last minute, sudden dumping of infomercial media into the media buying marketplace, usually due to an agency canceling unprofitable media at the minute.

flight: term used by short-form media buyers to describe a specific number of spots to air during a three, six, twelve week or more period on a specific TV station or cable network.

footprint: the process of using comparables to develop a media test strategy based on a similarly positioned and targeted product that has previously succeeded in the infomercial marketplace. Footprinting involves analyzing the preceding infomercial's media buying execution: markets, stations and time slots that the infomercial repeatedly aired in.

format: the creative concept governing the overall structure of an infomercial. Classic formats include: documercial, storymercial, talk show, studio demonstration, lecture presentation, and video magazine.

frequency: refers to both the number of times an infomercial will play in a specific TV market over a specified time period and the number of times the average individual will see the same commercial. The latter definition is most applicable to the spot television ad industry and is a measure of the depth of an image ad campaign.

fulfillment: term generally used to describe the warehousing, packaging, labeling, shipping and tracking functions of an infomercial product. These responsibilities are typically subcontracted to fulfillment company specialists. Some fulfillment houses also offer inbound telephone customer service.

fulfillment house: facility designed to handle product warehousing, packaging, labeling, shipping and tracking functions of an infomercial product.

full-disclosure agency: ad agency that collects broadcast affidavits (confirming media time purchase price and run time/dates) from the TV stations and networks from which it buys, and discloses the affidavits to its clients. This proves to clients that the agency is not marking up the media time and taking more than their maximum 15% commission.

G

grazing: same as **channel surfing**.

gross buy: the total amount paid by an agency client for media time. It is the sum of the net buy (amount paid the media outlet), plus the agency commission.

gross profit: on an individual product, refers to the dollar figure derived from subtracting COG from average retail (or wholesale) price. If a product has a COG of $25 and retails for $100, its single-piece gross profit is $75. For infomercial proforma calculations, the gross profit is the retail price less COG and other direct marketing costs, not including media expenses.

gross profit margin: quoted as a percentage and calculated by dividing the product's single piece gross profit by the product's retail price. For example a product with COG of $25, a gross profit of $75 and a retail price of $100 has a gross profit margin of 75%.

gross rating points (GRPs): generally not used by infomercial media buyers, GRP represents the number of rating points, in aggregate, that a media campaign will generate. Traditional spot advertisers use GRPs as a campaign goal. For example, 150 GRPs means that a specific commercial over the life of its run in a local TV market will accrue 150 total rating points of a targeted demographic group. If the spot runs 15 times during two weeks in programs with an average 10 rating, it will achieve a GRP of 150. This is not an unduplicated audience. Reach (×) Frequency = GRPs.

guaranteed CPO: a guarantee that a media agency gives its client that the cost per order for a specific infomercial telecast will not exceed a certain dollar amount. If the actual CPO does exceed the guaranteed CPO, the agency is responsible for paying the difference.

H

home shopping: term now used to describe live, 24-hour per day home shopping television networks such as HSN, QVC and Value Vision.

home shopping format: infomercial program structure that mimics live home shopping—using a simple set, a single product presenter sitting next to the product and often taking testimonial "phone-ins." Although they appear to be "live," these programs are pre-recorded.

Home Shopping Network: commonly known as HSN or Home Shopping Club. The Florida-based, 24-hour per day, live, satellite-fed, cable network purveyor of goods and services. Launched in 1984, HSN was the first shopping network; it went national in 1986.

homes using television (HUTS): The number of homes watching television at any particular time divided by the total number of homes with television, reflected as a percentage.

household: for media buyers, a home with one or more televisions.

I

impression: the experience, impact of watching a TV commercial.

inbound call handler/telemarketer: telephone service companies with multiple WATTS lines and operators who take infomercial/DRTV orders and answer questions using scripts provided by infomercial marketers. These companies are paid either by the call or by the second for connect time.

inbound telemarketing: service provided to infomercial marketers of receiving inbound phone calls from viewers who want to order the advertised product or ask for more information.

independent broadcast station(s) (indy, indies): any broadcast TV station that is not affiliated with a network such as ABC, CBS, NBC, Fox, UPN, and WB.

independent infomercial producer: specializes in filming or videotaping infomercial productions.

infomercial: any television commercial longer than two minutes.

infomercial retail multiple (IRM): The multiple used to predict retail sales generated by an infomercial media campaign. The multiple usually is a number between 1 and 5. If the multiple is 4, then for every product sold in the infomercial, it is predicted (or realized) that 4 of the same product will be sold at retail stores.

inquiry: a DRTV commercial generated telephone response that doesn't result in an order. Most inquiries ask about product price, payment plan, competing products, and product content. Inquiries are distinguished from orders and problem calls.

interactive television (ITV): any television programming that stimulates an immediate response in the form of a telephone call or pushing a button on an interactive controller. The latter will be commonplace by the mid-twenty-first century. Interactive TV will combine a household's phone, fax, computer, stereo and security systems and television into one electronic communications center or "telecomp."

interconnect: local cable systems connected together by wire or microwave to telecast shared commercials or programs simultaneously.

Internet: worldwide network of computer networks and online services, used to enhance the marketing mix of infomercial and other direct marketers. Infomercials are natural advertising formats to make a smooth transition to on-line selling once video/film can be downloaded in real time.

inventor: original creator of the product or service to be marketed via infomercial.

K

kiosk: stand-alone structures in public space (malls, airports) outfitted with computers, TVs, and VCRs, and used to advertise products and services.

knock-off: a like-category product that quickly follows another successful infomercial product. This is common in infomercials and

DRTV as it is in all marketing. In infomercials, there have been as many as five similar products on air at the same time. Example: juicers, food dehydrators, steppers, miracle mops, teeth whiteners, and Ab exercisers.

L

lead-in: the half hour program that immediately precedes your infomercial.

lead generation: a two-step offer where the viewer is asked to call a toll-free phone number for more information. The inbound telemarketer captures the "lead's" name, address and phone number. The fulfillment house then sends, free of charge, information in the form of letters, brochures, videotapes and/or product samples. If the lead doesn't respond within a short time (e.g., two weeks), additional information is sent. As many as five or six mailings may be sent the lead, attempting to procure an order. The advertiser may follow up a lead, additionally or exclusively, with outbound telemarketing.

lead-out: the half-hour program that immediately follows an infomercial.

leads: see **lead generation**.

lecture format: infomercial program structure that generally features a charismatic speaker addressing an audience about his/her infomercial product. Examples: Susan Powter, Covert Bailey, Gary Cochran, Richard Simmons.

linear editing: also known as analog editing. This refers to editing analog video in a linear fashion, adding one image after another into a long string of video cuts. The disadvantage of linear editing is that if you change the length of a cut five minutes into a 30-minute infomercial, you then have to re-edit everything that followed the change.

light table: a translucent plastic table shaped like a curved "L" on which products are positioned for beauty shots. The plastic allows for special, soft lighting effects from beneath and behind the product.

local access: generally a specific channel on local cable systems set aside for the local community to program as they see fit. Some cable systems sell infomercial time on their local access channel.

local cable: one of over 11,000 local cable systems servicing communities large and small. Most often owned by large MSOs, but because they are often locally operated, it is possible to buy infomercial media time on a local, community-by-community basis.

logging: the act of recording the good takes and shots and their time code start and stop points. This is the first stage of post production—sifting through the many hours of field-shot footage to locate the best shots for the rough, off-line edit.

long form: any television commercial longer than two minutes. This was the accepted term for an infomercial from 1984 until "infomercial" came into vogue in 1988.

low power TV (LPTV): type of broadcast station with a very low power signal that limits the broadcast radius to less than five miles. The FCC began selling LPTV licenses in the early 1980s, but few have gone on the air and fewer still are significantly profitable. LPTV infomercial time is extremely cheap . . . because few people are watching. Similar to cable local access infomercial time.

M

make-good: an infomercial telecast provided by the station or network, often at reduced or no cost, to compensate for a station mistake or poor results from a previous media purchase.

manufacturer: company that manufactures DRTV products in quantities large enough to meet infomercial demand.

margin: see **gross profit margin**.

market: for television advertisers, a distinct geographic area surrounding a city or cities that is the area of dominant influence for the city's broadcast TV stations. See "area of dominant influence."

mark-up: a ratio (3-to-1, 5-to-1) derived by dividing a product's retail price by its cost of goods (COG). A product costing $20 to manufacture and package that retails for $100 has a mark-up of 5-to-1. Because of rising media costs, the benchmark product mark-up for infomercial products has increased from 3-to-1 in 1984 to 5-to-1 in 1994.

mass rally format: infomercial program format that mirrors a mass rally. Often shot in large auditoriums with an enthusiastic audience of thousands. "Herbal Life" was the first to successfully use this format in 1984, where Herbal Life's top sales people and top dieters would preach the gospel on stage in front of the throng.

master: the original, final edit version of a completed infomercial.

media agency: An infomercial agency that provides only media buying and analysis services.

media analysis: the time-consuming task of reviewing the profitability of each infomercial telecast to determine whether to buy the specific time slot again or to cancel. Also, to review all telecasts in aggregate to determine trends, strengths, weaknesses and enhance predictability.

media: the air time that a cable network or broadcast station has available to sell for commercial insertion.

media buy: usually refers to the amount paid for one or more time slots/spots over a period of time. "The client's media buy for the month of September was $1,847,372."

media buyer: Infomercial agency that handles media buying and tracks results. Also, the individual who personally negotiates and purchases media time.

media cost: the price paid for a specific time slot or "flight" (group) of spots on cable and broadcast stations.

media efficiency ratio (MER): the number that is a snapshot of an infomercial's overall success or failure. The ratio is derived by dividing total sales (resulting from a particular telecast or telecasts) by the media cost. For example, if you buy a half hour for $1000 and generate $3000 in sales, the MER is 3. Sales/Media Cost = MER

media time: any time on a TV station or cable network available for programming or commercials.

MER: see **media efficiency ratio**.

merchant account: agreement between a company selling a product and the credit card company responsible for collecting the sale. Marketers have merchant accounts with Visa, Master Card, AMEX, etc. Companies new to direct marketing often have a difficult time getting merchant accounts because of the risks in long distance credit card transactions.

merchant account discount fee: the percentage of every dollar that the credit card companies charge the marketer for financing their credit card transactions. Typical fees range from 1% to 4%.

merchant account vendor: Credit card vendors hired by infomercial/DRTV agencies or infomercial marketers to authorize and process infomercial credit card transactions for a fee. New infomercial projects are closely scrutinized by merchant bankers because of the risk involved in long-distance credit card transactions.

minimercial: a DRTV commercial longer than two minutes but less than ten.

mock-up: the creation of preliminary product packaging (brochures, video cassette boxes, product labels and boxes) for the purposes of filming/taping to meet production deadlines. Often a new product infomercial will be scheduled for completion before product package manufacturing has been completed. The product beauty shots are therefore filmed with mock-ups.

money back guarantee (MBG): the promise a marketer gives a consumer to refund all or part of the purchase price within a given time period, typically 30 days.

money shot: the one scene in a DRTV commercial that "says it all" and excites viewers to call. For example, the Ginsu knife cutting through a can, then slicing through a tomato like butter.

MOS: term used to describe the lack of audio at specific points of a script, from a German acronym that means "without sound."

MSO: see **multiple system operator**.

multiple payments: offer technique of breaking the retail price into smaller amounts to be paid in monthly installments via credit card or advertiser-sponsored financing. "Pay in three easy installments of only $24.95." First tested in 1989 and now common, multiple payments can boost response by as much as 25%. If the product price is $100 or less, the percentage of purchasers opting for multiple payments can be as low as 25%. Percentage increases as total retail price rises. Soloflex holds the record for most installments: "39 payments of $39."

multiple product offer: technique of offering two, three or more products in the same infomercial. The varying products can be in the same product category (single shows devoted to dolls, video tapes, kitchen appliances) or different categories (single show showcasing a tool, automotive, kitchen and self-help products). The latter format has never proven profitable for a non-retail driving infomercial. A risky venture, this gives a prospective buyer too much to think about resulting in no buying decision.

multiple system operator (MSO): a corporation that owns and operates multiple local cable franchises. Largest MSOs are TCI, Time-Warner, Comcast, Cox, and Continental.

N

national cable: cable network that broadcasts its signal via satellite to numerous local cable systems. There are over 100 national cable networks, but only half of them reach 25 million or more TV households.

national sales manager (NSM): the TV station sales person responsible for selling commercial time to national (not local) advertisers such as McDonald's, Coke, GM and nationally distributed infomercials.

net audience: synonym for **reach**.

net buy: actual amount paid to a TV station or cable network for media time. The net buy is typically 15% less than the gross buy, which reflects the commission paid the agency for its media-buying services.

NIMA International: trade association founded in 1990 comprised of infomercial product manufacturers, distributors, producers, writers, directors, agencies, media buyers, telemarketers, fulfillment houses, TV stations, cable networks, home shopping and other electronic media.

no charge: free infomercial telecast given by a station or network to a media buying agency for a variety of different reasons. Buyers get no charges as payment for station mistakes (telecasting the wrong version of an infomercial) or as a bonus for buying a significant amount of time on the station.

nondisclosure agency: ad agency that buys media without revealing to their clients the exact price they pay for it. Broadcast affidavits are not disclosed to the client. There is the potential here for the agency to make significantly more than 15 percent commission. For example, an agency might pay $750 net to a station and sell it to their client for $1250 for a 40 percent commission.

non-linear editing: same as digital editing, this refers to the ability to manipulate sound and images in random order. If you change the length of a shot five minutes into a completed 30-minute infomercial, all shots adjust accordingly thereafter and do not have to be re-edited.

NSM: See **national sales manager**.

O

off-line editing: the electronic assembly of an infomercial's varied elements (images, audio, graphics) in a rough, preliminary manner. Off-line editing is usually done on less expensive electronic equipment to reduce hourly cost since most decisions involve much trial and error. The look of the program is created here.

on-camera: a script denotation for a person or thing to appear in the filmed or taped image.

one-step offer: an infomercial/DRTV offer that requests the viewer call the 800/888 number (or write) now and purchase the featured product with his/her credit card.

one time only (OTO): an infomercial time slot that is not available on a regular basis but will be sold just this one time.

OTO: see **one time only**.

one-timers: infomercial product consumers who buy the first product in a continuity program (books, music, skin and hair care) and do not order again.

on-line editing: the final electronic assembly of an infomercial's diverse production elements on high-end, top quality equipment at expensive hourly rates. The off-line edit version is generally translated directly to the on-line edit session for mastering on 1-inch videotape.

on-line services: computer commercial on-line services such as America Online, CompuServe and Prodigy now offer sales and promotional arenas (or "shopping malls"), which some infomercial marketers use to promote their campaigns. (See also **Internet** and **World Wide Web**.)

orders: telephone calls to an infomercial's inbound telemarketing company that result in a product order, as opposed to inquiries and problem calls.

owned and operated (O and O): TV station that is owned by a major network (ABC, NBC, CBS, FOX). Networks can own just a limited number of stations.

outbound telemarketer: service company that contracts with an infomercial/DRTV marketer to provide trained staff who make outbound sales calls to prospective product buyers. May handle back-end sales, inquiry conversions, credit card upsells and cross-sells.

P

people meter: Nielsen electronic device that records television-viewing habits in about 5,000 homes.

per inquiry (PI): primarily small broadcast stations' policy of accepting infomercial media payments in the form of a percentage of sales. The stations/networks essentially become the direct marketer's partner and receive 20% to 35% of total sales generated from the telecasts. PIs were a common practice until DRTV time became tight in the 1980s. Same as **per order**.

per order: see **per inquiry**.

phone-in: a live, testimonial phone caller to a home shopping network product presenter who discusses the merits of using the product currently being sold.

pod: term used to describe the body segments of an infomercial preceding and following a call to action. There are generally three pods per infomercial, each about six to eight minutes in length.

post production: electronic assembling of video, audio and graphics via off-line and on-line editing.

pre-emption: removal, at a TV station or cable network's discretion, of a scheduled infomercial to be replaced by another infomercial, entertainment program or special report.

premium: similar to bonus, a product or service added to the core product offer to enhance value.

pre-production: organizational stage that precedes infomercial production. This involves research, location scouting, set design, production crew hiring, testimonial pre-interviews, production scheduling and more.

preventive products: products that "prevent" a negative experience from possibly happening some time in the future (security devices, fire alarms, etc.). Rarely successful in DRTV marketing. To motivate an immediate response, successful DRTV products must showcase benefits that immediately contribute positively to the consumer's life. There are exceptions to this rule, though rare.

problem call: an infomercial-generated telephone call requesting assistance in solving a problem such as delay in product delivery, product doesn't work, request for refund, etc. Problem calls are different from *orders* and *inquiries.*

producer: person responsible for the organization, management and execution of an infomercial production. Responsibilities include scheduling, hiring free-lance personnel, budgeting, etc.

product sourcer: hired by infomercial marketers to seek out new products that fit the profile for infomercial success.

production: the film or videotaping of infomercial script elements.

production company: company that executes the filming or taping of a commercial production.

"Product is King": common knowledge among infomercial producers that focusing on product features and benefits, not entertainment, is what motivates an immediate response.

product shots: similar to beauty shots, the display shot of the product(s) in an appealing setting.

proforma: a financial spreadsheet, based on certain marketing assumptions, which details the flow of expenses and revenues over time and calculates projected profits and loss.

program length advertisement (PLA): adopted by the Madison Avenue advertising community as the preferred name for infomercials in an attempt to make them respectable to Fortune 500 companies.

public relations firm: may be hired by infomercial agencies to promote infomercials to television networks, keep industry publications abreast of marketing progress and/or to enhance current or prospective retail relations.

Q

QVC: stands for "Quality Value Convenience," the 24-hour per day, live home shopping network, similar to HSN. Launched in 1986, QVC also programs the spinoff channel Q2.

R

radiomercial: long-form commercial on radio, five to 30 minutes in length.

rating: the percentage of people or homes that watch a specific TV program based on the total population or homes with television, whether watching or not. Rating = HUT (×) Share.

reach: the number of different people or homes that see a specific commercial at least once. Reach measures the breadth of an ad campaign.

reactivation program: typically an outbound telemarketing campaign designed to reactivate continuity program consumers who have ceased ordering.

repeaters: term usually used to describe multiple purchase consumers of live home shopping networks and/or faithful continuity program subscribers.

reps: station sales representatives.

response: term often used interchangeably with "results" to an infomercial telecast.

retail driver: see **driving retail**.

retail price: in infomercials and DRTV, the retail price is the advertised offer price.

retail sales multiplier: same as Infomercial Retail Multiple (IRM).

returns: number of units, dollar amount or percentage of total sales that are returned to the direct marketer for a refund.

returns and allowances: a projected or actual percentage of total sales returned for refunds.

roll-in: a pre-taped video segment, 30 seconds to three minutes in length, that is played back and inserted during the taping of a live telecast.

roll-out: stage of an infomercial media campaign, after a successful media test, where the infomercial plays on an ever-increasing number of TV stations and cable networks nationwide. A roll-out can mean buying thousands of telecasts, up to $2 million of media per month with telecasts in nearly all 212 television markets. Typically this maximum media spending level is reached through a gradual expansion over 2 to 4 months.

run of station (ROS): short-form commercial media time is purchased at a discount because stations retain the right to insert them wherever they choose within certain broad time periods, e.g. 12 noon to 4 P.M. The station determines the run time.

S

saver program: similar to **reactivation program**.

self-improvement product: any product or service that provides benefits of improving an individual's financial status, occupation, relationships, self-esteem, memory, physical and mental health. Such products often have excellent mark-ups of as much as 15 to 1 but rarely succeed unless the benefits are visually concrete (e.g., diet products). Tony Robbins "Personal Power" is an exception. His success can be attributed primarily to his charismatic TV persona.

selling cycle: infomercials generally have three pods, each of which is a selling cycle that details the same basic selling information but is packaged somewhat differently. The matching elements in each cycle are: features, benefits, credibility, substantiation, guarantee, offer and call to action.

"send check" address: the address in the billboard for those who wish to pay by check.

share: percentage of households using television who are watching a specific program. The share is always higher than the rating. 10% of all TV homes might be watching Program X. But because only 50% of all TV homes are watching TV at this particular time, Program X's share is 20%. Share is a measurement of a program's relative strength versus its immediate competition on other channels.

shipping and handling (S&H): the cost to consumer, stated on the billboard, which is in addition to the stated product price.

S&H: see **shipping and handling**.

short form: any DRTV commercial that is two minutes or less in length.

signpost: term used to describe an on-camera spokesperson who introduces a storymercial's fictional segments and reappears periodically to remind the viewer of key product benefits.

sit-commercial: infomercial program structure that mimics a situation comedy.

60s, 90s, and 120s: refers to the length (in seconds) of short-form commercials. 60s and 90s are easier to buy media for than 120s. 10s, 15s and 30s are the domain primarily of image/awareness advertisers—generally not effective for short-form DRTV.

spill-in: percentage of viewership in a specific market that is directed to TV stations originating outside of the market.

spin: synonym for airing.

"spin 'til you win": an agreement between TV station and media buyer to telecast an infomercial as many times as necessary in a specified period of time to achieve a predetermined cost per order. Similar to per inquiry except the station gets paid a known amount up-front.

spot: advertisers in the infomercial business refer to any image/awareness, non-DRTV commercial (generally five to 60-seconds in length) as a spot commercial. Traditional advertisers (non-DRTV) define the "spot" market as the purchase of advertising on local broadcast TV stations, market by market.

Standard Rate and Data Service (SRDS): a widely used publication that details information about broadcast TV stations management, personnel, county coverage and commercial rates.

station reps: companies, such as Petry or Katzy, that represent local broadcast stations in the sale of airtime to national advertisers.

story board: a series of sketches or rough artwork with accompanying description of action and audio that approximates what the infomercial will look like.

storymercial: the infomercial program format that uses actors to tell a fictional story that showcases the featured product.

submaster: the assembly of certain video and audio on a tape that later will be incorporated into the final edit master.

success rate/ratio: the ratio of infomercial "winners to losers," which is often quoted for the industry as a whole (1984—one in three; 1996—one in 10) or for specific infomercial companies, directors, writers. The ratio has risen over the past 10 years primarily because of increased media rates and competition.

super: graphics and text that is superimposed over other video/film.

superstation: local broadcast television station that also sends its signal via satellite to numerous local cable systems to increase viewership. Examples include WTBS, WGN, WOR.

sweeps: four-week period held four times per year by Nielsen where all U.S. television stations are measured for viewership levels and demographic breakdown.

sweetening: post-production process of mixing audio and music for the final edited master.

syndication: production of independent, non-network programming distributed to local broadcast stations and cable networks and paid for by cash or bartered commercial time.

T

tag page: same as **billboard**.

talk show format: infomercial program format that mimics a talk show.

tape duplicator: companies that duplicate master infomercials. Adds 800/888 numbers for tracking and distributes to television stations and cable networks for telecasting.

telecomp: term used to describe the electronic communications center of the twenty-first century, combining a home's television, fax, radio, stereo system, computer, phone and security system in one all-inclusive console.

telemarketing: the use of the telephone to receive and make phone calls to capture sales.

telephone service rep (TSR): trained telephone operator making and receiving infomercial-related phone calls to create sales.

telethon: infomercial program format that mimics a PBS or Jerry Lewis telethon with product presenters standing in front of a bank of telephone operators taking "live" calls to order the featured product.

test media: any media time slots where an infomercial has never run or has not run for at least the preceding four weeks.

time code: the numbers ascribed to every frame of video and recorded on the address track or an audio channel of the videotape. Each frame (30 frames per second) will have a distinct number attached to it defining hour/minute/second/frame, such as 02:47:21:28 which means: 2 hours, 47 minutes, 21 seconds and 28 frames.

tonality: the "look and feel" of a commercial as reflected in its sets, lighting, camera movement, image quality, casting and message.

treatment: a two- to six-page exposition on what an infomercial will look like and communicate. This is the first stage of script writing.

transactional TV: another Madison Avenue name for infomercials or DRTV.

TSR: see **telephone service representative**.

tube camera: the technology (slowly becoming extinct) within video cameras using three tubes to capture and transmit the image.

two-step offer: also called lead generator (see **lead generation**), an infomercial offer that requests the viewer call an 800/888 number (or write) and ask for more information (video or brochure) after which they are considered a lead and pursued via mail or phone for the actual order.

U

unduplicated audience: synonym for **reach**.

upsell: any product that is additionally offered to an infomercial product purchaser at the time of their initial telephone order. Inbound telemarketers, after taking the key product-ordering information, will often offer the caller one or two related products, which are typically discounted. For example, a music CD at half price; three months of a cosmetic for the cost of two; an additional key product at half price, etc.

USBC (United States Broadcast Markets): any Nielsen TV market that doesn't have signal and viewership spill over into Canada.

V

video magazine: infomercial program format that is documentary in form, but lighter in style. Often uses male/female cohosts with multiple on-location shoots. Similar to *PM Magazine.*

voice over: the unseen narrator's voice.

W

wall: an unseen, unpredictable "wall" of resistance to any further infomercial campaign expansion. Response can begin to drop off dramatically, so media spending drops.

wobble zone: response levels prior to "hitting the wall" that are consistently around ad allowable while spending levels are maintained. In this "wobble zone" the CPO fluctuates under and around the ad allowable.

World Wide Web (WWW): the commercial context of the Internet where infomercial marketers can post product and company information by creating a commercial Web site or home page, which online computer users/consumers can access at their convenience.

Z

zapping: avoiding commercial viewing by changing channels with a remote control.

zipping: avoiding commercial viewing while watching VCR-recorded programs by fast-forwarding through the commercials.

Index

Q

R

S

TITLES OF INTEREST IN MARKETING, DIRECT MARKETING, AND SALES PROMOTION

SUCCESSFUL DIRECT MARKETING METHODS, by Bob Stone
PROFITABLE DIRECT MARKETING, by Jim Kobs
INTEGRATED DIRECT MARKETING, by Ernan Roman
BEYOND 2000: THE FUTURE OF DIRECT MARKETING, by Jerry I. Reitman
POWER DIRECT MARKETING, by "Rocket" Ray Jutkins
CREATIVE STRATEGY IN DIRECT MARKETING, by Susan K. Jones
SECRETS OF SUCCESSFUL DIRECT MAIL, by Richard V. Benson
STRATEGIC DATABASE MARKETING, by Rob Jackson and Paul Wang
HOW TO PROFIT THROUGH CATALOG MARKETING, by Katie Muldoon
DIRECT RESPONSE TELEVISION, by Frank Brady and J. Angel Vasquez
DIRECT MARKETING THROUGH BROADCASE MEDIA, by Alvin Eicoff
SUCCESSFUL TELEMARKETING, by Bob Stone and John Wyman
BUSINESS TO BUSINESS DIRECT MARKETING, by Robert Bly
COMMONSENSE DIRECT MARKETING, by Drayton Bird
DIRECT MARKETING CHECKLISTS, by John Stockwell and Henry Shaw
INTEGRATED MARKETING COMMUNICATIONS, by Don E. Schultz, Stanley I. Tannenbaum, and Robert F. Lauterborn
GREEN MARKETING, by Jacquelyn Ottman
MARKETING CORPORATE IMAGE: THE COMPANY AS YOUR NUMBER ONE PRODUCT by James R. Gregory with Jack G. Wiechmann
HOW TO CREATE SUCCESSFUL CATALOGS, by Maxwell Sroge
101 TIPS FOR MORE PROFITABLE CATALOGS, by Maxwell Sroge
SALES PROMOTION ESSENTIALS by Don E. Schultz, William A. Robinson and Lisa A. Petrison
PROMOTIONAL MARKETING, by William A. Robinson and Christine Hauri
BEST SALES PROMOTIONS, by William A. Robinson
INSIDE THE LEADING MAIL ORDER HOUSES, by Maxwell Sroge
NEW PRODUCT DEVELOPMENT, by George Gruenwald
NEW PRODUCT DEVELOPMENT CHECKLISTS, by George Gruenwald
CLASSIC FAILURES IN PRODUCT MARKETING, by Donald W. Hendon
HOW TO TURN CUSTOMER SERVICE INTO CUSTOMER SALES, by Bernard Katz
ADVERTISING & MARKETING CHECKLISTS, by Ron Kaatz
BRAND MARKETING, by William M. Weilbacher
MARKETING WITHOUT MONEY, by Nicholas E. Bade
THE 1-DAY MARKETING PLAN, by Roman A. Hiebing, Jr. and Scott W. Cooper
HOW TO WRITE A SUCCESSFUL MARKETING PLAN by Roman G. Hiebing, Jr. and Scott W. Cooper
DEVELOPING, IMPLEMENTING, AND MANAGING EFFECTIVE MARKETING PLANS by Hal Goetsch
HOW TO EVALUATE AND IMPROVE YOUR MARKETING DEPARTMENT by Keith Sparling and Gerard Earls
SELLING TO A SEGMENTED MARKET, by Chester A. Swenson
MARKET-ORIENTED PRICING, by Michael Morris and Gene Morris
STATE-OF-THE-ART MARKETING RESEARCH, by A.B. Blankenship and George E. Breen
AMA HANDBOOK FOR CUSTOMER SATISFACTION, by Alan Dutka
WAS THERE A PEPSI GENERATION BEFORE PEPSI DISCOVERED IT? by Stanley C. Hollander and Richard Germain
BUSINESS TO BUSINESS COMMUNICATIONS HANDBOOK, by Fred Messner
MANAGING SALES LEADS: HOW TO TURN EVERY PROSPECT INTO A CUSTOMER by Robert Donath, Richard Crocker, Carol Dixon and James Obermeyer
AMA MARKETING TOOLBOX (SERIES), by David Parmerlee
AMA COMPLETE GUIDE TO SMALL BUSINESS MARKETING, by Kenneth J. Cook
AMA COMPLETE GUIDE TO STRATEGIC PLANNING FOR SMALL BUSINESS, by Kenneth J. Cook
AMA COMPLETE GUIDE TO SMALL BUSINESS ADVERTISING, by Joe Vitale
HOW TO GET THE MOST OUT OF TRADE SHOWS, by Steve Miller
HOW TO GET THE MOST OUT OF SALES MEETINGS, by James Dance
STRATEGIC MARKET PLANNING, by Robert J. Hamper and L. Sue Baugh

For further information or a current catalog, write:
NTC Business Books
a division of *NTC Publishing Group*
4255 West Touhy Avenue
Lincolnwood, Illinois 60646-1975 U.S.A.